Priest in Deep Water

Priest in Deep Water

*Charles Plomer Hopkins
and the 1911 Seamen's Strike*

R.W.H. Miller

The Lutterworth Press

The Lutterworth Press
P.O. Box 60
Cambridge
CB1 2NT
UK

www.lutterworth.com
publishing@lutterworth.com

ISBN: 978 0 7188 9232 6

British Library Cataloguing in Publication Data
A catalogue record is available from the British Library

Contents

Abbreviations

ACS	Additional Clergy Society
AGM	Annual General Meeting
BFSFSBU	British and Foreign Seamen's Friend Society and Bethel Union
BSS	British Sailors' Society
BSU	British Seafarers' Union
COS	Charity Organisation Society (from 1946 known as the FWA (below))
CPH	Charles Plomer Hopkins
CTS	Catholic Truth Society
F&GP	Finance & General Purposes Committee
FWA	Family Welfare Association
ICOSU	International Committee of Seamen's Unions
ISF	International Shipping Federation
IT(W)F	International Transport (Workers') Federation
MtoS	The Missions to Seamen (now Mission to Seafarers)
NESSOA	North of England Steamship Owners' Association
NMB	National Maritime Board
NSFU	National Sailors' and Firemen's Union
NTWF	National Transport Workers' Federation
NUS	National Union of Seamen
OSP	Order of St Paul
RGWB	Rangoon Gazette Weekly Budget
SAWCM	St Andrew's Waterside Church Mission (also referred to as SAWM in some references)
SFSSP	Seamen's Friendly Society of St Paul
SPG	Society for the Propagation of the Gospel
SSP	Society of St Paul
SVP	Society of St Vincent de Paul
TNA	The National Archive
TUC	Trades Union Congress
USPG	United Society for the Propagation of the Gospel
WNA	Winter North Atlantic

Preface

This book is an introduction to the remarkable life of Charles Plomer Hopkins. It started life as a thesis.[1] I have reduced the number of footnotes, adjusted the text to make it readable, added the results of further research and completely restructured the whole. Those who need more detail will find it in the thesis, together with a full bibliography.

The book straddles the twin subjects of trade unionism among seafarers and the Christian sea apostolate. Trade unionism has been dealt with extensively by others, the sea apostolate less so, but neither with any particular attention to Hopkins. In combining the two disciplines I have tried to indicate the background to industrial organisation for those who study the sea apostolate, and vice versa. I first encountered Hopkins in Peter Anson's *Call of the Cloister* in 1964. As I tried to discover more about Hopkins it became apparent that here was an important but forgotten man, and somebody Anson neither understood nor knew much about.

A major problem has been in sourcing Hopkins. I used the archives of the National Union of Seamen and the Shipping Federation in Warwick University's Modern Records Centre. Documents kept there appear in footnotes with the prefix 'Mss'. Alton Abbey, which Hopkins founded, seemed an obvious and promising source of information but proved reluctant to open its archives for me until the first abbot allowed me to see copies of Hopkins's publication, *The Messenger*, at the Abbey. I managed to read as far as 1912 in the time available. Dom Andrew Johnson, the Abbey librarian, generously made a copy of his own study available, which was then in its early stages. I have made little progress with Alton Abbey since the first abbot's departure. *The Nautical Guildsman, Shipmates,* and others of Hopkins's work are in the British Library. I am grateful to the Archbishop of Canterbury and the Librarian of Lambeth Palace Library for allowing me to see those records of Archbishop Davidson which refer to Hopkins. The Family Welfare Association kindly gave permission for me to see files in the Greater London Records Office. Society for the Propagation of the Gospel papers held at Rhodes House Library, Oxford, contain correspondence with colonial bishops. Many references to Hopkins were found in *Proceedings* and some newspapers held in the India Office Library. Most newspapers were consulted at the Newspaper Library, Colindale, in North London. St Andrew's Waterside Church Mission records were made available by The Missions to Seamen (now The Mission to Seafarers).

There have been frustrations. It seems that many documents relating to Hopkins and his work in the field of seamen's welfare were thrown away at Alton Abbey in the 1950s. Japanese action during the Second World War accounted for the absence of Rangoon church papers. I failed to find a complete run of Calcutta newspapers. Surviving records of Holy Trinity parish, Shoreditch, carry no mention of Hopkins, so it has not been possible to verify his version of events during his stay there. Union records for the period before and during the strike are at best patchy and often non-existent. Havelock Wilson, the Union President, ended volume one of his autobiography just as he met Hopkins... but never wrote volume two.

There have been pleasures, too. I record my thanks to those who have been specially helpful. Dr Tony Mason of Warwick University supervised the original thesis. He also suggested the title of this work. The late Joseph Kyaw Zan of Burma confirmed for me the destruction of Rangoon church records. Stephen Friend of what was then the University College of Ripon and York St John pointed me towards FWA records. The late Fr Gabriel Sanford CR checked community records at Mirfield for me. The Rev. Canon N. Panter generously provided an extract from the diary of his late father, The Rev. C.E. Panter. Dr Herma Barz provided translations from the German. Alton Abbey's first abbot could not have been more helpful. The Diocese of Southwell granted study leave. The Rev. Canon Dr Michael Austin gave patient encouragement. Dr David M. Williams of Leicester University indicated various nineteenth century leaflets. Hopkins's grand-niece, Mrs Janet Rees, explained details about the family. Abner K. Pratt II kindly helped by investigating records at Cape Cod. Dr Alston Kennerley, Plymouth University, provided the reference to Hopkins in Shalimar and has been a constant source of advice, encouragement and friendship. I am also grateful to Dr Jan Setterington, Plymouth University, for her helpful comments. The final text would have been much worse without the editorial skills of Elaine Proudlove and Rachel Baguley.

Introduction

Here are accusations of sexual impropriety, murder, financial mal-practice and other alarms, set against a backdrop of the British Empire, the Raj, and the Catholic revival in the nineteenth-century Church of England. Charles Plomer Hopkins, a Victorian church organist, called by circumstance to a seamen's chaplaincy on the Indian sub-continent, eventually achieved an unlikely apotheosis in his announcement and leadership of the first and, so far, only international seamen's strike. The reader will perceive immediately that this is not the usual career path of most Anglican, or indeed any, clergy. The extraordinary effect of Hopkins's ministry among seafarers on his own and other churches is only now beginning to be appreciated. His influence was profound. His troubles, often of his own manufacture, were great. It seemed apt to entitle his life story Priest in Deep Water, its ambiguity encapsulating both the general thrust of his ministry and the particular troubles by which it was dogged.

Charles Plomer Hopkins, referred to as CPH when it is neces-sary to avoid confusion with his father, also Charles Hopkins, was born in 1861 and died in 1922. He is a figure largely forgotten or ignored and seldom understood by historians who have sought to document the struggle by seamen to obtain union recognition from their employers. Most people who know his name have met it either as a footnote in such work or outside maritime literature altogether. Fortunately Hopkins has an entry in the latest edition of the *Dictionary of National Biography*, which may improve his place in future studies. Some of the misunderstanding seems to have arisen from dependence on the Labour politician, Emmanuel Shinwell. Shinwell was a self-publicist who had been removed from office in

the National Sailors' and Firemen's Union by Hopkins shortly after
the seamen's strike of 1911, which may account for Shinwell's
tone in his memoirs, *Conflict Without Malice* (1955):

> the 'Rev' Charles P Hopkins .... was in his own words as
> a witness at a later court hearing a volunteer 'sky pilot',
> who clad himself in a semi-clerical, semi-nautical garb
> consisting of a discreet black habit with a blue seamen's
> jersey and a gold crucifix. He was a newcomer, having
> become a trustee of the union that summer, though an
> old crony of Wilson's ....

Shinwell gives us little of use. When Hopkins wore his habit (full
and Benedictine) on a platform, it was precisely because it was not
discreet. Shinwell here combines it with Hopkins's more usual garb,
which he was wearing when he met the seamen's leader, Havelock
Wilson, around or before 1900, of seaman's jersey, clerical collar,
pectoral cross (as Superior of the Order of St Paul), jacket and cheese
cutter cap. It was the young Shinwell who was the newcomer to the
movement. Those who follow Shinwell, such as Wailey and Clegg,
failed to realise that Hopkins was genuinely a priest and a religious
(that is, a member of a religious community, living under vows),
with a fine record of service to seafarers.

To find Hopkins it is necessary to look elsewhere. Compton
MacKenzie is a primary source and wrote with accuracy. Material
from his books will appear in the text; suffice it to say here that
his second *Octave* of autobiography gives his experience as a
neighbour of life at Alton Abbey, while his novel *The Altar Steps*
depicts Hopkins at some length, but as a priest serving the army.
Hopkins also appears in a book by Shalimar who seems to have
met Hopkins when Shalimar was a midshipman visiting Calcutta
in the 1890s. Better known as a source, however, was Peter Anson,
whose principal interest in Hopkins was in Hopkins's linking of the
religious life (a life in a religious community in which members take
traditional vows, usually of poverty, chastity and obedience) with
the sea apostolate. Anson seems to have picked up Hopkins's name
through the writing of Fr Goldie SJ who in the 1890s and 1900s was
trying to promote Catholic work among merchant seamen and who
had been impressed by what he had heard of Hopkins's Calcutta
work. Equally, news of Hopkins's quasi-Benedictine community at
Alton and its work elsewhere probably reached Anson whilst he was

Charles Hopkins in middle life (from his
obituary in The Seaman, 3rd March, 1922).

a novice in the Benedictine community on Caldey Island. Anson
wrote an obituary of Hopkins shortly after the latter's death, but
strangely appeared to know nothing of his association with either
the seamen's strike or Union, even managing to get Hopkins's name
wrong. After the Second World War Anson compiled a major book
on the religious communities of the Church of England, The *Call
of the Cloister*, in which he included Hopkins and the Order of St
Paul, using, uncritically, information supplied by Alton Abbey. I have
dealt with his writing elsewhere.[1] We should be grateful to Anson for
keeping Hopkins's name alive. Anson wrote extensively on the sea
apostolate and is credited, with some justice, with reviving Catholic
work among seafarers, so it is curious that he understood so little
about Hopkins's very important contribution to that apostolate or to
the strike. Largely because of their dependence upon Anson rather
than upon primary sources, others who chronicle the development of
the sea apostolate have little to say about Hopkins. Even the doyen
of maritime missiologists, Roald Kverndal, provides him with only

the shortest of shrouds.[2]

If Hopkins is poorly served in religious or maritime titles, he fares little better in literature concerning the strike action. The fact that the 1911 strike, eventually, involved many larger groups than seamen has caused writers on contemporary industrial relations to neglect the seamen. In his book *John Burns* (1977), K.D. Brown blamed the strike on a specially hot summer. L.H. Powell, as a Federation official, wrote about the strike from the Federation's point of view in his book *The Shipping Federation* (1950) but mentioned Hopkins only in passing. An unusually balanced account is to be found in Barbara Tuchman's *The Proud Tower* (1962), which distinguishes the seamen from the other striking groups, examines why the political scene around 1910 made the strike imperative and places it against a background of anarchy, socialism and other contemporary movements. She makes no mention of Hopkins. The context she provides for Hopkins's bursts of socialist oratory makes them appear less extreme or odd than they would otherwise appear today.

Despite this neglect, it is possible to track Hopkins. The life that emerges effectively falls into three parts. His early years brought him into contact with merchant seamen and moulded his thinking. He came to see that seamen needed to be organised. The second part deals with his attempts to improve the lot of seamen, especially with regard to their organisation. The climax of this second period is his role in the 1911 strike. A third, post- climactic period followed with his occupation of a senior position in the Union's leadership in close association with its president, J. Havelock Wilson.

The story opens with Hopkins's American father, employed as a river pilot in Burma, sending the very young Charles from Burma to England aboard the *GEOLOGIST*, to be educated at his mother's Cornish home of Falmouth. Later CPH wrote in his book, *Altering Plimsoll's Mark*:

> My personal introduction to the load-line controversy took place on board the sailing ship *GEOLOGIST* in or about 1870, on my passage from India to England to school. The sailors called her a 'death-trap' and she all but drowned me on the main deck....

His father, familiar with visiting sailing ships, is unlikely to have consigned his eldest son to a coffin ship, though the *GEOLOGIST* was certainly a 'hard' ship. The concept of coffin ships is closely

associated with the campaign for greater safety at sea that was
championed by Samuel Plimsoll, MP. The Plimsoll campaign
spanned several decades and provided the background for Hopkins's
own campaign. Its full impact will begin to appear in Chapter Two.

After his schooling in Falmouth, the young Hopkins went on to
study music in London. In Chapter Two he then returns to Burma as the
cathedral organist in Rangoon, and becomes increasingly involved
with the local church's ministry to seafarers. Ordination and his
appointment as Port Chaplain may appear uncontroversial but almost
at once Hopkins is caught up in the case of a ship overloaded:

> My next personal experience ... took place in Rangoon,
> Burma, in or about 1884, when the load-line disc of
> the sailing ship *CASSIOPE* was raised by the captain's
> orders to enable more cargo to be taken aboard. She
> was lost with all hands ....

Hopkins tried to intervene but found his efforts unwelcome. The
subsequent furore was followed by his removal to the small, seasonal,
rice port of Akyab. His time there was meant to be an interlude but
is important enough to merit a separate chapter (Three) describing
how, having started another seamen's club, his thoughts began
to turn to the religious life as a means of providing a committed
ministry among seamen. His time in Akyab was ended by a serious
bout of malaria, its after-effects haunting him for the rest of his life,
and forcing his return to England.

Hopkins's brief stay in London (Chapter Four), ostensibly on
medical grounds, coincided with the growing unrest which would
culminate in the Dock Strike of 1889, though he seems in no way to
have been connected with this. He came to London under the influence
of a colourful and remarkable clergyman, the Rev. A. Osborne Jay,
founder of a small and ephemeral religious community in which
Hopkins very soon made his profession. Jay was Vicar of Holy
Trinity, Shoreditch, a very deprived London parish which responded
well to its vicar's unusual methods, some of which Hopkins would
adopt in his next appointment as Port Chaplain in Calcutta. Jay, and
surrounding clergy who were Christian Socialists, cast a little light
on the thinking he would have encountered in Shoreditch. Although
Hopkins cannot be directly associated with Christian Socialism, it is
part of the background against which he must be seen. Hopkins saw
his few months in London as pivotal to what would follow.

The second phase of Hopkins's life begins in Calcutta (Chapter
Five). Here he established his religious community, started his own
quasi-union in the guise of a Seamen's Guild, fought some thirty
cases involving seamen through the courts, and got involved with
Havelock Wilson's seamen's Union, apparently to the extent of
starting a local branch. The Calcutta period saw him return twice
to tour England in pursuit of recruits and cash. The presence of
two Jesuits among an 1893 Hastings audience which Hopkins
was addressing on one of these tours contributed substantially, if
indirectly, to the foundation of the modern ministry to seafarers of
the Roman Catholic Church. This chapter, inevitably a long one,
ends with his return to the United Kingdom in 1894 surrounded by
considerable controversy, mainly resulting from rumours of sexual
impropriety following a court case which seems to have been
arranged to blacken his name.

The years following his return (Chapter Six) were spent
consolidating the life of his community, which continued
its maritime work through priories established in Barry and
Greenwich. There is evidence to show that his brethren were
aware of developments within the seamen's union but nothing
to confirm contacts. Concurrently Hopkins fell seriously foul of
Church authority. His lack of tact, combined with the requirements
of the Colonial Clergy Act, placed him in a difficult position which
prevented him exercising a public priestly ministry. His meeting
with Havelock Wilson, the president of the seamen's Union, around
1900 seems to have afforded him an opening which the Church had
failed to provide. The mystery here is why, when there is evidence
to show him working for the NSFU in Calcutta, it should have
taken him so long to meet its president.

There are years between meeting Havelock Wilson and the
declaration of the strike in 1911 which are almost blank (Chapter
Seven). Hopkins became secretary of the International Committee of
Seamen's Unions in 1910, but his route to that position is only dimly
lit. The role made him privy to the plans for an international strike
which, in 1911, it was his privilege to announce, and then effectively
bring to a reasonable conclusion. The 1911 strike (Chapter Eight)
was prolonged by strikes of other workers associated with the
industry, which largely fall outside the scope of this book. These
two chapters are controversial and any interpretation of Hopkins's
and also of Wilson's role, and the relationship subsequently of the

NSFU with the main body of trades unionism, depends as much upon who is viewing as on what is seen. It seems to me that neither wished to have much to do with the other. Seamen were scattered across the globe and could add little weight to the claims of other unions. The Shipping Federation Ltd, or more familiarly the Shipping Federation, records refer variously to the Humber District and the Hull District for what is also called the North East Steam Ship Owners Association (NESSOA). In the text, to avoid confusion, I use either NESSOA or the Humber District.

The period after the strike I describe as Hopkins's third phase. He became a trustee of the NSFU, an elected delegate, and increasingly involved in Union affairs (Chapter Nine). Union records now begin to appear and reveal his activities as trustee and delegate. The impact of the First World War on the Union was substantial. Wartime demands for increasing numbers of crews and the issues surrounding their recruitment became meat and drink to Hopkins. After the war he was awarded the CBE in recognition of his work in this respect, acting effectively as the Union's liaison officer with government. In 1917 the National Maritime Board was formed with Hopkins as its first secretary jointly with Cuthbert Laws, the secretary of the once-hated Shipping Federation; hated because, according to L.H. Powell, it had been founded in 1890 as a 'fighting machine' to counter the increasing power of the Union.

It is my hope that Hopkins will be restored to the public mind and his major contribution to the welfare of merchant seamen, to the development of the maritime apostolate in the Anglican and Roman Catholic Churches, and to the restoration of the religious life to the Church of England, be recognised. It is a sad fact that the decline of the British merchant navy, the rise of flags of convenience and the increase in third world crews, mean that there is a need in the world for another Hopkins figure to speak for the oppressed. It is a matter for thanksgiving that the Church societies at work amongst seafarers no longer hold back when welfare issues and seamen's rights need attention.

Before looking at Hopkins's life in detail, it is necessary to look at the background against which his ministry was set. Essentially this is formed by the Merchant Shipping Acts, the seamen's Union, and the Church of England. If one were considering clergy generally, those three would probably be in the reverse order, but the peculiar circumstances which will unfold explain why the order is as it is.

Hopkins and the Merchant Shipping Acts

It is necessary to see Hopkins and his work in the light of the various Merchant Shipping Acts. The latter half of the nineteenth century saw, amongst other lesser legislation, the passing of three great Merchant Shipping Acts by the British Parliament in 1854, 1876 and 1894, the latter consolidating the many smaller Acts preceding it. Although Hopkins had to familiarise himself with local variations in the Indian Merchant Shipping Acts, it is these three Acts which were of prime importance to him, to the Union and to the seaman. The Act of 1854, as those that followed, was fought through in the teeth of owner opposition as, for the first time, an attempt was made to regulate conditions under which men sailed.[3] It dealt with ship registration, minimum provisions and training, and made a modest gesture towards safety. Steamships, especially passenger vessels, were subject to inspection and fines could be imposed if regulations were infringed. Seamen were now to be discharged with an indication of character and those discharged abroad for medical reasons were no longer simply to be cast adrift. Complaints could be made and further fines imposed for bad stores. The Act's failure to achieve much is evidenced by the need for Samuel Plimsoll's campaign and from the horror stories which Havelock Wilson would retell in his autobiography. To these will be added Hopkins's Rangoon experiences.

Of particular interest in the 1854 Act was the section on discipline. Any seaman deserting after signing-on was liable to a maximum of twelve weeks' imprisonment with hard labour and the forfeiture of his possessions left on board ship. After signing-on, neglect or refusal to join a ship within twenty-four hours of sailing attracted a maximum of ten weeks' imprisonment. Plimsoll was to bring these injustices to public attention in 1873, graphically illustrating his book *OUR SEAMEN – an Appeal* with photographs of overloaded or otherwise unseaworthy 'coffin ships', the crews of which could be imprisoned, owing to the provisions of this Act, for refusing to sail in them. That such severe penalties were thought necessary indicates that masters had difficulty obtaining crews, which in turn reflects the harshness of life at sea at this time. One of Plimsoll's strong points was to argue that if passenger ships could not put to sea without a certificate and with the remedy of trial by jury for loss of life or injury at sea, there was no good reason why such a system could not also be applied to cargo ships. Owing much to Plimsoll's pressure, a Royal Commission reported in 1873 on unseaworthy ships.[4] Its findings were mixed. Their impact can be measured in part by seeing what changes they brought about in the working conditions of the men. The government introduced the Unseaworthy Ships Act in 1875 which, through the pressure of shipowners, left the load line to be placed at the owner's discretion.

The 1854 Act was considerably altered by that of 1876 and more so in 1894, largely through

Samuel Plimsoll (1824-1898).

Plimsoll's efforts. He was a West Country man who had been brought up to be familiar with the men who carried the cargoes of coal which were his father's business. He stood at Derby as a Liberal on the reform of the 1854 Act and was returned as its MP in 1868.[5] He failed in his attempt to get a bill introduced at this time.[6] To this end, he brought out a sensational book, *OUR SEAMEN – an Appeal*, in 1873, which pressed for a Royal Commission and highlighted a number of scandals, giving examples of ships overloaded, badly stowed or undermanned, none of which was covered by existing legislation. Plimsoll catalogued examples of deficient engine power, defective construction and improper lengthening, comparing the rules, or their lack, unfavourably with the abundance of regulations covering public safety in other industries. He blamed many evils on the growth of marine insurance during the nineteenth century. In earlier centuries owners had had to take care of their ships. Now, insured ships were underwritten by so many people that none stood to lose a large sum when a ship was lost. To get so many underwriters to unite in a prosecution of a shipowner was difficult, as it could cost each more in legal fees than any individual underwriter had

pledged and was bedeviled by the problem of collecting as witnesses
a crew dispersed around the world which would, if collected, need
to be kept together until a case came before the courts. In short, any
hope of the insurance world uniting against a bad shipowner was
all but impossible. Plimsoll also proposed legislation for the proper
measurement and registration of ships, their inspection before putting
to sea, and insurance, together with strict rules regarding loading
in connection both with loose (e.g. grain) and deck (e.g. timber)
cargoes. More particularly, though, in regard to what was to become
his lasting memorial, Plimsoll suggested changes to the eponymous
load line as well as the draught of every vessel which was to be
clearly displayed at foot intervals on stem and stern of every ship.
His publication had a remarkable influence and sold many copies.
In the resulting parliamentary debate he withdrew his bill in favour
of one sponsored by the government, produced in response to the
depth of feeling in the country aroused by Plimsoll's book, which
he thought would have better success.[7] In the event it became the
1876 Act, emasculated in comparison with his own proposals. He
was well aware of the influence of the shipowners in Parliament.
Hopkins's later recording of injustice at sea shows how necessary
Plimsoll's efforts had been, and how much remained to be done.

Discussion at the committee stage of the Act of 1876 illustrated
very well some of the conditions under which the contemporary
seaman laboured. Gorst, the MP for Chatham, for example, pressed
for the removal of the clauses relating to imprisonment and
forfeiture where breach of contract did not involve injury to ship
or danger to life and also for arrest without warrant, in each case
often the result of the system whereby men were signed-on before
they had seen the ship on which they were to serve. Some of the
discussion in the making of the Act tried to relate the position of
seamen to recent legislation about masters and servants or to the
safety of passengers or to the delay of the mails, all of which might
at least give the seaman in regard to imprisonment parity with
the gasworker. Although an Act forbidding the imprisonment of a
workman for breach of contract had been passed nine years earlier,
the committee was able to hear of an instance where two seamen
had been imprisoned with hard labour through being counted absent
while they slept in their bunks on board ship after a night of hard
work! All other workmen were exempt from imprisonment (seamen
at this time were not 'workmen'[8] in law) for non-fulfillment of

contract, except in exceptional circumstances – only gas and water companies could deal with an employee in this way, and that was for the good of the public rather than the good of the employer. To justify these penalties by the need for discipline at sea was to forget that in each case the provision in the law affected only men ashore. Gorst denied that seamen were in need of special legislation through any peculiar recklessness or immaturity ('Poor Jack'). If a man refused to honour a contract it was either because he was a bad seaman or because the ship was bad; to insist on the former going to sea was against the interest of the owner and the latter case meant a choice between prison or drowning. Under the Act of 1854 a seaman needed the support of 25% of the crew, whom he may have met only at the point of sail, to be able to demand a survey of his ship. There is a parallel here with the railway where there were strict safety regulations, sometimes honoured in the breach, where a man could be fined or face dismissal for hesitating over taking a train which might be defective. Hopkins's Guild Rules would stress the importance of honouring contracts.

Another issue dealt with in committee concerned the abolition of advance notes, a system whereby some of a man's wages were advanced before the voyage, allowing the possibility of considerable abuse and imprisonment for debt for the man who failed to board his ship. Pay could be lost at the end of a voyage through the crimping system, where the crimp made his living by persuading men to desert ship before selling them on, often drugged or drunk, to other ships in need of crews. Some officers deliberately made life so unpleasant for a crew before entering port that the men would desert on arrival and so forfeit their accrued wages. This sordid business was intricately bound up with the operation of seamen's boarding houses and dockside taverns.

The 1876 Act dealt with the matter of unseaworthy ships. It permitted the positioning on each ship of Plimsoll's mark at the shipowner's discretion though its subsequent adjustment was forbidden.[9] Hopkins later recorded hearing the master of the *CALLIOPE* proposing to move his mark so that more cargo could be taken. A recent commission had found that many ships were lost through unseaworthiness but more were lost through unseaworthy crews, a state of affairs which could be blamed upon existing law, for good shipowners found little difficulty in crewing with able men and seldom felt the need to exercise their full powers. Where ships were found to be unseaworthy, this could, in many cases, be related to the increase in insurance of ships, and unseaworthy ships attracted poor crews.

A difficulty lay in defining what it meant to send a ship to sea 'wilfully' in a poor condition. Plimsoll argued that no ship should put to sea in an unseaworthy condition, wilfully or otherwise. There should be a system of inspection before departure: afterwards was too late. This need not mean that every ship should be inspected but only those which were unclassified at Lloyd's and similar registers. If a ship was to be detained, it cost the owners, for whom time was money. It was discussed whether crews could be protected by anonymity, like passengers, when reporting unseaworthiness. Plimsoll's experience had been to be sued for libel for naming a ship as unseaworthy and, since seamen could also be sued, the power to report unseaworthiness which had been adopted in 1871 had been withdrawn in 1873 as impractical.

The 1876 Act also dealt in detail with the matter of ships' provisions. Hopkins was to prosecute in a number of cases in Calcutta where poor provisions were involved. His own account of six-month-old pork in the cask, open in the tropics for weeks with only the brine being changed, will be given at the appropriate point. Plimsoll cited seven-year-old meat being returned to the naval dockyards at Gibraltar or Malta where it was sold off by the dockyards to parties who put it in fresh pickle before selling it on as stores to merchant ships. He threatened to buy some when it was next on sale at Plymouth or Portsmouth and send portions to every member of Her Majesty's Government, with a Benjamin's portion (i.e. the largest, from the Bible story) for the Prime Minister. He asked for the Board of Trade to check provisions.[10] Plimsoll was to continue his fight for better conditions for many years. There is a story that on one occasion, an old seaman presented Plimsoll with his dinner of dried salt junk (meat), which had been carved to represent a sailing ship, complete in every detail (a skill practised by many men of the time on this staple of their diet). He was to use it when campaigning about scurvy and its source: salt meat and lack of vegetables.

The 1876 Act included many items on which Hopkins and Havelock Wilson were to continue the campaign. In it, sending an unseaworthy ship to sea became a misdemeanour not punishable on summary conviction, meaning that it had to go to the Crown Court rather than magistrates. A survey could be ordered by the Board of

Trade and business conducted in open court, with costs against a guilty owner 'recoverable as salvage is recoverable'. It gave power to require of complainants security against frivolous complaints, but with no deposit required if a quarter of the crew (not less than three) complained. Owners' losses in consequence could be recovered from the complainant. These regulations applied even to foreign ships in British waters. It takes little imagination to see that a seaman would still be in a peculiar position if he did complain and why he would need the support of people like Hopkins to stand by him in his complaint. There remained the danger of owners closing ranks when a man who had complained sought further employment.

The 1876 Act also dealt with cargoes. In particular, grain cargoes, so liable to shift, and timber were regulated. Bow and load lines were to show the level of the deck above water. In short, many improvements were included in the Act and a comparison with Plimsoll's pamphlet reveals the measure of his success. He did not, however, stop campaigning, believing that the best protection for

Month	Railway servants	Miners	Factory & workshop operatives	Seamen
January	63	82	55	359
February	31	60	33	316
March	39	53	36	195
April	32	63	35	242
May	41	78	46	120
June	36	349	29	139

Industrial fatalities January-June 1894. Source: *Seamen's Chronicle*, 25th August, 1894.

seamen lay in fair legislation. Havelock Wilson was to assist him
in his later years, and, in part, assumed his parliamentary mantle.[11]
Hopkins, too, was to play his part. Once Hopkins started printing
his community magazine, *The Messenger*, more people were to
discover that this legislation, improvement that it was, was far from
satisfactory.

How successful was the legislation of 1854, 1876 and 1894?
Certainly some regulations did not in practice have the effect they
intended. For instance, the Act of 1854 required lime juice to be
provided as part of a man's rations as its anti-scorbutic effect was
in no doubt. The loss of man-hours aboard ship due to scurvy
was considerable. Nevertheless, so many owners bought the lime
juice required by this Act of such inferior quality or resorted to
its watering-down so readily that another Merchant Shipping Act
(1867) was necessary to require owners to buy lime juice from a
bonded warehouse to ensure quality and efficacy.[12] Despite this
further Act, the incidence of scurvy increased annually from 1873
because owners now reduced fresh provisions to offset the provision
of lime juice.

The 1876 Act tied up many loose ends but, as shown by Hopkins's
articles in *The Messenger* in 1893, it left work to be done. Its particular
weakness in the matter of the men's protection, both ashore and at
sea, has been illustrated. The seaman's financial position was little
improved. As regards pay, a man setting out on a two-year voyage
needed some means of getting money to his dependents during his
time away. Similarly, at the end of such a voyage, after paying-off a
man would be carrying a lot of money, making him an easy prey for
land sharks. Voluntary and statutory provision to meet this problem
has been presented in great detail by Kennerley.[13] It is also powerfully
demonstrated by comparing the seaman's industrial mortality rate
with that of workmen in other industries. The physical conditions
under which seamen laboured were always harsh. Some aspects of
life at sea could not be altered, such as storm or ice; others could.
The Seamen's Chronicle (25th August, 1894), the official organ of
the National Amalgamated Sailors' and Firemen's Union, gave these
figures for industrial fatalities during the first six months of the year
(chart on p. 23).[14]

That Hopkins's Order of St Paul was aware of the contents of
the *Chronicle* at this time is evidenced by a letter published by
the *Chronicle* from Brother Austin OSP on 10th November, 1894

(appealing for donations to help destitute sailors at Barry).

Two further areas affected by contemporary legislation need attention. The toughness of life at sea has been indicated, at least generally, above. That it affected all equally is only partly true; some were in a peculiar position: the apprentices. It will become apparent that Hopkins's ministry to sailors, at least in its early years and particularly in Rangoon, was especially to this group. They are also significant for the special legislation which related to them. The second area is connected and concerns the wider issue of training seafarers.[15]

Throughout the nineteenth century a debate had persisted whether government or owners should be responsible for training apprentices, young men training to be officers. In the early part of the century there was no requirement that an officer should be certificated. The government's interest in this came about because of the need of the Royal Navy to have access to a pool of trained men. The Merchant Navy needed its supply of officers to be constantly replenished too. An Act of 1835 required ships to carry apprentices in proportion to tonnage and, in 1849, compulsory apprenticeship was abolished. In 1845 there had been 15,704 apprentices but when the 1854 Act put the onus on owners, numbers of apprentices began to dwindle alarmingly: in 1894 there were only 2,164 according to the Registrar General's Returns. The 1876 Act required that apprentices be boys aged at least twelve and that they should be healthy and strong. A boy was to be bound to a master who 'is to be a proper person for the purpose', and must be brought before the master at the time of the crew's engagement. The boy's parents would usually pay £50 for his indentures. Of this, he would receive, as pay, £8 for the first year, £9 for the second, £10 for the third, and £13 for the final year. If his money restricted his activity, the indentures did so further. He could be required to do anything by the master whom he

> faithfully shall serve, his Secrets keep, his lawful com-
> mands everywhere gladly do.... He shall not commit
> fornication nor contract Matrimony ... he shall not play
> at Cards, Dice Tables or any other unlawful games,
> whereby his said master may have loss.

He might not buy or sell without permission, 'haunt Taverns, or Playhouses' and must furnish his own 'Sea Bedding, Wearing Apparel and other necessaries'.[16] He was neither seaman nor officer.

His hours of work, his free time, his instruction, his welfare, all depended upon the master. In a less than gentle age, the poor ship's apprentice was often the subject of great brutality. His only escape would be a few hours ashore, again at the whim of the master, where he had no friends, and plenty of people willing to take the little money he had. Small wonder that Hopkins's Indian priories were full of apprentices glad of a haven.

With regard to training, the link between bad seamen and lost ships was obvious and the 1873 commission had already highlighted bad seamanship as a significant factor in the total losses. Owners seldom lost out as their ships were well insured, but it was hard to argue against the need for good crews. Hugh Falkus summarised the changes brought about by legislation during the century:

> In the second half of the century a more rigorous approach was adopted towards the training of ship's officers. By 1888, for example, the Board of Trade standards required that a second mate be no younger than seventeen, but with four years at sea – so that sea-going at the age of thirteen was envisaged! The second mate, furthermore, had to be capable of finding his latitude from meridian altitude, and his longitude from sun sights and chronometer.[17]

In short, it will be seen that there was, behind Hopkins's efforts to better the lot of apprentices, a groundswell so that he is not to be seen as unique but rather as part of a general movement. His initial efforts seem to have been entirely independent of Plimsoll's campaign in Parliament, but Rangoon and Calcutta were well supplied with English newspapers, and both ports would have had ships with crews abuzz with news of those attempts at home to improve conditions of life at sea. Hopkins would surely have been encouraged, even prompted by this news. When it is discovered, as will be shown, that he initiated some thirty actions on behalf of seamen in the courts of Calcutta, the reader is only surprised that others were not doing the same. That, in spite of all the legislation, he could initiate thirty cases suggests that the denunciation of all shipowners by some Union activists was at least understandable. There were exceptional shipping owners, many of whom put by what they would have spent on insurance in order to spend it on their vessels, but for many, profit seems to have been the driving force.

The 1894 Merchant Shipping Act was a consolidation bill, an

amalgamation of all the many Acts of recent years into one tidier Act. It comprised 748 sections and twenty-two schedules, and absorbed the content of forty-eight statutes, which it repealed or amended.[18] It was the subject of much discussion in Parliament through 1893 and into 1894. A quick look at the index in *Hansard* shows how many horror stories were brought forward even during its passage. One will suffice to illustrate the point that, despite the progress which had been made in the area of seamen's welfare since Plimsoll's original bill, much remained to be done. On 10th July, 1894 the House of Commons heard of the case of the *HELVETIA*, sadly by no means unusual. Three days earlier the Cardiff Stipendiary Magistrate had condemned the captain of the *HELVETIA* for prematurely abandoning his ship, suspended his certificate for two years and censured the *HELVETIA*'s owner. The ship, twenty-nine years old, had been bought for £5,000. After being laid up for twelve months she was insured for 'a sum much in excess of her cost and value' and then sent to sea without survey or repair. Within five days of sailing she was in great danger off Cornwall. She signalled for tugs. Her owner and agents were telegraphed and telegraphed again, both messages being ignored. Finally, after twelve hours she was towed into Cardiff with 15 feet of water in her hold. She was surveyed and repaired (superficially in the court's opinion) and her insurance increased. She put to sea again, only to be abandoned 'under suspicious circumstances' three days later and 'is supposed to have ultimately foundered', the evidence by now being at the bottom of the sea.

Hopkins, the Seamen's Union and the Shipping Federation

My references to the 'Union', capitalised to ensure it is not confused with another union, hide three successive manifestations of the same organisation that began as the National Amalgamated Sailors' and Firemen's Union of Great Britain and Ireland, founded at a public meeting on 18th August, 1887 and eventually became the National Union of Seamen. It started in the North East of England when Havelock Wilson, after a spell at sea, became very active within a Sunderland union which, due to contemporary attitudes and legislation, was more of a protection and benefit society than one which campaigned. Havelock Wilson extended the number of branches of this Sunderland union, trying to bring them and some of the other

few existing unions into one organisation.[19] Local committees felt
that this was going too far, so Havelock Wilson, determined that
there should be a national union for seamen, founded one with the
lengthy title given above. The Union's telegraphic address kept pace
with these changes. Originally it was AGITATORS, LONDON but
by 1910 it had modified to SEAROVING.LONDON.

The Union had from its earliest days been connected with
individual clergy. At a general meeting on 26th September, 1887,
an invitation from the local incumbent, The Rev. Edgar Lambert,
to 'the Continued Harvest Thanksgiving on Wednesday night' was
accepted and prayers were said in the Union reading rooms, which
were sometimes sublet to Mr Lambert.[20] The North East was an
area where Havelock Wilson was well known, and it is not without
interest that it was to be in the North East that the North of England
Steamship Owners' Association created the breakthrough in the 1911
strike. It may be significant that the Union was formed at just the time
when Hopkins was being moved in Burma from Rangoon to Akyab
because of his stormy relationship with the local shipowners. That is
to say, his organisation and the Union were developing concurrently
and it may have helped Hopkins in later years to appreciate what
Havelock Wilson had achieved and how, and the necessity for his
achievement.

The 1880s were a significant period in union development.
Before 1871 there had been the legal freedom to organise but no
corresponding freedom to pursue the objectives of trade unionism.
'The mere threat to strike was held to be "molestation", "intimidation"
or "obstruction" of an employer engaged in his lawful business'.[21]
Now there was a rapid growth of 'New Unions' (a 'method of mutual
insurance' as the Webbs called it[22]) with a centralised and business-
like financial administration and firm control by the executive over
strikes and strike pay. Centralisation of control within the new
unions also made greater co-ordination among them possible. In
other words, new unionism, of which Havelock Wilson's foundation
was a manifestation, was a foretaste of the type of unionism which is
familiar today and ceased to be purely a benefit society.

Havelock Wilson's infant Union was beset by many difficulties
which were – and are – peculiar to seamen. Others had found
before him that men who were likely to disappear at any time and
remain away, sometimes for years, were difficult to organise. There
was also the problem of who could be a member in an hierarchical

industry: did all seamen include the officers? There was no right of membership conceded by the shipowners and it took a brave supporter to carry the Union message to his shipmates when his job might be lost for supporting the Union. If it was hard to recruit members, the exercise of control was harder yet. The seamen's Union was forced to rely more than any other union on the paid official. This meant a constant drain on its hard-to-collect finances. It was in the role of a local organiser that Hopkins had first been in touch with Havelock Wilson, writing from Calcutta. At their first meeting in London some five or six years later Havelock Wilson had hoped to recruit Hopkins as a local Union organiser before realising his identity and Hopkins seems at first to have adopted that role. G.D.H. Cole was to write,

> it is reasonable to say that in or about 1889 Trade Unionism became, for the first time since the collapse of 1834, a movement open to every kind of manual worker, with a tendency to spread beyond manual trades into the field of blackcoat and professional employment. [23]

That said, it is a fact that almost no ship's officers became members of the Union.

1889 was the year of the great Dock Strike. It was at this time that Ben Tillett, Tom Mann and Tom McCarthy came to the fore as organisers and Havelock Wilson gained their acquaintance in his support for the 1889 Dock Strike through money, men and oratory. He gained too the respect of Tom Mann, who disagreed with many of his ideas, but was to become a valued helper during the 1911 strike. The seamen's Union had started with a membership of a few thousand. Numbers were always difficult to give with accuracy. The paid-up membership was easy to define but failed to differentiate between those who were unable to pay because of absence at sea, sometimes for several years, and those whose membership had lapsed through a conscious but unrecorded decision to leave the Union. At the end of the Dock Strike the seamen's Union claimed 65,000 members. The figure varies according to the method of calculation but, even if short of the real figure, nevertheless suggests a remarkable growth. [24] Unfortunately, it was not a figure which the Union was able to maintain. The Dock Strike started in August 1889, having been preceded by more local and less successful actions. [25] There had been some 500 strikes in the preceding year in the United Kingdom and in the docks, particularly at Tilbury where there had been a strike of some 500 men on 22nd October, 1888. Recent successes by seamen in a number of docks is thought to have given the strike impetus. In turn, the Dock Strike encouraged seamen to join their Union. Tillett, the strike leader, had been a merchant seaman and already knew Havelock Wilson. It is significant that Hopkins was present in the East End of London at this period of unrest which, although it included Will Thorne and his gas workers, revolved around that industry in which Hopkins was most involved.[26] On his return to Calcutta, Hopkins apparently wrote to Havelock Wilson about starting a Calcutta branch of the Union.[27]

If the Union in 1889 stood alongside the other main unions of the period, Havelock Wilson's independent line ensured that that would not remain the case. As the labour movement associated itself increasingly with socialism, Havelock Wilson remained an unreconstructed Liberal. Nor was his Union's increased number of members maintained. As a direct result of the 1889 strike the owners formed the Shipping Federation on 2nd September, 1890 and began to bring very considerable pressure to bear upon the seamen's Union. Havelock Wilson was hard pressed to keep it intact in the face of this new opposition. The Federation pressed him financially by, for example, getting creditors to call in debts or by questioning the lack of accounts, a method which served the Federation well over the years.[28] It also used its influence throughout the docks and allied industries where it was the principal employer through its members. It was to bring in restrictive conditions, such as the requirement to sign-on at the Federation office and the introduction of Federation medical tests, which in 1911 would become negotiating points. It used its considerable weight in Parliament, where a number of its members had seats,[29] to influence legislation, giving Plimsoll a hard time in his fight to obtain improved conditions for seamen through the legislative process. It issued its own ticket, which became a powerful means of control, carrying with it various benefits to the man who sold, in the Union's view, himself to the Federation. It also imported where necessary large numbers of blacklegs to break up strikes and always retained the threat to employ cheap labour from abroad. It did not hesitate to take Havelock Wilson to court, his first appearance being in April 1889 for attempting to persuade two seamen to desert. In 1893 Havelock Wilson told Parliament that the Federation acted in an illegal manner, employing people to libel leaders of trade unions and to join workmen's organisations to create dissension in the ranks. He accused the Federation of paying men to lie on oath at his trial in Cardiff in 1891 where he was accused of incitement to riot and unlawful assembly. That Havelock Wilson was of a litigious disposition is clear, for he initiated a number of cases and not always wisely. This was a serious drain on Union finances but, in his defence, in many of those cases he was a man sorely provoked. In this he was doing the same thing at the same time as Hopkins in Calcutta. There is no doubt that the Federation was out to 'get' Havelock Wilson.

Havelock Wilson's reluctance to publish accounts may have been as much to do with not wishing to reveal to the Federation his true membership figure as with their parlous condition. They were parlous, partly because of the shortage of money coming in but also because, it would seem, of poor bookkeeping. In young unions, short on leadership, what leadership there was often lacked financial expertise and made an easy target. In Havelock Wilson's case, he was working all hours just to keep the Union in existence. In danger of being sued by serious creditors in 1894, he suddenly placed the Union into voluntary liquidation to avoid giving the Federation the pleasure of doing it for him. Within a very short time he had reconstituted the Union, this time as the National Sailors' and Firemen's Union of Great Britain and Ireland (NSFU). It was in this union that Hopkins would take his place. The Union's third change of name, to the National Union of Seamen, lay well beyond Hopkins's lifetime. Today it has been subsumed into a larger transport union.

The next two decades of trade union history were to bring significant changes to all unions, with adjustment first to the Taff Vale Judgment and then to the Osborne Judgment. However, by 1910 there were some two million trade union members nationally representing something like every fifth man involved in manual labour, though considerably fewer women. A number of trades had a much higher density of union membership than the seamen. Indeed, because the seamen's Union had such a scattered membership it was hard for it to find a place among the other, land-based, unions. An increasing militancy is detectable throughout the period, and is revealed also in the emergence of the Labour Party (1906).[30] In part it can be traced to the spread of syndicalism, which is associated with the name of Tom Mann. Where unions had attempted to build up strength through their reserves and through collective bargaining, syndicalism advocated direct action and the general strike, with unions organised to seize power from the State. Though it is important to note the movement, it had little effect upon the seamen, except to distance the NSFU further from other unions, partly because of Havelock Wilson's style of leadership and partly because of the difficulty of organising a scattered membership. Hermann Jochade of the ITWF believed that syndicalism played no part in the NSFU and thought that it would find little wider recognition, arguing instead for centralism to meet the threat of the centrally organised shipowners.[31] In later years Havelock Wilson was often accused of being in the shipowners' pocket, mainly because he consistently argued for collective bargaining rather than direct action. The conciliation board, which Havelock Wilson had campaigned for since the inception of the Union, was intended to be an important instrument for collective bargaining. It needs to be said, though, that whole-industry unionism was rendered impracticable amongst seamen because of the divisions between officers and men.

The effect of the 1911 strike upon the NSFU was dramatic. According to one source, NSFU membership rose from a doubtful 55,000 in June 1911 to 160,000 by the end of August and 220,000 by the spring of 1912. For a union which had limped along with a membership of thousands and with many of those members overdue in their payment of union dues because of absence abroad, this was success indeed.[32] *The Seaman* (January 1912) quoted Edmund Cathery, general secretary, at the NSFU Annual Meeting as saying that the NSFU had added 77,000 new members in the whole of 1911 and that 'I am closing the year without any financial worry and with a substantial balance at our bankers'. Different sources give different totals of membership but all agree that the increase had been substantial. This was a novel situation for a union which had gone bankrupt in the 1890s and narrowly avoided liquidation on frequent and more recent occasions. Tupper claimed that when Havelock Wilson had recruited him just before the 1911 strike the Union had £6..13s in the bank.[33] Cathery's estimate of new members since the start of the strike on 14th June, 1911 is probably more reliable if less sensational and stands at 35,000, giving a weekly increase of income from £150 to over £1,000. He could also argue that sailors' wages had increased eight or ten pounds a month, a state of affairs which some would dispute and which failed to persist into 1912.[34]

The demand for a conciliation board was not an original one. The railwaymen had fought long and hard to achieve one. Ernest Bevin in

Bristol in 1911, when his dockers' union was a year old, was able to tell his AGM in September 1911 that he had, within six months, got the employers and workers together to form a joint arbitration board for the carters; within the same year he managed a similar agreement for the warehousemen.[35] Seamen were familiar with dock politics and could see what ought to be possible. The NSFU's principal aim in being recognised was the establishment of such a conciliation board. The Federation was very keen not to grant one precisely because it would be tantamount to recognition of the NSFU. A united workforce was not to its liking. Havelock Wilson's earliest approach to the Federation for some sort of agreement seems to have been in early 1891, but the Federation's response is not recorded.[36] The Federation had been formed by a majority of the leading shipowners after the 1889 Dock Strike when the embryonic Union had flexed its muscles and owners had found that it had a certain strength. In the ensuing years the Federation had used every opportunity to discredit the Union and its founder. At one point, Havelock Wilson did spend six weeks in jail, but largely through his own litigation.[37] He also spent some months recruiting members in America in a successful attempt to avoid British creditors. Over the years the battle had been a hard one, not least in Parliament, where Havelock Wilson had become MP for Middlesbrough. By the time of Hopkins's death, a quasi-conciliation board had been achieved.

Hopkins and the Church of England

Hopkins is peculiar among significant religious figures in that little evidence of his religious upbringing survives. I have failed to trace details of his baptism. He never mentions a conversion experience, or a particular turning point. However, his continuation in the Church despite his experience of its official face speaks eloquently of his commitment. For a time he was in demand as a preacher, but little survives from his sermons. Apart from his involvement in the production of the OSP's *Prayer Book for Catholic Seamen*, which has to be assumed from his signature, it has to be admitted that we have more clues to indicate his political views than his religious ones. Frustrating as this is, it is necessary to remember that here was a man who could fill a church with sailors receiving Holy Communion; here too was a religious and the founder of a religious community.

It is quite clear that he was an advanced High Churchman. In Burma he ordered eucharistic vestments, introduced a *Missa Cantata* and encouraged the use of the confessional (perhaps a source of irritation to his bishop). It is tempting to source this churchmanship to his Cornish upbringing; Cornwall as a county tended towards Anglo-Catholicism, offset by a strong Methodist tradition. However, he could just as easily have discovered ritualism in London while at Trinity College. Perhaps his welcome on his return to London hints at this. His friendship with his archdeacon and with Dr John Marks, whose churchmanship was less advanced than his own but nevertheless highly developed, suggests that here was no narrowness. Marks translated the *Book of Common Prayer* into Burmese. Either or both were, like Hopkins, strongly attached to the *Book of Common Prayer*, though Hopkins was sometimes (unfairly, for there is not a shred of evidence) accused of Romanism. His *Prayer Book for Catholic Seamen* is very similar to one produced by Lord Halifax's circle, the *English Catholic Prayer Book*, perhaps the use of common material saving the re-invention of the wheel. That, too, pointed away from Rome.[38]

Clergy of the Church of England in the colonies were less bound by the traditions and canons of the English church. Bishops were fewer to offend and at a greater distance. People abroad could not invoke the Public Worship Acts which limited in England what could be done with the liturgy. The Diocese of Rangoon received grants from the SPG, and Hopkins subsequently from the St Andrew's Waterside Mission, both of which organisations were in the Anglo-Catholic mould. Once he had established his community, his chapels would have been extra-diocesan, allowing freedom to follow the tradition of his choice.

As a founder of a religious order he falls within a Christian minority. The only answer to why he founded a religious order will be shown, initially, to have been expediency. None of the limited number of Anglican communities of the time, some of whom helped him in his work, provided the structure he sought. His time in Burma introduced him to a few Roman Catholic orders but in the most part his contacts were with Anglicans. He stayed with the (Anglican) Brotherhood of the Epiphany on his way back to England, in India he met the (Anglican) Cowley Fathers and the (Anglican) Clewer Sisters were responsible for the Calcutta hospital to which he was chaplain. The real puzzle is why he should make his profession in one of the most obscure of Anglican orders, that of St Paul, a small and ephemeral parish brotherhood. Nor is it clear why for his own Rule he should turn to the Rule of St Benedict when more active models were available, for example, in the Franciscans and Dominicans and a wealth of nineteenth-century French foundations. The Benedictine tradition of hospitality can hardly be a sufficient explanation. A small clue might be his friendship with Fr Ignatius OSB of Llanthony, whom he was known to admire and who, like Marks, was something of an ecclesiastical gadfly, though much further from the establishment, having put himself beyond the pale by accepting Holy Orders from a 'wandering' bishop.

Hopkins, on arriving in Hampshire, was careful to obtain the diocesan bishop's approval in the correct way. As his local Bishop (later Archbishop) Randall Davidson sat on the Church of England's Commission charged with examining the religious life in preparation for the Lambeth Conference of 1897, he might be supposed to have been sympathetic. Such was not the case, and Davidson's response curtailed Hopkins's ministry and prevented the ordination of other OSP members. This the bishop was able to do under the Colonial Clergy Act. Many of Hopkins's troubles can be traced to this Act. It was intended to prevent men from going abroad to be ordained under conditions sometimes less than stringent and then returning home to a comfortable benefice in the gift of the family, without first fulfilling certain conditions. Anyone not having held an English curacy or other preferment required the written permission of either archbishop (Canterbury or York) to minister in England and Wales at all. Such permission was only granted if the minister in question assented to the Thirty-nine Articles and the *Book of Common Prayer*, the use of which was also a prerequisite. Any further preferment required the diocesan bishop's written approval and a previously held curacy or equivalent in England or Wales of at least two years: effectively a process of incardination. Failure to observe these conditions, for example by preaching in a church without episcopal approval, would attract fines on the preacher of £10 and on the incumbent of the church preached in £10. Where examples survive of the sums taken in collection when Hopkins was preaching, they often fail to reach the amount which would have been the fine. There was also the question of taking the Oath of Allegiance to the sovereign, but since Hopkins's recognition had not reached this point, the problem of American citizenship, which was still his, did not arise. Where he had only been visiting England to raise funds and recruits his Letters Commendatory sufficed, requiring only the archbishop's signature for a limited period. The appropriate chapter details the consequences.

The revival of the religious life in the Church of England has been dealt with at length by Peter Anson.[39] Early communities picked their Rules from where they would, according to expediency. When Hopkins founded his order it was for practical reasons, whereas most of his contemporary founders, doing their founding in England, felt that they were restoring to the Church of England an essential part of its Catholicity which had been lost at the Reformation. Nevertheless he was part of a general movement: almost contemporary with his foundation were, among the orders for men, the Society of the Divine Compassion, founded in 1894 in the East End of London, and the Caldey (as they became after starting in London's Isle of Dogs) Benedictines of 1896. As male foundations went, Hopkins's was sixth in the revival.

1

Early Contacts with Sailors

Charles Plomer Hopkins was born in Brewster, Massachusetts, probably at the home of his paternal grandparents (an address presently unknown) on 7th March, 1861.[1] His American origins would catch up with him briefly in 1907 in an unexpected way, but otherwise impacted little on his life, for he was never to visit the country again. His father, Charles, an American, was described in 1860 as a mariner and later as a master mariner, probably with an American ticket. From the mid 1860s he worked at Bassein in Burma as one of eight river pilots. His mother, Elizabeth Jane Plomer Roberts, was English, hailing from Cornwall. The Plomer in her children's baptismal entries is sometimes given the alternative spelling of Plummer, which indicates its pronunciation. Plomer was a family name from her side of the family, usually given to the eldest son.

CPH's parents were married in the Falmouth parish church of Charles, King and Martyr, on 1st January, 1860. The church register gives Elizabeth's age as seventeen and Charles's as 'full', meaning over twenty-one. It looks like a tale of the young girl swept off her feet by a handsome sailor. Whatever the circumstances, she married with her father's approval, for he signed the register as a witness. Charles is described as a bachelor, the son of Edward Hopkins, mechanic; Elizabeth is noted as a spinster, the daughter of Samuel Plomer Roberts, salesman (though succeeding census details suggest a succession of jobs). The officiating clergyman was the rector, The Rev. W.J. Coope, a priest of sufficiently advanced churchmanship to alter the register to the effect that they were married, not as the register would have it, 'according to the Rites and Ceremonies of the Established Church', but 'of the Catholic Church'. The wedding, however, was undoubtedly Anglican. Coope recorded that they were married by licence (the groom, as a sailor, would have had difficulty establishing the residence required by banns), writing it in the space for banns. A question arises over his recording of Charles as a bachelor, as there is a family tradition that Charles was a widower. If the tradition is correct, it would explain the existence of Mary Ann, described as CPH's older (by about five years) sister, who will appear later as an important presence in his life.

Few details survive from CPH's early life other than those in his own memoir.[2] It is possible to check details of his several voyages[3] and also to a lesser extent of his schooling.[4] Before he was a year old, he was brought from Brewster to England, to settle for a while in Falmouth, near his mother's relatives. Then in June 1867 his mother, together with the three[5] children, Mary Ann (probably born 1856), Charles, and younger sister Margaret ('Maggie'),[6] boarded the *HELENSLIE* in Glasgow to join their father in Bassein. Burma was to be his parents' home for many years.

The passage to Rangoon via the Cape of Good Hope took roughly 140 days; the excitement of a six-year-old, one used to seeing the ships at Falmouth, actually to find himself on board one and bound for his first big adventure, may be imagined. Six years old is too young to comprehend the time and distance at sea, or the mystery of Burma, but probably old enough to know that he was going to see his father. The *HELENSLIE* was a sailing ship able to carry a small number of passengers. Her outward cargo was a general one. Her return cargo would be rice, loaded in Rangoon, in sacks destined for Bremen. The young Charles would see more of the life of the crew as a passenger on a cargo ship than he would if the ship had been primarily for passengers. The ship sailed from Glasgow on 2nd June, arriving in Burma on 20th November, 1867.

In 1869 it was decided that Charles and Mary Ann were to be sent back to England for their education. Their time together away from their parents would account for their closeness in later years. Mary appears in Hopkins's story repeatedly, even after her marriage, when she would become Mrs Baker. The pair travelled from Burma on the *GEOLOGIST*, taking cargo from Bassein (his father's port as river pilot) to Cork. CPH would later speak of the kindness of the men in the foc's'le who sang and danced to amuse him and to lift the sadness of this, his first journey without either parent. As an adult he would write of the important bearing this voyage had on his later concern for the welfare of seamen.

What can be discovered of this voyage? It was in no way unusual for children to be sent home from the colonies for their education. Where such children became, later, the subject of a biography, it would be unusual for the biographer to examine the voyage to England in any detail. However, this was no ordinary voyage: it was to colour the whole of CPH's career. An examination of the *GEOLOGIST*'s official log shows that it had sailed from London via Hong Kong for Burma. The experiences of the crew, according to that log, were ones which CPH, in later life, would find all too familiar. Henry Coppin, the ship's carpenter, accidentally fell overboard and was drowned on 4th November, 1869. Sailor Frederick Lister caught fever, was treated 'according to the direction given in the Ship's Captain's Medical Guide', but died after 23 days of suffering. Lister's burial, at the mouth of the Bassein River on 2nd June, 1870 was witnessed by the young Charles.

Towards Cork, the aptly named Able Seaman Richard Shipman was logged for

> misconduct such as swearing, whistling, singing and dancing during his watch on deck, and when the rest were at work, also for the dilatory manner in which he has throughout continued, and still continues to carry out any order … has never once been punished, fearing a worse result, deeming it prudent for the interest to bear with it as much as possible ….

Shipman had been logged on the voyage out, in January, as being sick and unfit for work with swelled testicles. CPH's recollection of the level of violence on board makes it a possibility that the swelled testicles resulted from some roughly administered form of 'justice' rather than the after-effects of a visit ashore. Perhaps Edwin Foster, second mate, recipient of much of Shipman's behaviour, administered punishment which failed to find its way into the log. Then, Shipman was logged again, this time with more detail, for endangering the ship by failing to sound the ship's foghorn at five-minute intervals in a visibility of less than the ship's length.

A ship's log is an official record. Entries in it are supposed to be accurate, entered by agreement, witnessed if necessary. Before being entered in the log ('logged'), which was a last resort, a man would have been disciplined in less formal ways by the mates. A 'bully' captain might give short shrift to a crew member's objections to such informal punishment where a fairer man would abide by the

Person logged	Number of entries
Lister's illness and death	25
Shipman's behaviour	11
Shipman's illness	9
Coppins' death	2
Reprimands to Allen	5
Misbehaviour of Johnson & Mills	3
Reprimands to Hall	2
Reprimands to Meehan	7
Reprimands to Macaulay	4
Reprimand to Brown	1

A summary of sixty-eight entries in the *GEOLOGIST*'s log for this voyage

law and admit them to the log. For Shipman, perhaps, one could read Everyman! A summary of sixty-eight entries in the *GEOLOGIST*'s log for this voyage makes for interesting reading.[7]

In one entry Mills admitted stealing one of the ship's fowls intended for the saloon table. This need not indicate a 'hungry ship' but the other entries confirm that it was a 'hard' one: Charlie Wills, logged on 4th December, 1869 as having 'knocked down the Mate and gripped him by the throat in a very brutal manner', declared 'he would rather be in prison for 3 months than in such a floating workhouse as this...'. Supposing the log's assertion that the attack was unprovoked to be correct, the reader remains with the impression that the *GEOLOGIST* was, at least with this crew, not a happy ship.

Hopkins, more than once and many years later, wrote of this

voyage in a way which suggested its etching into his memories of childhood. This extract from *The Messenger* (August 1899) is indicative of his state of mind and of what had then impressed this river pilot's son:

> Most of my early childhood was spent among ships and sailors. The circumstances of my birth made something of a sailor of me, and these voyages placed me in a truly nautical atmosphere, and made a regular little wanderer of me at a very early and impressionable age. Shall I ever forget saying goodbye to mother and father, as the ship's boat lay ready at the landing stage to take my little sister and myself off to the great ship which was to carry us away to live among strangers for years and years? And shall I ever forget the great large-hearted tenderness of the big grizzly bearded horny-handed seamen as they handed me up the gangway of the *GEOLOGIST*, and afterwards tried in a hundred different ways to ease my little heart of its great aching, and to wipe away the tears that would come, though I tried so hard to keep them back. For had I not promised mother to be a 'little man'? In this, my first great trouble, the sailors helped me on my way.

Hopkins senior, as a river pilot, should, and probably would, have been well aware of the reputations of the visiting masters and their ships, and taken account of them when finding a ship to convey his children. Children were often sent back to England, both for their education and their health. Burma was considered a very unhealthy place, especially for children, to the point where eyebrows might be raised at their remaining with their parents. What may have been slightly unusual was the decision of these parents to send only the two oldest children to England for their education. The 'little sister' of whom Hopkins wrote would have been around thirteen at this time, a seniority which may well have been a source of comfort, both to his parents as they left the pair on board ship and to the lonely Hopkins on this voyage.

Hopkins wrote also of his impressions aboard the *GEOLOGIST*. He witnessed the burial of Henry Coppins at the mouth of the Bassein River on 2nd June, 1870. In 1899 Hopkins wrote,

I was not supposed to associate with the men for'ard,
but I did. And on the occasion of one of my stolen
visits, I discovered this man lying in his bunk. He told
me he was 'very bad'; and as I knelt on the sea- chest
at the side of his bunk, he put up his hand and touched
my face. What for, I didn't know. I know now. He
was hungry for a little sympathy and love. I promised
him some biscuits and sweets, for mother had put a
big consignment on board for me, and then crept away.
But my good intentions were frustrated by one of the
officers; and didn't I hate him for it ....
The sick man had been brought forward, and had been
placed in one of the cabin state rooms; for by then those
in authority had realised that he was seriously ill, and
I was able to get to him more easily.... With two nice
little packets in my hands, I got into my friend's cabin. I
had given him what I had promised, and had just pushed
the packets under his pillow, when the loud voice of the
officer roared:'What are you doing in here youngster?'
Then, without waiting for a reply, he put his hand under
the pillow and drew out the two packets, and promptly
threw them out of the open port. And I crept away and
had a good cry.... Then I was told that he was dead, but
I was not allowed to see him until they brought the body
out on the deck, already sewed up in canvas ready for
burial. Then I ... kept my eyes on the Union Jack which
covered the body. Then suddenly they seemed to tilt it
up and let it go, and I saw it shoot out from the side of
the ship and sink.

No doubt the officers were not pleased to have a river pilot's son
to keep an eye on as an extra duty; nor want him contracting fever,
the causes of which were still not understood, if that was Coppins's
complaint; nor yet disturbing a sick man. A small boy would not have
appreciated this and the strength of Hopkins's feelings remained
with him into adulthood and are reflected in this article. It may be
this experience which lay behind the elaborate funeral rites he would
prescribe for members of his future seamen's guild. However, here
Hopkins was writing to wring the hearts and pockets of genteel
landsfolk and may be forgiven for writing his story to the best effect.

Allowing for all of this, the impression of a 'hard' ship is confirmed by further details from the log. A later entry, whilst the ship was discharging in Bassein on 26th March, 1870, concerns Ordinary Seaman John Meehan who

> proceeded after some delay at 6.00 p.m.... to flatly refuse to do any more. When stopped by the Mate from coming down the gangway, Meehan ran and took a belaying pin from the Mizzen mast, swearing and making a rush at the Mate, saying he would 'stave the Mate's skull in'.

The mate warded off the blow. However, on 3rd May Meehan was up before the captain and the Port Commissioner, complaining that the mate had slapped him in the face. He was fined for persistent insolence and subsequently deserted ship along with Macauley. A 'hard' ship, indeed. Hopkins traced his concern for the men of the sea to his time spent on this ship. These log entries explain all too well why the voyage should have made such an impression on him. This was the ship which brought him to England and to school.

A few details of Hopkins's schooling survive. That he was returned to Cornwall is certain, as is the fact that he received his schooling there. It has always been understood that Hopkins was sent back to Cornwall so that he could stay with his mother's family, with whom he had previously stayed as a small child along with his mother, rather than with strangers. This understanding is entirely logical and nothing, such as the unhappiness Rudyard Kipling and many other children of Empire sent home for their education remembered, survives in his later writing to suggest that this was a specially unhappy time. He seems to have entered Falmouth Grammar School at the age of eight. It is not known whether this was through another's patronage or with his fees paid by his parents. It would not be unreasonable to wonder if the decision to send only the first two children home for their education might have been prompted by a kind offer from within the family to educate the pair.

In fact, we have no record of a family offer of any kind. Instead, according to the 1871 census, Hopkins was boarded, along with his sister, at 2 Dunstanville Villas in the Budock area of Falmouth and within walking distance of the school. At this address he was the only male in the household and the youngest member by a couple

Dunstanville Villas on Falmouth
Harbour front. No. 2 is on the left.
(Source: author.)

of years. He was in the care of the householder, Jane Martin, aged sixty-two in 1871, described as a school mistress, and her daughter Ellen, aged thirty-two, described as a teacher of music. The entry does not indicate whether they taught at the Grammar School. Apart from his sister Mary Ann and himself, the other boarders were a Cornish girl, Nellie Bunt, Mary Ann's junior by one year, and Bertha Phillips from London, two years older than young Charles. There was a resident general servant, Bessie Smith. As the youngest member of the household and the only male, Hopkins may have had a gentler treatment than might otherwise have been the case. It is tempting to wonder what part thirteen years away from his family in an all-female environment played in his later foundation of the Order of St Paul, effectively a family substitute. And might the presence of a music teacher in the household be what led him to an organ console in Rangoon, so many years later?

The briefest record of his school time survives in his obituary in the school magazine which says only that he

> received his early education at the school…. Few of us
> knew him as an Old Boy, but still we all take our hats
> off to one who so gloriously enhanced the traditions of
> our school….

Falmouth Grammar School was not ancient. It had been founded in the early part of the nineteenth century, supported by the subscribers whose sons it educated. The school had all but foundered until rescued by a clergyman named Bennett, the long-serving headmaster of Hopkins's school days. There is nothing to suggest where, if anywhere, Mary Ann was educated. The school was divided into four forms with pupils joining or leaving the school at no prescribed age. The number of pupils was not great, probably under a hundred, of whom forty were boarders (the latter being a useful source of income for the headmaster). Perhaps Hopkins was not numbered among those boarders to keep him together with Mary Ann, but their presence in the school means that his own status as a boarder – albeit elsewhere – would not have marked him out as unusual. The school afforded a significant amount of its timetable to Scripture. Pupils also studied English, Mathematics, Drawing, History and Geography, with the opportunity to add French, German, Latin and Greek, as the school claimed. There is some evidence from Hopkins's later correspondence that he studied German, probably here, but also in Heidelberg after leaving school. His later need for coaching in Greek when in Rangoon suggests that ancient languages did not feature in his timetable. The headmaster circulated local newspapers every December with the names of the school's prize winners, together with the reports of visiting examiners and the names of pupils successfully gaining admission to Oxford or Cambridge universities. Pupils were listed by surname, undistinguished even by an initial. The name Hopkins appears in 1875 as the winner of Class Four's second prize for French, a prize which brought the reward of 3s..6d for its recipient, and in second place again for the school Drawing Prize (7s..6d); in 1877 as winning the Class One Drawing Prize and the school Essay Prize. If this Hopkins is 'our' Hopkins, it is likely that he left the school around the age of sixteen, for his name appears in no subsequent prize list.

Falmouth may hold the key to Hopkins's later religious views. At the time of his arrival in the town the incumbent of the parish church, scene of his parents' marriage, was still The Rev. W.J. Coope, who was the officiant at that ceremony. He was now on sick leave with his services conducted by his assistant curates in a manner prescribed by Coope. Coope was receiving considerable publicity for his ritualism in the *Falmouth and Penryn Weekly Times*, the paper describing his church as 'among the most notorious of the Tractarian churches of the West of England' and Coope as 'an advanced Puseyite'. The Hopkins children for whom baptismal records have been found (Charles not among them) were all baptised in the Church of England, though it seems his mother was of Baptist stock,[8] so Hopkins may be supposed to have been sent or taken to the parish church, where the 'fantastic extreme of ritual' (the Easter High Mass as described was particularly splendid) would surely attract his attention. Coope was followed as rector in July 1870 by his son-in-law, The Rev. J. Baly, a more moderate man who, the paper reported, 'has views upon Church government and Church doctrine different from those which for many years alienated... the inhabitants of Falmouth'. His services attracted such numbers that seating, within a month of his arrival, became a problem. In 1872, Baly left the parish to become Archdeacon of Calcutta (a position he no longer occupied by the time Hopkins accepted the Calcutta port chaplaincy).

The local newspaper is a fair barometer when assessing the atmosphere in ecclesiastical Falmouth, which was typical, if rather more extreme, of ecclesiastical Cornwall. The Established Church showed a strong Tractarian (sometimes called 'High' church) influence in the face of a range of popular nonconformity; the Baptists, Congregationalists and various types of Methodist (Methodism was strong in Cornwall) were much in evidence in the town. By 1878 the town again had an absentee incumbent, successor to Mr Baly. The rector drew a generous salary of £700 a year from special Town Rates so his absence added nothing to his popularity. The relationship between town, absent rector and congregation had deteriorated, as reported in the local paper, to a point where an assistant curate, chairing a meeting to solve the church's music problems, was told firmly by those present that no money would be forthcoming unless the rector, who could well afford it, was prepared to head a list of subscribers. This was the talk of the town just about the time Hopkins was leaving school and Falmouth for further study (presumably of the organ) at Trinity College of Music in London. There is no record of his being anywhere near the Falmouth parish church organ console but it is hard to believe that his first attempts on the instrument were not undertaken here, with or without a resident organist.

There is another point of interest in Falmouth: the Royal Cornwall Sailors' Home (BFSS). The local papers recorded the work of the Shipwrecked Mariners' Society and of The Missions to Seamen (for the Church of England) Harbour Chaplain, details of whose annual meetings were reported regularly. In 1877, Agnes Weston, variously called the Sailors' Friend or the mother of the Royal Navy, was billed to speak at the Town Hall. None of this is surprising in a maritime town; 'Falmouth for orders' was a common instruction to ships awaiting precise orders in the days before radio. It meant,

however, that Falmouth's inhabitants, perhaps even the young
Hopkins, would be unusually aware of the agencies for welfare work
among seafarers.

His time in Falmouth seems to have been followed by a spell in
Germany, perhaps to consolidate the German he had learned at school,
perhaps to study music, for by this time his musical ability must have
been apparent. His obituary in the London *Times* mentions without
explanation a visit to Osnabruck, while his obituary in *The Seaman*
refers to Heidelberg. A photograph at Alton Abbey of the young, fresh-
faced Hopkins has the mark of a Heidelberg photographer. How long
he was there is not known, nor is the date of his return to London where
The Seaman's obituary has him studying music at Trinity College.
There is no reason to doubt this claim but it has not been possible to
confirm as Trinity College has no records for this period.

His time in London seems to have finished sometime in 1882,
which is the first year he is listed as resident in Rangoon. He, or others
for him, had obtained the post of organist at Rangoon Cathedral. It
is hard to imagine what his bond with his parents might be after such
a long absence but his return to Rangoon must surely have been
prompted by a desire to revisit what was, in his mind at least, home.
It is not said whether Mary Ann returned at the same time. We might
wonder if it felt at times to Mary and Charles as if they had been
cast aside as news came of the arrival of yet another brother or sister.
Their contact in the intervening years with 'home' would largely
have been by letter. Perhaps regular letters shortened the distance
between parents and children. Their mother had been in England
in 1880⁹ with three of their younger siblings, so it is possible to
imagine some sort of reunion. Nothing seems to survive to throw
more light on this period.

In 1882 Hopkins was twenty-one years old. His return to Burma
would have involved another lengthy sea voyage. If the sea voyage
and his time spent at Trinity College, London (assuming a stay in
Germany of summer months) are subtracted from his age on arrival
in Rangoon, it suggests that he left Falmouth at the age of seventeen.
More children (ten in total) were to be born to his parents, so the
family to which he returned was, although settled from the point of
view of work and housing, one still in the making. We do not know
if he visited them in Bassein before taking up his appointment in
Rangoon, brief though such a visit must have been, but it is hard
to imagine that he did not. In the small world of British Burma the

name of Hopkins would be well known. Anyone unfamiliar with it had only to glance at *Thacker's Indian Directory* to discover Hopkins senior's job and pay scale. The same directory subsequently lists also CPH's various jobs, his changes of address and the names of those living with him. So CPH, newly arrived in Rangoon, would hardly be a stranger to those around him, unfamiliar as they might be to him.

2

Port Chaplain in Rangoon

Rangoon was the centre of the part of Burma which was administered by the British, ceded to them after the first Burmese War in 1824. Hopkins had a flat in Dalhousie Street. Later he moved to a flat at 15 Phayre Street, which he seems to have shared with a J. Jackson, at least for part of his time there. Phayre Street was named after the first Commissioner of Pegu (Pegu was ceded after the Second Burmese War in 1852), later Chief Commissioner of British Burma, and as such was a reminder of how recently the British had settled the country. So were the reports in the local English-language newspaper of the presence of dacoits, the word from Hindi for bandits. Rangoon was the third port of the Indian Empire. In the short time that the British had been in Burma, an extensive administration had been established and within it a place had been created for the Church of England. A bishop and archdeacons were appointed, paid by the Bengal Government, as well as a number of chaplains, whose primary task was to minister to the large expatriate community. Missionary society grants and a local Additional Clergy Fund, derived in part from the sale of church land at an optimum moment, the profit being invested, enabled a ministry to smaller communities, and to natives.

A visitor in 1882, reading his newspaper, would discover in Rangoon an increasing range of comforts. Advertisements could be responded to by telephone. By calling 9 he could contact the Carriage Building Company. Number 119 would allow him to book a room at Jordan's Hotel, which advertised 'FIRST CLASS ACCOMMODATION FOR FAMILIES AND SINGLE GENTLEMEN'. He could order from the Burma Ice and Aerated Water Company soda water, lemonade, tonic, gingerade, Hot Tom and Ginger Ale to be delivered. He could read about decorations, royal deaths, and Queen Victoria's Jubilee.

Many of the advertisements were concerned with health, or rather, the lack of it. Rangoon was not a healthy place. Readers were invited to buy 'Little Oriental Balm', for example, to cure rheumatics, lumbago, sciatica, neuralgia, headaches, colds, sprains, bruises, stings, bronchitis, sore throat and asthma. This list was perhaps indicative of the sort of ailments experienced by residents, but with one notable omission: malaria.

Hopkins had certainly been appointed Cathedral Organist by 1883, though *Thacker's Indian Directory* dates his residence from 1882. The cathedral organ had been installed as recently as 1881, an event which may have precipitated his appointment. Official papers documenting this process reveal not only how the organ was purchased but also how bound together Church and State were at this time:

> The Department of Finance and Commerce … refusing
> to exempt from Customs Duty … an organ imported for
> the use of the Pro-Cathedral at Rangoon … the property
> of the Government, the Governor-General is pleased to
> sanction grant-in-aid equal to the amount of customs
> duty leviable … instead of a refund of the duty.[1]

Thacker described Hopkins as music master at the two diocesan schools, one for boys, the other for girls. The diocese was always short of money and his salary would not have been generous; this was a way of supplementing it.

The Bishop of Rangoon, Dr Titcomb, having had a bad fall early in 1881, was replaced as bishop by Dr Strachan (a medical doctor) in June 1882, making Hopkins and the new bishop, in a sense, Rangoon contemporaries. One of Strachan's concerns was the River Chaplaincy, which he hoped could be financed from the Additional Clergy Fund, together with donations 'from the leading mercantile houses' and a grant of £70 passage money.[2]

The appointment of a seamen's chaplain, which is what this referred to, was expected early in 1883. The bishop seems to have made only a little progress with the appointment in the first half of 1883, though it is not clear whether his difficulty lay in finding the salary or the candidate. There was a local Sailors' Home which had been run by Methodists. By 1883 it had passed out of religious control altogether, leaving work among seamen open to all. By June it was becoming clear that obtaining a salary was the principal problem, for in that month it was discovered that the promised subsidy from the Port Trust had fallen through. The appointment was proving a difficult one.

There is nothing to suggest during this time that either a seamen's chaplaincy or ordination had been in Hopkins's mind, though he claimed years later that on his way to and from the cathedral he would sometimes have a word with passing apprentices and sailors. There would be nothing unusual in his doing that. He acquitted himself well enough in the organist's job to be offered at some point in 1883 the post of organist and choirmaster at Madras Cathedral, a promotion offering a higher salary. Initially he was inclined to accept, but later changed his mind. The reason for this change of mind is usually ascribed to his sudden discovery of a vocation to minister to merchant seamen. His own account is quoted at length below but this must be compared with those parts of the Hopkins story which can be verified.

The Indian Churchman in August 1883 noted unspecified progress towards a Port Chaplaincy. The progress seems not to have involved Hopkins for his work in establishing the nucleus of a choir school ('so much needed in Rangoon') was commended in another item: 'the energetic organist W. [*sic*] Hopkins ... already has a goodly number of his choir boys residing with him attending the Diocesan School as day scholars'. No evidence survives of a resident choir school and Hopkins does not mention it when writing about this time in his life, though his mention of an anthem at Evensong (below) indicates the presence of some sort of a choir. His 'well-earned promotion' as organist of St George's Cathedral, Madras, was commented upon in October 1883, when it was noted that he had had to work against unspecified 'difficulties that might well have daunted a less able and determined man ...'. In spite of this 'he has raised the musical services ... to a very high state of effectiveness and *his work as a sub-deacon in the parish* [my italics] has been exceedingly diligent and useful ...'. The pro-cathedral, to which he had been organist, served the town parish and it was this he served as sub-deacon, effectively a sort of lay reader. Equally, it could have been Rangoon's form of probation for those seeking Holy Orders (*Thacker* mentions at least one other sub-deacon).

The Rev C.E. Panter, a naval chaplain, visiting Rangoon in January 1884, wrote in his diary after meeting Hopkins on the first day of his visit:

> Hopkins the port-chaplain came off; he was organist
> at the Cath[edral] & plays beautifully; he has been at
> London University; he wanted to be ordained 3 months
> ago but was not old enough, so this B[isho]p made him
> sub-deacon, by holding hands over, but not on his head;
> he is nearly 23 now.

The role of sub-deacon was not at the time something recognised in the Church of England and may indicate the bishop's churchmanship or Hopkins's understanding of what took place at what must have involved some sort of licensing. Panter spent some time with Hopkins reading New Testament Greek and a book of doctrine, which Panter referred to as Pearson (presumably John Pearson's *Exposition of the Creed*) in an attempt to help him in his preparation for Holy Orders.

Hopkins seems to have been a success in the town parish. If the bishop had put him there as a kind of pre-ordination placement, perhaps to give him necessary experience, or to obtain a report on his character and ability, we may assume he was satisfied. Either way, it was the parish in which he was employed. His duties as organist, though it is not said, may have been combined with his new duties. There is no hint whether the placement was full or part-time. In June 1883 *The Indian Churchman* implied that Hopkins had been a sub-deacon for some months when it reported that he had recently held a 'Flower Service; the first of its kind in Rangoon. It was attended by over 50 children, rich and poor, each with a pretty bouquet which was afterwards sent to the hospital'. That Hopkins could omit his admission to the sub-diaconate and his services beyond the organ in this parish from his memoirs, which admittedly were slanted towards his work with seamen, encourages caution in approaching his own account of his call to the port chaplaincy.

The seamen's chaplaincy, which the bishop was soon to offer Hopkins, continued to exercise the bishop's ingenuity in the matter of obtaining proper funding. In early 1883 he had arranged an ecclesiastical grant of Rs100 per month towards the chaplain's salary. In March 1883, perhaps at the bishop's prompting, the vice chairman of the Rangoon Port Commissioners sought sanction for the disbursement of a similar sum for the same purpose, the bishop also approaching the same authority in November 1883, and again in March and December 1884. The repetition of the bishop's applications illustrates the difficulty he was experiencing in finding the port chaplain's salary and in extracting money from the Port Commissioners. He had experienced no similar difficulty when appointing and financing a railway chaplain in 1882. Nothing explains the present difficulties, but it is important to remember that they preceded and continued during Hopkins's appointment as port chaplain and so cannot be described as personal to Hopkins, a point which will have increasing significance as the story unfolds.

Panter's reference to Hopkins's wanting to be ordained three months previously (October 1883?) finds support in what is known about the bishop's plans for the port chaplaincy. In October 1883 the bishop had intimated to the appropriate authorities that The Rev. C.C.N. Bazely, Officiating Port Chaplain, would shortly vacate the appointment and that he proposed to appoint Mr C. Hopkins, a sub-deacon, to undertake the duties of the office. *The Indian Churchman* announced the appointment on 20th October, 1883. If Hopkins's version of events, which is given below, is substantially correct, his encounter with the archdeacon, to whom he attributed the suggestion of his appointment to the seamen's chaplaincy, must have preceded that date and probably by more than the lag between announcement and publication in the paper. The paper noted that Hopkins had refused the Madras organist's post 'and has resolved to remain here, the bishop having appointed him to minister as Port Chaplain and accepted him as candidate for Holy Orders', which suggests that the bestowal of the sub-diaconate should be understood as an indication of episcopal recognition of his candidacy. It is unlikely that Bazely had been anything other than a part-time port chaplain and it is possible that Hopkins's appointment was not at first full-time.

The financing of the port chaplaincy remained a problem. *Thacker* continued to list Hopkins as having musical duties even after ordination, though material in the directory was not always up-to-date, in part due to communications and in part to the nature of an annual directory. He was certainly back at the organ console playing for a wedding in October 1884, but this may equally have been a favour for a friend as much as an indication that the organist's post remained vacant or perhaps that Hopkins was supplementing his income. By 1885 the bishop was having to pay him from Church Lands funds (the source of funding was to become crucial when Hopkins's departure from Burma became a matter of urgency) and having to defend this payment to the Secretary for the Home Department of the Government of India:

The grant to the Port Chaplain supplements the pittance which he now receives from the State, and enables him to live, with economy, in an expensive place like Rangoon. I should deeply regret losing the services of a Chaplain in this large and important port. During the past season more than 3,000 sailors have attended the services, with an average of 76% at each service.[3] I can bear personal testimony to the very excellent and useful work of the present Port Chaplain.

Letters from the Society for the Propagation of the Gospel (SPG) in London to the bishop show that the Diocese of Rangoon was in financial straits at this time, overdrawn in 1886 by £75 and in 1887 by £390. The need for financial stringency affected not only the Port Chaplaincy. The Diocesan School, of which Hopkins's confidante Marks was Warden, ran at a permanent loss.

The only detailed account of this key period in Hopkins's life is his own in *The Messenger*. Enough information has now been given for this to be weighed. His words show it to have been a deeply emotional point in his life, perhaps the nearest thing in his writing to an experience of religious conversion. That being so, it is worth quoting him at length, with the caveat that the words postdate the event by many years and had most likely been honed in the telling to countless audiences in the meantime, perhaps giving another incidental but powerful insight into his platform style to put beside his account of his voyage on the *GEOLOGIST*.

> One Sunday morning, after service was done, something – not duty – kept me longer than usual at the organ, and when I looked about me the Cathedral was quite empty. I closed the organ and passed out of God's House, to come face to face with a big crowd of excited natives surrounding six young Englishmen in the uniform of merchant apprentices. As I came up, the crowd dispersed and two of the lads managed to slip away. The other four were so drunk that they were sitting or lying on the ground in the blazing sun.
>
> To leave them as and where they were would have been cruel, and so, with the help of one or two natives, I got them into a gharry and took them home with me. My home was a bachelor's flat by the riverside, and not

far from the Cathedral. Here I had the fellows taken in hand by my bearer, who made them as comfortable as he could in the spare bedroom, where they slept off their debauch. At about half past four in the afternoon, my bearer came to say that they were awake, and I told him to see that they were provided with everything for a wash up, and to supply them with clean clothes as well, if necessary.

After a time, my young friends came forward, looking extremely uncomfortable and shy, and I had the difficult task before me of putting them, as much as possible, at their ease. I did not want them to go away, and so invited them to sit down for some refreshments. They all accepted my invitation, and as I made no reference whatever to the plight from which I had rescued them, they gradually gave signs of being more at ease, and chatted quite freely with me and amongst themselves.

At six-thirty I had to be at the Cathedral for Evensong, so as the time approached I went, as was my custom, to the piano to try over the service and the anthem. In a few minutes one of the boys was at my side humming over the music. I asked him if he were at all musical. 'Oh, yes', he replied, 'I love it and am an old cathedral chorister'. This boy and two others went to the Cathedral with me. After Evensong we went home for dinner, and found the other lad who did not go to church waiting for our return. We had a merry little dinner party to ourselves, and a very happy evening afterwards; the recounting of my own sea experiences seemed to interest and amuse them immensely.

It was long after eleven o'clock when they took their departure and it was when saying goodbye that I broached the subject of their morning's plight. We were standing by the front door and in my hand I had the hand of the chorister that had been. 'Now tell me', I said, 'how was it that I found you in that terrible state outside the Cathedral this morning?' After some hesitation, one of them said: 'Well, Sir, being Sunday, we had the whole day off and came ashore. But we had no friends

to come to see, so we strolled about the town. Then we
met some of the men, and they invited us to go into one
of the saloons to have a drink. We did not like to say no,
and so went in. After having a drink at their expense,
we thought we were bound to ask them to have one at
ours, and so it went on, and after getting back outside,
we began to feel queer, and made back for the ship, and
– well, then you found us.'

'Well', I said, 'just because you have no friends in this
place and have not anywhere to go, do not get drinking
again. I'm an acquaintance at any rate, so come and see
me whenever you like.'

They came on Monday, they came on Tuesday, and
yet again on Wednesday; and on that occasion they asked
if they might bring some of the other fellows too on
Thursday. I said yes; from that day my flat was overrun
with apprentices all day on Sundays and on every other
evening through the week. That was how I think my
call came.

The internal evidence of this passage is compelling in spite of
the oratorical ring of the final paragraph. Contemporary medical
records[4] describe similar problems of drunkenness in the bazaar,
while details of apprentice life and the men's responses to Hopkins's
offer of hospitality tally with journals from the period. The presence
of a bearer and the amount of hospitality Hopkins seems to have
dispensed, as well as the pony mentioned below, suggest he had a
sufficient income to make ends meet. The problem with this passage
lies in the dating.

It seems that Hopkins thereafter was seldom without apprentices
in his flat. One evening, he said, he had invited Archdeacon Blyth
and his wife to supper, wondering, perhaps mischievously, what
they would make of the fifteen or so apprentices amongst whom
they found themselves. The numbers suggest a fairly large flat. The
presence of so many makes one wonder if Hopkins was not trying to
stake a claim for the seamen's chaplaincy, the vacancy of which must
have been common knowledge amongst the cathedral community of
which Hopkins was a part. He implies otherwise. It seems that the
Blyths fitted in very well. Hopkins wrote in the August 1899 issue
of *The Messenger*,

> The Archdeacon seemed very meditative during the
> latter part of the evening and ... expressed a wish that
> I would go to see him the next day.... It was suggested
> that God might be calling me to undertake a definite
> work amongst our sailors, and I was to think it over.

Hopkins gives no hint that at this stage he was aware of the parlous state of the River Chaplaincy finances, though details of them were available in contemporaneously published documents.

Hopkins now had to make his choice between the seamen and the Madras organist's post, the latter giving a higher and more secure salary. Before declining the Madras offer he took counsel from his friend Dr John Marks, Warden of St John's College, the diocesan school for boys which had some 500 students of various nationalities. Marks, as a Lambeth Doctor of Divinity, treasurer and secretary of the SPG Orphan Home, honorary chaplain to Bishop Titcomb, and preacher of ordination sermons, with long years of service in the diocese, seems just the wise person that Hopkins should consult.[5] Hopkins had helped him at the College with his youngsters by preparing them for Confirmation, helping with a Sung Eucharist and establishing a devotional guild – of which there were a number in Rangoon. A closer look at Marks reveals that here Hopkins was being drawn to a type whose attraction would be repeated later in his life. Archdeacon Blyth would write in 1892 of Marks: 'Marks is the great difficulty of the diocese; he is no real missionary. All the clergy in the Diocese are united against him; or, more justly, he against them'.[6] Successive episcopal letters from Rangoon reveal that this opinion of Marks was shared by more than one bishop. That said, the official SPG records[7] publish a very favourable opinion from Bishop Titcomb, mention that Marks's career was a notable one, and indicate that his successes in the educational field led directly or indirectly to a number of other foundations. A contemporary account of a meeting with Marks by The Rev. C.E. Panter, given below, confirms the general opinion. Yet from Marks, Hopkins sought advice. It is not now possible to say whether Marks was right, either in his view of the diocese, or in his advice to Hopkins, which seems to have been that Hopkins should withdraw from the Madras appointment and seek Holy Orders. This Hopkins did.

Theological colleges in the Anglican Church in the 1880s were rare. Candidates for Holy Orders usually undertook supervised

reading before writing essays to satisfy the bishop's examining
chaplain. Hopkins commenced reading under the personal
supervision of Archdeacon Blyth, whilst, it seems, continuing in his
organist's post. Panter's diary (below) gives a glimpse of Hopkins
both at study and at the organ. Bishop Strachan made him deacon
on 9th March, 1884, two days after his twenty-third birthday, the
minimum possible age. That receipt of Colonial Orders, that is,
ordination by a colonial bishop, might be a problem can hardly have
crossed his mind at this stage. Ordination to the priesthood followed
on 20th December, 1885, eighteen months rather than the more
customary year after his reception of the diaconate. The bishop's
attempts to obtain funds to appoint a River Chaplain, and Hopkins's
settled position as it appears in the Panter diary in January 1884,
suggests that his interview with Archdeacon Blyth had taken place
sometime in the Autumn of 1883, if not earlier, which is why his
account of inviting the archdeacon and his wife to his flat appears
disingenuous. It may be that the formal appointment as Chaplain did
not come until he was in Holy Orders but that he was doing the work
whilst still a 'sub- deacon' is certain from the Panter diary (below).
It should be remembered that Hopkins was writing at a much later
date and without reference to contemporary documents; memory
sometimes recalls how matters ought to have been.

   The Panter diary offers an independent and contemporary glimpse
of his work pre- ordination but apparently after his appointment as
Port Chaplain. Panter's ship, HMS *BRITAIN*, anchored off Rangoon
post office on the morning of 5th January, 1884, and Hopkins 'the
port-chaplain came off… went ashore with him in our boat, his
followed; saw his large place with registry office and reading-room &
apprentices'. 'His large place' appears to have been the local sailors'
home. Here Panter confirmed his appointment as Port Chaplain
pre-ordination. Later the same day Panter, Hopkins, and Hopkins's
older sister, now Mrs Baker, rode ponies before dining together. The
next day Panter met Hopkins in the cathedral at Holy Communion,
afterwards taking him back to his ship by gig. Hopkins preached for
him and stayed with some captains from other vessels for lunch.

   The two men had now become sufficiently friendly for Hopkins
on 7th January to take Panter sight-seeing, and to the Pegu Club and
the Gymkhana; the next day to 'his place', lending Panter his pony.
On the 10th they studied Greek together before going ashore to the
Pegu Club. Panter noted the tension in local church life caused by the

introduction of ritualistic church furnishings; the Catholic movement in the Church of England was extending to Burma. The implication is that he and Hopkins were part of this movement – which has already been encountered in Falmouth parish church during the 1870s – and it may account in part for their ready friendship. Panter recorded a trivial but revealing story, an indication of Hopkins's position in local society: over dinner in the evening, discussing the visiting cards they had left during the day, Hopkins recalled 'how a woman returned his card in an envelope saying, "I think you dropped this in our house by accident"'. On the 11th, they studied doctrine together before going ashore to call upon more dignitaries, in this case the Roman Catholic bishop (out), and Mrs Strachan, Bishop Strachan's wife (at home). Supper at the Sailors' Home allowed Panter to note that the introduction of alcohol had led to the secession by a determined and dissenting few to build an alternative, alcohol-free, 'Sailors' Rest', perhaps the one appearing in local papers as being under Methodist auspices. On the 12th Hopkins and the archdeacon went aboard HMS *BRITAIN* for lunch, before Hopkins and Panter went ashore with the masters of several vessels in port for a railway trip. Whether this trip was one of Hopkins's regular entertainments as Port Chaplain is not stated, but it would have an appeal for his sailors.

Sunday, 13th January saw both men in the cathedral for morning services, with Hopkins playing the organ. In the evening Hopkins took Panter's service ('crowded'), presumably on board ship, before giving Panter supper. On the Monday they called on Marks, Panter recording that his school had '500 boys of all nations.... He has Lambeth D.D. f[ro]m [Archbishop] Tait; the SPG paid the £120 for it; his boys gave him the hood. He showed me the parchment and seal.... B[isho]p Wordsworth once introduced him publicly as "future B[isho]p of Rangoon"'. In showing how Marks had shared his doctorate (then four years' old), and his other achievements, and compliments received, even on such a brief acquaintance, Panter gave enough to reveal, subtly but very clearly, Marks's character. Marks was not invited to join them for a dinner party at the mess of the XIth Madras Infantry. The dinner party delayed Panter's collection of his 'goods' from Hopkins before getting a boat off at 1.00 a.m.. Panter and HMS *BRITAIN* sailed later that morning at 7.00 a.m., with Panter returning the books he had borrowed from Hopkins via the pilot boat. And so ended a packed week, important

because it is one of the few independent pictures that survives of
Hopkins in Burma.

We learn from Panter's diary that Hopkins's base was indeed
the Sailors' Home, which was separate from the Port Chaplaincy.
The latter was governed by a committee quite typical of its day. Its
president was the bishop, with the archdeacon as his vice president.
The honorary treasurer and secretary was a government official:
the Port Officer. The remainder of the committee consisted of port
officials and representatives of commercial and shipping companies,
a group of worthies intended to ensure that the chaplain's position
was more secure than that of his opposite number at the nearby
Methodist Mission, which (according to the *Rangoon Times*) was
run by 'a highly respectable lady, lately widowed … the coffee
supplied is superior …. The number of customers is now said to be
steadily increasing'. The Port Chaplaincy committee was supposed
to provide a link with the port industry: those in commerce helping
his work by subscription and those in the port by facilitating
his progress. The committee was primarily concerned with the
chaplaincy and its finances, while Hopkins involved himself mostly
in pastoral matters. Unfortunately, his view of his duties soon
diverged from that of his committee.

What may have been the first clash (references to this event
occur at different times and places) appears to have arisen when
Hopkins, as he claimed, raised a question of financial injustice to
his men. I have, however, failed to find independent verification
of Hopkins's role in the affair. Certainly very early in his ministry
Hopkins became aware that seamen paid locally were receiving
only Rs10 in exchange for the pound sterling. He claimed when
speaking around England in 1893[8] that he protested vigorously at
an exchange rate that was very much in favour of the ship owner,
and that his efforts 'and correspondence with members of the House
of Commons and others had enabled the sailor to obtain 15 rupees
8 annas to the 20 s[hillings]'. It can be imagined that the loss of
income for those charged with paying the seaman caused by this
50% increase in the exchange rate was considerable. On a sailing
ship, crews' wages formed the largest part of the costs of a voyage.
Hopkins's intervention would do nothing to increase his popularity
with the shipping community. There is an ambiguity about the date
of this reference which makes it impossible to be certain whether
it lay at the root of his troubles in Rangoon or later in Calcutta; in

either port it would explain the hostility shown to him by those in authority. It is entirely possible that he first became aware of the problem in Rangoon, but it is certain from contemporary evidence that his major battle on the subject took place later in Calcutta. His obituary in *The Seaman* ascribes the incident to Calcutta. In any event the 1894 Merchant Shipping Act remedied the situation and set out an appropriate method for calculating sailors' wages.

The rate of exchange was a relatively local issue. Matters came to a head over an international problem: overloading. Since the publication of Samuel Plimsoll's book, *OUR SEAMEN – an Appeal*, in 1873, overloading had been a highly emotive and widely publicised issue. Hopkins later recorded that he watched a ship [9] being overloaded in harbour, overhearing the chief officer ask the captain to inspect the, by now, submerged load line beyond which further loading would render the ship unsafe. In spite of Plimsoll's vigorous campaign, the placing of the load line was still a matter for individual masters to decide, though it was illegal to exceed the line, once placed. Perhaps because the master knew that the ship would ride higher at sea in the salt sea water than in the relatively fresh water of the harbour, he ordered loading to continue. Then he ordered the carpenter to go over the side and paint the load line higher. The ship subsequently foundered off Mauritius with all hands lost. What made this loss at sea particularly unusual was that Hopkins later received a letter from the father of one of the drowned apprentices who said that his son had written before departure (probably mentioning time spent with Hopkins if the father's letter is to be explained) hinting at overloading. Hopkins was asked if he was able to confirm this impression. To obtain evidence after a vessel had sunk was extremely difficult; dead men tell no tales, while survivors, if any, are soon scattered across the globe. Hopkins can hardly have been unaware of Plimsoll's brilliant press campaign, nor of the shipboard talk of visiting seamen, to whom it was of intense interest. Here was an issue which united crews and chaplain.

Hopkins was still a novice in the port, feeling his way. In a quandary about what action to take, he turned first to his bishop and then his archdeacon, both of whom expressed shock, while pointing out the difficulties. The civil authorities, on being approached, told him strongly that it was none of his business as a parson. He was so disheartened that he claimed to have considered resigning his Orders. Instead, he did two things. He wrote to the mourning father that he had no information to give and he asked the bishop to relieve him of the Port Chaplaincy. However, he was overtaken by events when the Third Burmese War broke out. Although it lasted only ten days, the increase in troops it brought to Upper Burma (from 14,000 to 25,000 in December 1886) demanded of the diocese an increase in chaplains. Hopkins acted as an Honorary Naval Chaplain, fulfilling his duties in Rangoon. He was later commended for his services by Admiral Sir Frank Richards.[10]

At the end of this brief war, Hopkins again found himself in deep water, at loggerheads with his committee for other reasons. Committee members were probably aware of their chaplain's tendency to resort to litigation. Though there are no details available, it is known that Hopkins was (in his words) active before the law in Rangoon and this would not have increased his popularity with the committee. Members may also have suspected his hand in other matters: long after, Hopkins admitted advising an apprentice to desert, which while a serious offense in the apprentice was even more so in Hopkins. The spark for his disagreement with the committee, or the committee's with him, which ignited the tinder involved a relatively trivial thing: the purchase of a launch to aid his visiting of ships.

The *Indian Churchman* of 6th September, 1884 noted that Hopkins was working 'zealously' and that friends and supporters were thinking of providing him with a steam launch to enable him to go about the harbour from ship to ship. In time, the object was achieved, and the *ST GEORGE* was purchased. Along with other vessels it was commandeered by the military during the few days of the Third Burmese War. At first, the government remuneration of Rs300 per month was paid to Hopkins, for whom the boat had been provided, not by the chaplaincy, but by friends. By its provision the committee had been spared the expense of continually hiring rowing boats for ship visitation. Now, it insisted that the monthly Rs300 should be paid to it, which it could easily do, since the Rs300 was government remuneration, and there were government members among the committee membership. It claimed the money as compensation for the loss of what was maintained to be its asset. In a way the boat had become part of the chaplaincy, but Hopkins could not see it in this light. He would have been very well aware of the financial straits of the committee, year after year. The committee no doubt did its sums and found that Rs300 was almost equivalent to the chaplain's monthly salary, and stood its ground. Things came to such a head that Hopkins seems to have declared independence and separated his work from the committee.[11]

Apparently in an attempt to let tempers cool, the bishop asked Hopkins to go to Akyab, a small port in the province of Arakan, Lower Burma, to undertake a six-months' chaplaincy to the local expatriates. Hopkins must have wondered what his welcome would be, for in such a small community his reputation would surely have preceded him. The port officials in Akyab, a seasonal rice port, would have been among the first to hear of the disagreement which underlay his removal from Rangoon. What would they have heard? It may not have been the Hopkins version which appeared in *The Messenger* (February 1900):

> The 'goings-on' of the Port Chaplain – *my 'goings-on'* – were pretty freely discussed in the [Rangoon] Shipping Office. The master had the ear of the Port Officer, who was Secretary of the Seamen's Mission; and the Port Officer had the ear of the Bishop. Clouds commenced to gather, and there were one or two stormy interviews between the Secretary of the Seamen's Mission and myself. I claimed the right to take the whole sailor – not the spiritual part only – under my care; and I absolutely refused to abandon my efforts to improve his temporal surroundings, or to cease my endeavours to protect him [Hopkins's italics].

This vintage nugget makes it no clearer which issue – boat, exchange rate, litigation, or all of them – led to the final break, but a break there surely was. And if such things were possible when Hopkins was chaplain in a large port, what might the outcome be on finding himself in such a small port and tight community as Akyab?

3

Hopkins in Akyab

Hopkins's portrayal of the situation before his departure from Rangoon for Akyab sounds on the one hand highly plausible, on the other, rather muddled. He claimed much later in *The Messenger* that his modest attempt to run his work for sailors from the Phayre Street flat, with the help of his sister Mary Ann, had the approval of the bishop and the archdeacon. At the same time he accepted that the diocesan committee under which it would properly be placed was not prepared to accept it, perhaps because some of its members were also to be found on the Seamen's Chaplaincy committee. When it is remembered that the bishop and archdeacon were members of both committees his claim to having their approval appears rather odd.

To be sent to Akyab, according to Peter Anson in his *Call of the Cloister*, was a sign of the bishop's displeasure and an attempt to remove Hopkins from the centre of maritime activity [1]. Either view needs to be approached with caution. In a sense, he was being given his own church (not a usual sign of episcopal displeasure) and here especially so, as Akyab was an opportunity for Hopkins to prove himself in a situation far from his bishop, and therefore from supervision. The appointment also, far from removing him from sailors, placed him in another port. Later he would write of being sent out to relieve a sick chaplain, which is more plausible if he understood his appointment to be for six months only. However, his subsequent actions suggest that he saw his removal as being more permanent. This may be why, as he said, his first action on being appointed was to cable the All Saints' Sisters at Bombay for a complete set of eucharistic vestments, the first, he later claimed, in the Anglican Church in Burma.

Hopkins went to Akyab in June 1886. The chaplaincy which he was now to serve was a 'parish' of some 250 miles by 105 miles, no small area but with the population centred on Akyab in the Arakan Division. His base was St Mark's church in Akyab, but he served too an old military church at Kyauk-Pyu (or Khyouk Phu), a small port in the north of Ramree Island. Commercial residents of Akyab may have wondered what sort of man they were getting. Word had gone round that his presence was to be temporary. His first work was not among seamen, but only because of the seasonal nature of this port: Akyab depended heavily on the rice trade. In the absence of ships, Hopkins concentrated on the people ashore, who were, according to *Thacker*, a divisional population of 359,706, a figure predominantly composed of native Burmese, spread over 5,535 square miles.

If Hopkins's appointment was indeed for six months, his period at Akyab outlasted that of all previous chaplains, the regular turnover of whom, usually and correctly ascribed to ill health, encouraged the view that Akyab was a seasonal chaplaincy. Although he had resisted the diseases of Rangoon, here he was not to be so fortunate. Neither port was a healthy place and local diseases were not pleasant. In Akyab 247 Europeans died from cholera alone in 1885, 103 in 1886. Figures for Rangoon are more comprehensive and indicate the unhealthiness of the whole country. Deaths were classified by fever, bowel complaints, smallpox and cholera. Fever claimed 1,419 lives in 1883, bowel complaints, 435, smallpox 152, and cholera 20. One old Burma hand described the Arakan Division as the unhealthiest area in Burma, and within that Division, Kyauk-pyu as its worst, the military sanitorium there abandoned because of the prevalence of malaria.[2] In Hopkins's day the causes of fever were not well understood. Sir Ronald Ross (1857-1932), in the Indian Medical Service from 1881, was to discover in 1897-8 (well after Hopkins had come 'home') the connection between mosquitos and blood parasites, and thus the cause of malaria. Its incidence in Akyab, a town but recently and rapidly developed, with less than adequate drainage, would have been greater; it was an ever-present threat to which Hopkins would succumb.

Mention has been made of Hopkins's ordering a set of vestments. If his ministry in Rangoon had left them in any doubt, this was an action which would identify him firmly in the eyes of the bishop and others with the Ritualist party which was causing such a stir in the wider Anglican Church. It is another clue to his theological views to add to his discussions with Panter about church ornaments and his assistance of Marks with a Sung Eucharist. And yet there is an ambiguity about the churchmanship of the church in Akyab, when Hopkins's claims are compared with other sources. Though the 1885 Christmas services under his predecessor, The Rev. Mr Wintour, were fully choral, and the church furnished with flowers, candles and hangings, Hopkins claimed to have been the one who introduced a fully choral service; he claimed too to have made the choral service a weekly event. Nor was the scope of his choral service limited to St Mark's Church. The local paper (14 June 1887) referred to 'Mr Hopkins, who has lately been showing High Church tendencies, and on this occasion introduced what is certainly a novelty in Akyab – a choral funeral service in the cemetery... has not given general satisfaction.'

'High Church' leanings were not to everyone's taste. The expression refers to what was originally a high regard for *The Book of Common Prayer*, one of the Church of England's foundational documents, as opposed to a low regard and therefore casual use of the same book. High Church clergy were also known as Tractarians (named from a series of Tracts for the Times). These tracts written earlier in the nineteenth century had introduced a generation to the Catholic treasures, lost for centuries, of the Prayer Book, and the successors of the Tractarians, amongst whom we must now number Hopkins, imported into the worship of their churches many of the practices associated with the Church of Rome, so becoming known as Ritualists, later as Anglo-Catholics. These clergy were controversial and often had to seek, if there was access to no comfortable family benefice, employment in parishes with mean circumstances and small incomes. Such men, therefore, were often to be found in the slum and mission parishes of the Church. Some chose these parishes because Anglo-Catholic theology was strongly incarnational, believing that the God who took flesh was to be found particularly among the poor. Others went knowing that any attempt to introduce elaborate ritual would produce few protests while bringing colour to otherwise drab lives. The vestments, incense and other imports had a strong didactic role for people otherwise ill-educated, revealing the Holy Communion as something more than a memorial meal. Hopkins's probable experience of such ritual in his time at Falmouth has been touched on in an earlier chapter. These parishes often became a seedbed for Christian Socialism, which will find its place in the next chapter. Bishops of the period, as bishops of any period, preferred not to preside over controversy and many were strongly anti-Ritualist.

Hopkins's first year, then, was not without its difficulties. When compared with his subsequent start in Calcutta, the similarities will confirm that this was largely due to matters of churchmanship. We must also allow, however, for a lack of tact. The *Indian Churchman* (22nd November, 1884), whilst Hopkins was still in Rangoon, had implied as much when referring to the annual report of Hopkins's Rangoon Port Chaplaincy Committee as rather personal (he being at loggerheads with the committee at the time). It noted that Hopkins's own report had 'evoked much adverse and harsh criticism.... It will ... teach him to do what he feels right and wise, and to talk of it afterwards, rather than to submit his plans to public criticism'. The editor clearly believed Hopkins to be less than judicious in his words and actions.

Socially, Hopkins was proving an asset in Akyab. He was a single, slim and attractive young man, according to contemporary photographs which survive at Alton Abbey, with the added attraction of being able to play the piano and to sing: highly desirable qualities at a time and in a place where people made their own entertainment. And there was plenty of entertainment in Akyab of the home-grown variety. The season included several 'calico balls', fancy dress balls (on 24th January, 1887 it was reported that he went dressed as 'a R.C. priest', the reporter perhaps confused by Hopkins's cassock), and in 1887, many celebrations of Queen Victoria's Jubilee, which Hopkins had made the subject of his first sermon in 1887. Such events were written up in the *Rangoon Gazette Weekly Budget* (RGWB),of which many copies survive in London's Newspaper Library at Colindale. The same paper reports him away in February on duty at Kyauk-Pyu: it seems that during this tour he was invited, by whom is unsaid, to minister to local Buddhists, processing into the village preceded by a cross and a banner of our Lady and Child; later he appears to have baptised some natives. For part of this tour he was accompanied by the choir which he had formed in Akyab soon after his arrival. The tour appears to be the only instance known to us of his ministry to the native people of Burma. His primary concern was for expatriates and his seamen and it may have been the latter who drew him to Kyauk-Pyu.

Back in Akyab, it is apparent from the local press that Hopkins was again working among seamen.

> About a fortnight ago the British steamer *BEDOUIN*
> arrived in port with a case of smallpox on board ... the
> poor sick man was brought ashore and put into a small
> hut in the hospital compound. So far as I know, the only
> European who attended him was the Rev Mr Hopkins,
> who, I believe has made a report to the Government about
> the cruel way in which this poor sailor was neglected.

Here is another instance of Hopkins's willingness to complain or
'report' to authority. At this time there was a general campaign in
Akyab to improve medical attention. The newspaper reporter filled
his report with details of the campaign at the expense of this particular
incident, leaving us with little more about the sick man. Elsewhere,
and later in *The Messenger*, a very sad account of the sailor's plight
is given, Hopkins apparently being the only person concerned for his
welfare. The incident gives a strong indication of Hopkins's genuine
sense of compassion, as well as of his comprehension of the 1876
Merchant Shipping Act which required sick seamen who had been
put ashore to have provision made by the ship's master.

Hopkins's six months in Akyab passed with no sign of the bishop
wishing him to move, and indeed he was able to find out through the
local commissioner, Colonel Strover, whose friendship he enjoyed,
that he was not going to be moved. Colonel Strover and his wife
attended St Mark's church. Mrs Strover was to help him with a
sick seaman, probably the one mentioned above, while Colonel
Strover helped by using his influence generally. For example, the
colonel was president of the local Gymkhana Club, a position of
great social usefulness. The colonel and his wife seemed happy to
meet seamen who conventionally would be considered their social
inferiors. Support of this kind was valuable and extended in several
directions. Having survived the calico ball of 1887, a Cinderella
dance, and various other terpsichorean delights, Hopkins was to
be found at the August concert for St Mark's charities playing a
Mendelsohn duet, singing with Mrs Strover, and later, singing on his
own. It is not hard to picture members of the Gymkhana Club in the
audience. One of the beneficiaries of this concert would be the new
recreation rooms which Hopkins had obtained for the use of seamen
on finding he was to remain in Akyab. No details of the rooms
seem to have survived. They are variously referred to as reading
and recreation rooms. The difference is of little consequence. With

the rooms went a committee, presumably one of his own choosing, with whom he was soon to be at odds.

Hopkins's work was expanding in a number of directions and he was keen to find paid help, particularly with visiting seamen and to run the reading rooms. The Strovers were prepared to help in raising funds to this end. Several people were considered. One possible helper, found as a result of an advertisement which Hopkins had seen in *The Church Times* (a weekly paper popular with Ritualists), proved inadequate and was found other employment to help him work his passage home. Another recruit embezzled money. Hopkins was forced to consider seriously the problem of how to maintain his work for seamen with inadequate funds and with people uncommitted to the task. Perhaps, too, he wanted a way forward which would make him less dependent upon a local committee.

In May 1887 the local paper carried this interesting paragraph:

> There is evidently a screw loose in the appointment of the Port Chaplain. His report is flatly contradicted by his Committee, and washing dirty linen in public is not usually held to be the best way of getting support. With a resident Bishop one would have thought that such differences would have been smoothed over....

It is not clear from the papers that survive what was the nature of this particular trouble between chaplain and committee. The detail is probably unimportant beyond its revelation of Hopkins's willingness to plough a solitary furrow. The reference to the bishop may refer to the days when Rangoon had no bishop of its own but was under the more distant Bishop of Calcutta, the Rangoon Diocese being a relatively recent foundation. The important point of the article is its confirmation of Hopkins's work among sailors.

In August a further paragraph appeared, again with no indication of what was afoot. The subject was probably considered too well-known to local expatriates to give more detail.

> From the Rangoon papers we are able to see what charges the local correspondent of the *Rangoon Times* has to make against our padre, also what your correspondent Ramree has to say about Akyab people generally. I have read ... Mr Hopkins' contribution in self defense to the *Provincial News*. I do not think that the affair has

> brought out the best side of Akyab at all, and therefore
> think that I had better say nothing about it, and only
> express the hope that Mr Hopkins will remain with us
> yet, and that all concerned may be better from this sore
> when it has healed.

The article's tone suggests that Hopkins had his sympathisers. The
reference to the *Provincial News* reveals that his work and troubles
would be known in Calcutta, city of the metropolitan bishop. If the
Bishop of Calcutta read the *Provincial News*, such news items were
not enough to prevent his invitation to Hopkins to accept the Port
Chaplaincy of Calcutta little more than a year later.

For Hopkins, close on the heels of this trouble, whatever it was,
came fever. He evidently went on sick leave, for the local paper's
Akyab correspondent noted his return to Akyab in October (whence
is not said) aboard the *COCONADA*, adding, 'he looks much better
for the change'. But his return was brief and controversial, and his
enemies were not slow to find fault. The fancy dress ball of January
1888 was the cause of this item:

> The only sad thing in connection with [the ball] is the
> action of *The Advertiser.* Our Padre has become the Editor
> of the Weekly News and in his zeal for the welfare of that
> paper made notes on the ball and issued a special edition
> next morning, and thus got ahead of his contemporary.
> Here is what his esteemed contemporary says:-
>
> We can imagine nothing more unbecoming,
> improper, unreverential or infra dig than for a clergyman
> to strut about ballrooms in the sacred garb that ought
> to be regarded with respect. To see one dressed in that
> clerical garb, strut about ballrooms, notebook in hand,
> taking notes of frivolous costumes, cannot but inspire
> disgust in all right-minded persons. Yet such was the
> sight we saw last Wednesday night... a sight we never
> saw before though... we have seen dancing dervishes.
>
> ... even the veriest child will allow that Mr Hopkins
> on Wednesday evening did not at all resemble a dancing
> dervish.

The passage offers an example of Hopkins going into print, which
he would do with increasing frequency. It also reminds the reader,

indirectly, that he was a man to inspire strong feelings.

The social round was not to last for long. Hopkins left Akyab again at the end of January 1888 by steamer for Calcutta for a further month's leave. This would be just before Akyab's busy season and the arrival of the rice ships. His own version of events is that he left to consult an eye doctor for a childhood eye condition which had been aggravated by the malaria. The rest of his life would be marked by attacks of blindness and fever. In Calcutta he stayed for a while with the Oxford Mission brotherhood, and here his thoughts began to turn to the religious life as a solution to the twin problems of inadequate funds and uncommitted staff for work among seamen. The Oxford Mission brethren had their own particular charism and it was not one to which Hopkins was in any way drawn, but the idea of a life under vows did seem a way forward.

The only newspaper (the RGWB) which it has been possible to trace now became sympathetic to Hopkins, either because he was a sick man, or because his work spoke for itself:

> 11 May 1888. AKYAB – While neglect, and indolence in management, effectually closed our Seamen's Institute at Rangoon, undaunted energy and practical enthusiasm opened another at Akyab, and we are pleased to learn that it is much appreciated, and paying its way. Opened at 7 a.m. daily, it is, says a circular lying before us, to be closed at the discretion of the manager (Mr Cecil W Forder). Refreshments minus alcoholic liquors are always to be had, and a breakfast, tiffin or dinner, at 12, 8 or 16 annas respectively. We learn from an outside source, that at the close of one of the entertainments, recently given at the Institute, a shipmaster, in order to testify his approval of the good work being done, stepped forward and presented the Chaplain with a cheque for Rs 50. We devoutly wish that every seaport in the East, had a Chaplain of the stamp of our esteemed friend who ministers at Akyab.

Internal evidence suggests that some of the information, especially the reference to the shipmaster, must have derived from Hopkins, who never missed a chance to draw the attention of an audience to this sort of recognition, especially when he was becoming a figure of controversy to many of the visiting captains. Other authorities to be cited in later articles would include the Lieutenant Governor of Bengal and the Chief of the Calcutta Police. Almost incidentally, a picture emerges of the daily pattern of the Seamen's Institute and Reading Rooms, which were to be open on demand, closing when the port was quiet.

The same issue of the paper carried the information that Hopkins had swooned after Evensong in church on Easter Day. He was taken to the house of a parishioner nearby. The local doctor had ordered his departure from Akyab at once, either on furlough or at least for a change. The paper lamented this interruption to Hopkins's excellent work. His departure, however, was not immediate. A week later (17th May, 1888) the RGWB's Akyab correspondent was again writing that Hopkins's health was being seriously undermined by repeated attacks of 'Arakan fever'.

To make Hopkins's leave possible some parishioners got up a fancy fair to raise funds. This was necessary because the Additional Clergy Society was not retaining his services and he was therefore without pay. Worse: because he had been recruited in Burma, the Society would not be paying his passage home to England. The *Provincial News* noted that,

> a Clergy Society ought to be more considerate and we
> hope it will reconsider its present decision and grant
> a free passage home well earned by being a victim of
> Arakan fever.... However willing the Society may be to
> grant Mr Hopkins ... we are very much afraid that sheer
> inability on account of want of funds will prevent it ....

This illustrates all too well the state of the finances of the diocese.

The RGWB reported again on 31st July – some twelve weeks later – that Hopkins was expected to leave Akyab very shortly, being sufficiently ill for his church services to be conducted by laymen (who could read the offices of Morning and Evening Prayer). A week later a Mrs Duffing handed Hopkins Rs261, the proceeds of the fancy fair. Akyab people were very sympathetic and appealed to the bishop: '... it is very strange that the ACS should wish to get rid of a priest who is the only man to have done well in Akyab – filling the Church and Schools – and is well-liked by the people'. The bishop was memorialised on 4th September, but without effect. In spite of controversy, during his two years in Akyab Hopkins had managed, if the press is not mistaken, to endear himself to his people. Through their generosity his passage to, and stay in, London became possible. Donations seem to have come not just from his own denomination. A total of Rs300, equivalent to a month's salary, assisted him on his way, the delay in his departure allowing more time for late donations.

The local paper reported the wedding of his second sister, Maggie 'daughter of Captain and Mrs Hopkins of Bassein and Falmouth', on 9th October, 1888, giving an additional reason for delay. The bridegroom was John Shaw Brown, municipal engineer and secretary. The ceremony took place in St Mark's Church, Akyab, which was described as crowded with people 'and tastefully adorned with moss and evergreens'. The brother of the bride – CPH – officiated. 'After an impressive choral service, Mr Cecil Forder [manager of the Seamen's Institute] presiding at the harmonium, the party adjourned to the hospitable roof of Mr & Mrs George Brown for cake and wine...'. In the evening Captain Hopkins gave the couple a grand ball at the Municipal High School.

Two days later, Hopkins sailed for the United Kingdom. London, scene of his student days, was his destination. Medical attention, and perhaps an overdue holiday, would be his purpose. As the centre of the Empire, London offered specialised treatment for tropical diseases, both at the School for Hygiene and Tropical Medicine and at the Dreadnought Seamen's Hospital. But London was also an excellent centre for the making of wider Church contacts, and for furthering his plans for a religious community to work among seamen.

4

London Interlude
1888-1889

Hopkins set out for England on 11th October, 1888. From this point, for some months, he disappears from the newspapers; almost the only remaining information comes from his own account in *The Messenger*. How long he stayed in London is uncertain as the date of his departure for Calcutta is not known. Anson in *Call of the Cloister* claims that Hopkins was in the UK for the best part of a year, but this appears to have been Anson confusing his notes. By Hopkins's own account, he wrote to the Bishop of Rangoon and said that he was due to leave the UK on 12th February, 1889. Records at Alton Abbey give the date of his profession into the Society of St Paul at Shoreditch (when he took the religious name of Michael, which he seldom used) as 14th February, 1889, two days after his expected departure. His appointment as River Chaplain at Calcutta was dated 15th March, 1889, suggesting a February departure date at the latest, except that it does not necessarily follow that he was in Calcutta by 15th March, only that this was the date of his appointment. Whichever date is correct, his stay in England can barely have exceeded four months.

Hopkins appears to have used part of his time in London to see a doctor, who can hardly have approved his spending the rest of his time, or the time of his rest, in Shoreditch. It is a mystery why Hopkins should have chosen to place himself in the middle of the worst slum in London, vividly described by Sarah Wise in *The Blackest Streets*. It is possible that Hopkins's purpose in going to Shoreditch was to acquaint himself with the Society of St Paul (SSP), a small parish brotherhood which had been founded there. There is no evidence to connect Hopkins with any of the local clergy except

The Rev. A. Osborne Jay, whose controversial ministry Wise covers comprehensively, and who had brought together the members of the SSP to help in his work. Jay was Vicar of Holy Trinity, Shoreditch, a parish which no longer exists. He was a colourful figure, no stranger to controversy. Born in North India (his father had been personal chaplain to the Maharajah Duleep Singh),[1] which may suggest his link with Hopkins, he was two years older than Hopkins.[2] Jay may not have been a Christian Socialist but his views were not far removed from Christian Socialism. He was also a man with a gift for raising money. There is no doubt that he was a Ritualist, as were several of the surrounding clergy; others were alienated by his style of ministry. Various of his views and his original methods will be encountered again in Hopkins's own ministry in Calcutta. It will be seen that in Jay's own account of his career there are definite parallels with Hopkins's.

No church registers survive from Holy Trinity at this time so it is not possible to discover what, if anything, Hopkins did in the parish. However, Jay's history, in his own words, does survive in print. He was to write (and in a style not unlike that of Hopkins),

> I had served two curacies in the East End already; one
> of which had been under a well-known organizer at the
> Mother Church of East London, Old Stepney, and had
> learned much from him of the work and problems of
> our dreary streets. Subsequently I had been in charge
> of a great College Mission, which might indeed have
> lived on and greatly prospered but for the pettiness
> of those who could neither understand nor appreciate
> success. On the closing of this enterprise I had lived
> in a dismal street near Ratcliff Highway, close to
> the famous 'Tiger Bay', drawing a stipend from the
> Bishop of Bedford's fund as a temporary solatium for
> wounded feelings, and looking for fresh opportunities
> of work ....[3]

Jay's 'wounded feelings' suggest a man who could identify with Hopkins's recent experiences with the Rangoon Church authorities, the latter lacking the comfort of a solatium.[4]

By his own account, resisting the tempting offer of a country living, Jay accepted the parish of Holy Trinity, Shoreditch. A friend told him that nothing but the Last Trump would wake the area.

> I had been told before that the district of Holy Trinity,
> though it had been created in 1867, and already passed
> through the hands of two Vicars, was yet without any
> church. I was not, however, prepared for the state in
> which outside apathy had left it ....

At this time the parish had a population of 8,000, seventeen public houses, and a death rate four times that of the rest of London. The temporary church was a hay loft above a stable. Most of the population lived in rooms that had been sublet and let again so that there were often seven or eight people to a room. Jay moved into rented rooms, gently scented by the nearby stable, on 13th December, 1886. He set about rendering them as cheerful as possible.

Jay was soon able to open a multi-storey building much in advance of its time, with a basement gymnasium, ground floor parish room, church above, and rooms for himself. The church was built to seat 400, but took 250 in comfort. He also had a decent lodging house built. He was assisted by a curate and the Kilburn Sisters (an early female religious order of the Church of England), whose work may also have been of interest to Hopkins. Together they created a remarkable concern: 'The parish room could be used e.g. to feed 900 of the poorest children in the morning, 300 women to meet in the afternoon, and 500 men to congregate at night ...'. Jay reckoned he could fill his church twice over easily, and this only three years after his inaugural service which had been attended by just fourteen people.

Jay's appeals for help to the wealthy of London were aided by newspaper publicity. His thoughts were couched in topical terms; Mr Bazalgette's great London sewers and Embankment were the wonders of London construction at the time. It is worth quoting his views on the social gospel, echoes of which will appear in Hopkins's speeches and writing:

> I know the business of the church, and of religion, is
> to provide for the spiritual side of our nature, but then
> remember that it is my business if I take a walk on
> the Embankment to enjoy my promenade, and yet I
> see one drowning close by, must I not plunge in and
> save if possible? Will that be *ultra vires*, not doing my
> business?...

> I know it is not right for religion to neglect the soul
> for the sake of the body, or to forget to worship God in
> theories of improved sanitation, but I know as well that
> it is the plain, obvious duty of religion to do all that can
> be done towards social reformation and advancement.

He quoted Dr Pusey's (leader of the High Church party after John
Henry Newman joined the Roman Catholic Church) love of the East
Londoner and his fear 'more for the rich than for the most depraved
poor... for the more there is, the more responsibility'.

Shoreditch surely lacked light:

> In no quarter of 'Darkest London' is there a more evil or
> sorrowful record of the lives and squalors of a miserable
> and overcrowded population than in Western Bethnal
> Green and Shoreditch. In no part of the vast metropolis
> have the powers of evil more boldly challenged the
> labours of the city missionary and his fellow-evangelists
> and the civic authorities.[5]

Some Christians were very active in such areas. William Booth,
founder of the Salvation Army, had lately raised the consciousness
of the nation and of the Church with his book *In Darkest England*,
which moved the Salvation Army away from an exclusively
evangelical message towards a social gospel. It was as a response to
Booth's widely read book that Jay came to write an account of his
life in Shoreditch, *Life in Darkest London*. In it he suggested – with
evidence – that Booth was both late on the scene and ill-prepared
for the work he was doing. At the same time his work attracted
much criticism from ministers of other denominations working in
Shoreditch who felt that their own work was being ignored.

Among Jay's efforts to meet the needs of his parish was the
founding of a small parish brotherhood, the Society of St Paul. It had
a short life and seems to have largely died before 1900. Jay's *A Story
of Shoreditch*, published in 1896, speaks of a brother and a sister,
suggesting that, even in reduced form, the community was still in
existence then. The wearing of a cassock identified a member as a
bona fide parish volunteer. The form of address was one of Christian
courtesy. Strangely, there is no trumpeting of the SSP's extension to
India, which makes one wonder when and why Jay and Hopkins had
decided to go separate ways.

Another little venture I [Jay] originated a short time
after I came was the starting of a small working
Brotherhood. I had always felt that there were many
young men engaged in business who would gladly live
under a simple rule, and devote their spare evenings and
Sundays to church work. We called our society that of
St Paul, and each took a simple vow to remain in it if
possible, at any rate, one year. The Brothers, who are
called by their own or some other Christian name, wear
a simple kind of black habit, and keep a simple rule. We
took a house and furnished it, and installed in it at first
four Brothers, having also associates who lived in their
own houses, and came over to help us. As time went on
we found it wise to admit those only to our Society who
worked actively in the parish, and, indeed to concentrate
our efforts. At times, of course, we had some ludicrous
experiences with one or two Brothers... but on the
whole the scheme works admirably, and the Brothers
work so self-denyingly that they are not only useful, but
set a good example to many around them. They teach
in the Sunday School, sing in the choir, and help in the
club.

Much of the life of the parish revolved around the club; Jay's
descriptions of his annual birthday dinners for 300 club members are
striking. After leaving Shoreditch, Hopkins would write of arranging
teas in Calcutta for a thousand sitting. As this kind of event did not
appear in Hopkins's ministry whilst in Burma, it is hard to avoid the
conclusion that he must, if only in this respect, have been influenced
by what he saw of Jay's methods.

The very few Holy Trinity records which remain carry no mention
of Hopkins. Their sparsity means we have to speculate. Perhaps
Hopkins's eye trouble prevented his officiating at services during
his visit to Shoreditch. He cannot have escaped, however, constant
contact with the convivial Jay, and his musical talents would have
been popular with the clubmen. His own views on using hospitality
as a vehicle for religion could not have been better expressed than
in Jay's words:

It is sometimes asked of me, do you not aim at something
higher? Do you never speak of religion? Never in the

club, unless it is first mentioned to me…. Think of the indignation a bishop would feel if an official of the Athenaeum [the exclusive London club] were always attempting to convert him to the doctrines of Methodism or Mormonism.

He would also have felt in tune with Jay's political opinions:

We have done away with slavery. Why is poverty essential? That is a question which at present is beyond our answering. But it may be that the day will dawn when some great economist shall arise with the answer ready. Not, it is true, by tinkering ways or bribery methods, but in a bold, broad, comprehensive spirit, such as alone can perform the herculean task required.

It might be thought that the proximity of the London docks, and the industrial unrest in them, would be of interest to Hopkins. He cannot have escaped word of it, and this may be in part – together with the discussions he would overhear on ships in Calcutta – the reason why Havelock Wilson, founder-president of the seamen's union, noted 1889 as the year he first heard, by letter from Calcutta, from Hopkins. The details of this contact between Hopkins and Havelock Wilson disappear until perhaps as late as 1900, a mystery to be pursued in a later chapter. There is no reason why the two men should have met in London. At this time Havelock Wilson was in the North East of England where his young union was a very locally based affair, though soon to obtain a London office. The earliest *Minutes* book of the Union records both local and national *Minutes* together, indicating that local branch and national Union were operated by the same hands and largely in the North East. Hopkins's Christmas, one imagines, was spent in Shoreditch. In October and November of 1888 Havelock Wilson had been occupied with industrial action in South Wales. His natural place over Christmas would be at home in Sunderland. According to his memoirs, January and February of 1889 involved him in further such action, some of it in London, affording a very slight possibility of an encounter between the two, but with all the evidence pointing away from any meeting.[6] Neither ever suggested a meeting then and there is no explanation why, at that time, a relatively obscure leader of a very young union should meet an equally young and obscure priest from the diocese of Rangoon.

Hopkins's primary reason for going to Shoreditch, unless the Indian connection with Jay allowed him a welcome offer of accommodation in London, must remain his interest in its parish brotherhood. We have no clue how he had heard of it and it is impossible to guess how much of his time the brotherhood took. Today membership of a religious community would involve a lengthy period of probation, first as a postulant, then as a novice, followed by simple vows, with the possibility of life vows at the end of a total period which might take five or more years. In the early days of Anglican religious communities, with neither episcopal regulation nor official Church recognition, it was not unusual to find the new member, especially if he was a priest, receiving little training and only a short period, if any, of probation. In the case of the Shoreditch community, with its promise to serve but a year at a time, it is possible to suppose the very shortest period of probation. Hopkins's vows in February 1889 followed just such a short period in SSP, especially since he was to sail, according to Peter Anson (who does not cite his source and sometimes intrudes his own fancies in such matters), as SSP's provincial for the Indian subcontinent.

There is no evidence that any member of the SSP took permanent vows so those of Hopkins taken on 14th February, 1889, should probably be understood as an annually renewable promise. His period of preparation for his new condition can be extended a little if his excursion into the Akyab ball in a cassock, a choice of dress seriously misunderstood by the reporter who had been moved by its appearance to write of whirling dervishes, represented an early attempt to begin a life set apart by some sort of rule, but that is supposition. The title of provincial, if it was in fact bestowed, may have been intended to give him some sort of status, or at least to regularise his position, and to keep him in touch as the only priest-member of SSP. If that was the case, he seems to have lost touch with SSP in Shoreditch in less time than it had taken for him to become a member, whether by his own choice or, less likely as it seems to have survived for a few more years, by the demise of SSP. Jay's silence on Hopkins's membership of SSP remains a mystery.

Hopkins's time in Shoreditch came at the end of the period of heart-searching which had begun in Akyab. Since his stay away from Akyab with the Oxford Mission (Brotherhood of the Epiphany) in Calcutta in an initial attempt at convalescence, he had come to realise that a group of men held together by the religious life would be the best way of achieving his vision of Church work among seamen; a view confirmed by his difficulties in recruiting suitable staff for his seamen's club. This was farsighted at a time when opportunities for living that life in the Anglican Church were few, and little understood by most Anglicans. Hopkins had already encountered a number of Anglican religious: men of the Oxford Mission and of the Society of St John the Evangelist (which seems to have started work in India in 1874), together with various sisters. It would have been difficult for him to have avoided the Benedictine priest who served the Roman Catholics of Akyab. And perhaps he had encountered the Christian Brothers which local newspapers reveal as part of the Roman Catholic missionary effort in Burma. All of these groups are possible sources of inspiration for his attempt to adopt the religious life but none affords a clue why he should choose the SSP as his starting point.

We have hints but not answers. His close relationship with Archdeacon Blyth whilst he was in Rangoon, which would have continued in Akyab, would have ensured that the archdeacon's views on religious orders would have been known to him. In the relatively small world of the Anglo-Indian Church he would also have been aware of the views of the Bishop of Lucknow. The correspondence of both with SPG shows their sympathy with religious orders, principally on the grounds of expediency and economy in the mission field. The *Indian Church Quarterly Review* carried two articles in 1889 on 'The Community Life as a Missionary Method'. The same journal in the same year published an article on guilds and confraternities. Hopkins had been involved in Rangoon with the Guild of the Holy Trinity,[7] which seems to have been a devotional group. He would also have known, since its doings were often in the local press, of the Roman Catholic Society of St Vincent de Paul (SVP), not a Religious Order, but rather more than a guild, in which Catholic laymen committed themselves to serving groups in all kinds of need.[8]

In applying the religious life to the maritime apostolate, Hopkins had no precedent. No other community of religious (the members of such a community) had ever undertaken such work, nor any guild nor confraternity since the Reformation of which Hopkins would have heard. Rome has no history of religious doing such a thing until 1895, when the Augustinians of the Assumption began to work among deep sea fishermen, a ministry which can be traced back to a speech about his work made by Hopkins in Hastings in 1893. Throughout history individual religious had worked among seamen in various ways, but not *qua* religious. In the Church of England the only instance of anything remotely similar, of which it is unlikely that Hopkins had heard (though it was an order of which his contemporary and later friend, Father Ignatius of Llanthony, approved), was Priscilla Lydia Sellon's Society of the Holy and Undivided Trinity, lineal descendent of the first sisterhood in the Anglican Communion, founded in 1848 at Devonport. For a short time Miss Sellon's Sisters had run a college for sailor boys and a home for old sailors and their wives. It was said that the sailor boys were highly sought as entrants to the Royal Navy. Since this seems to have ceased in the 1860s it is hardly a fertile field in which to find Hopkins's inspiration.

We have noted thus far Hopkins's presence in London (officially on medical grounds), his encounter with Osborne Jay, the industrial unrest in the port, and his involvement with the SSP. There is one other possibility which cannot be passed over: that he took the opportunity to visit some of the welfare provisions for seafarers in the Port of London, and in particular the Sailors' Home in Well Street, situated just east of the Tower of London and near the Mercantile Marine Office where men signed on and off ships. This pioneer institution had been founded in 1829 by the Baptist George Charles Smith (1782-1863) as a refuge for destitute seamen and it became a model for other, albeit smaller, institutions serving sailors around the globe. By 1890 it had become an independent Church of England mission. It included the adjacent St Paul's Church for Seamen (1847) and had a staff of more than forty people. It provided four meals a day, hot baths, a tailor's shop, over 500 beds in individual small cabins, a savings bank, a barber, a daily visit from a surgeon, reading and smoking rooms, a library, and more.[9] It also housed a Navigation School. It is hard to imagine that Hopkins did not go to see this wonder for himself.

It remains to explain his return, not to the Diocese of Rangoon, but to the Diocese of Calcutta. The details are incomplete, as with each period of his life, but at some point during his stay in England (and in a period so short as four months, precision is probably not important) Hopkins received a letter, reproduced much later in *The Messenger*, from Bishop Strachan of Rangoon who, in spite of Hopkins's past difficulties and disagreements with his committees in Rangoon and Akyab, continued to appreciate Hopkins's undoubted ability to draw seamen to the Church. Bishop Strachan wrote:

I hope soon to be able to welcome you back to my
diocese. I shall be very glad to see you back here. You
did most excellent work as Port Chaplain in Rangoon,
and now I ask you to resume that appointment. I cannot
at present appoint you to any spiritual charge on shore
at Rangoon, because Mr Sisam is in charge of the East
Rangoon District and Mr Graham-de-Lancy is at present
legally the Assistant Chaplain at the Pro-Cathedral. But
I should like you to come out, take the Port Chaplaincy
and do what you can in pastoral work in the Town District
and I should regard your so doing as constituting a very
strong claim upon the Assistant Chaplaincy of the Pro-
Cathedral when that post becomes vacant or available.

Hopkins would have observed that the bishop was careful to get what
he could without committing himself to anything in return. There is
no hint of passage money or job security. Whatever he may have felt
on receipt of such an oleaginous letter after being cast adrift without
financial support so recently by its author, he had the satisfaction of
being able to reply, 'I have accepted the Port Chaplaincy of Calcutta,
which is attached to the parish of Kidderpore, and leave England
on the 12th of February'. With that, the Bishop of Rangoon had
to be content, for the offer to Hopkins had come from Rangoon's
metropolitan bishop.

The Bishop of Calcutta, Dr Johnson, was at this time in London on
furlough and so able to see Hopkins personally. After his interview
with Hopkins the bishop advised him that he would receive a
formal offer from his commissary. This offer appears to have been
a five- year contract with the promise of a free hand, which suggests
that Hopkins had not accepted the bishop's offer without making
conditions. He attributed the offer to the influence of the parish
priest of Kidderpore, The Rev. A. Saunders Dyer, who may also have
been his link with Jay and with whom he would be working in India.
Dyer would have been known to him at least in name as the editor
of *The Indian Church Quarterly Review*, which circulated widely
among Anglicans in India and Burma. (Dyer wasted no time in
getting Hopkins to write an article on his work, which would appear
in 1890.). It is possible that Hopkins also knew Dyer personally. It
would make a logical sequence of events, though one gleaned from
very slender hints here and there, if Hopkins received the Bishop of

Calcutta's offer before joining SSP, then agreed with the bishop to go to Calcutta for five years, expecting a priest from SSP to join him in 1890 to help with starting some sort of community life there. He certainly had hopes of recruiting such a priest once he had arrived in Calcutta but, in the event, one did not materialise.

The Calcutta Port Chaplaincy had had seven chaplains in the preceding fourteen years, each chaplain being followed by gaps of between six and nineteen months. It seems uninviting in retrospect, so much so that it is easy to imagine that Hopkins was offered the free hand and the five-year contract by a grateful, and possibly desperate, bishop. The bishop may have found it hard to credit that anyone should want such an appointment. The bishop's offer of a free hand, which we must assume carried with it a general assent to the starting of a quasi-religious community in Calcutta, would have had considerable attraction for Hopkins after his experiences in Rangoon and Akyab.

Ministry in Calcutta

Although appointed to the Chaplaincy, described correctly as the River Chaplaincy but more generally as the Port Chaplaincy, in Calcutta from 15th March, 1889, Hopkins did not start chaplaincy work full-time until the beginning of December 1889. Initially he was required to cover an absence at St Paul's Church, Scott's Lane, Calcutta. Even at this stage he seems to have been joined by others seeking to live a common life: Brother John (William Franks[1]), a former ship's cook, who would later leave to marry and manage the Calcutta Scandinavian seamen's club; Brother Stephen, who had an able seaman's discharge, and Brother Paul (Mr Butler), late of the Bengal Pilot Service. A Mr Bullen, a Merchant Navy officer, joined and took the habit in 1891.[2] How these men were recruited remains a mystery but their willingness to join Hopkins suggests his personality had a certain magnetism.

Hopkins recorded that within a fortnight of his arrival he was beset by a 'No Popery' demonstration. He was later to claim that this was the result of his introduction of a sung Mass and his advertising times for confessions. It would have been odd for him to have done this at a church where he was simply covering an absence. Neither point would have been a novelty in Calcutta but both could have been inflammatory. The cause of the demonstration could equally well have been the wearing of his habit in public, which, by the look of contemporary photographs, could not be mistaken for a simple cassock. However, in 1900 Hopkins would write,

> Every missionary, dissenter as well as Church, was
> recognised by the coat and collar he wore – the regulation
> clerical coat and collar! And every man, so coated and
> collared, was supposed to come for what he could in the

> way of a subscription; or to dispose of Bibles, Prayer
> Books and tracts. I never took a subscription list on
> board ship, nor did I take Bibles, Prayer Books or tracts
> to dispose of; and I wanted to disassociate myself from
> those who did. So I discarded the clerical collar and
> coat, and adopted a cassock and girdle instead.

Either way, his Anglo-Catholic credentials were established. It is probably better not to wonder how a cassock or habit lent itself to ship visiting, where access would be up a precarious gangway or a vertical monkey ladder.

It was agreed that the Seamen's Mission in Calcutta would give Hopkins a free hand, his salary, the assistance of two lay agents, house rent and a small establishment allowance for boat hire and necessary servants. As in Rangoon, money was to prove a continuing problem. The archdeacon had to ask formally for the appointment of Hopkins as Chaplain of the Calcutta Medical College Hospital at Rs100 per month in addition to the River Chaplaincy, a formal request made necessary by the Accountant General's objection to paying one man for two jobs. His Hospital Chaplaincy was confirmed from 1st August, 1889. The appointment was a sensible one as this was the hospital to which seamen were admitted.[3]

The Calcutta River Chaplaincy had experienced a number of problems in addition to its frequent turnover of chaplains. In 1886 the Scripture Reader had quarrelled with the chaplain, severed his connection, and set up his own institute under Methodist auspices. The chaplaincy had been attached to St John's Church, once Calcutta's cathedral, and the junior priest was committed to act as secretary of the Seamen's Mission at its quarterly meetings. This Seamen's Mission, which included Hopkins's work, had been founded as early as 1852. It had been extended in 1867 when the Government of Bengal gave an old ship for the purpose. The chaplain had been intended to live on board this ship and be paid Rs300 a month, as Hopkins was, but the source of this salary had been precarious for some years. It helps to place Hopkins's salary if it is known that at about this time the salary of the future Lord Inchcape, starting out as a clerk in Calcutta, was a similar sum, though with opportunities to add to it. It was also the salary of the local police inspector (all such salaries were published in *Thacker*). Its sterling value of some £35 per month gives no clue to its purchasing power. Hopkins's work was supposed to include ship- visiting on the river, superintending the coffee and reading rooms at 19 Lall Bazaar, holding weekday services on Fridays and holy days, Sunday services morning and evening, and classes for religious instruction. The congregation, described as 'not large', averaged between forty and sixty 'seafaring men', depending upon the number of ships in the river.[4] Hopkins was to find, when he arrived, some twenty communicants among them, and this figure he would increase considerably. Other provision for seamen in Calcutta included a Seamen's Institute at Clyde Road, Hastings, and the Calcutta Sailors' Home at 13 Strand Road.

Apparently the cries of 'No Popery' directed at Hopkins failed to deter the bishop from becoming the president of the Seamen's Friendly Society of St Paul (SFSSP) which Hopkins founded as the main instrument of his work. It was separate from the Seamen's Mission and River Chaplaincy, and distinct from the Order of St Paul (OSP), which was to be the title of his own community. SFSSP turned into a quasi-union and Hopkins would see it almost as the older brother of the National Sailors' and Firemen's Union (NSFU). Its headed note paper always gave its foundation date as 1889, when it was well-known that the NSFU dated from 1894. The three agencies, mission, OSP, and SFSSP, were intertwined to the point where they are sometimes impossible to distinguish, though, for convenience, Hopkins would claim to be acting under whichever seemed appropriate at the time. The bishop was also, *ex officio*, president of the Seamen's Mission with, by 1890, his archdeacon as secretary and vice president. The rest of the committee consisted of laymen of considerable influence: E.F. Longley (secretary of the Great Eastern Hotel Company), J. Lambert CIE (Commissioner of Police), W Pigott (probably of the firm, Pigott & Chapman), Captain Reed (the river surveyor), L Rose (representing MacKenzie Lyall & Co), Sir Alex Wilson Kt (Jardine Skinner & Co), and Captain Campbell IM (deputy director of the Indian marine dockyard). The treasurer was H. Pinkerton of Gillanders, Arbuthnott & Co, Bankers. These were powerful men and represented serious commercial interests.

Calcutta, situated on the River Hughli, was the premier port of the Indian subcontinent and the Port Commissioners were zealous in its development. Its trade had been affected in 1869 by the opening of the Suez Canal but it nevertheless continued to be an important centre of commerce.

	Vessels	**Tons**
Arrivals	811 steamers	1,353,089
	223 sailing ships	363,881
		Total 1,716,920
Departures	816 steamers	1,363,702
	236 sailing ships	373,966
		Total 1,737,668

Shipping movements in Calcutta, 1890. Source: *Times of India*.

A visiting ship's officer, R.A. Horn, who seems to have served all his time in steam, wrote in 1892,

> The grandest sight I see here is the long line of sailing ships moored in the river. Most of them being four masted and some of them the largest and finest ships afloat, it looks like a large cobweb to look up aloft but there are a lot of them been laying here for 8 to 10 months and still no chance of getting a cargo. Trade is very bad.[5]

The 1891 statistics show the ascendancy of steam. By 1895 the *Times of India* (7th June) was noting '70% of the ships which come up the Hughli every year are compelled to wait from one to six days in the river before they can approach the jetties to unload ...'. Delays waiting for a berth and delays in waiting for a cargo meant that ship owners were disinclined to be generous, and may go some way towards explaining the bishop's difficulty in finding the necessary finance for the River Chaplaincy. It was however these delays and those referred to by Mr Horn in his letter that gave Hopkins his opportunities to serve the seamen.

At first Hopkins lived in the parsonage house attached to St Paul's but, on the return of the incumbent, he had to move. The river chaplain's accommodation was unsuited to community life.

Hopkins settled for 17 Garden Reach, convenient for the point of arrival of most of the sailing ships and where coolies employed in the government scheme for labour in other colonies were loaded and unloaded. The house was set in a spacious garden, in the centre of which was a water tank. The garden seems to have been large enough for some sort of cricket and the tank for swimming lessons (few sailors could swim), both popular Sunday activities.[6] On two occasions sailors were found drowned there. The house was homely rather than smart and a large room was set aside for receiving sailors. It was furnished with a piano (which Hopkins considered indispensable) and a billiard table and was conveniently near to both chapel and Hopkins's study. The brethren had a community room off which their cells were situated. Successive volumes of *Thacker's Indian Directory* indicate the growth of the infant community: in 1891 there were four brothers with Hopkins, in 1894, seven. F. C. Hendry, a popular writer of sea stories, writing under his pen name of Shalimar, mentions Hopkins by name in his 'Pride at the Main Truck'.[7] Internal evidence suggests that Hendry visited Calcutta and its priory while an apprentice in the Merchant Navy in the 1890s. In his short story, Macrae, the senior apprentice

> had discovered an establishment called the Priory, run by Father Hopkins, where in addition to two services a day there was open house to all the apprentices in the port. The attraction of the Priory included games, a billiard table, a swimming tank, and well-cooked free meals.

For the seamen there was also the Seamen's Church, a former military building replacing the floating chapel which had ceased to be used in 1887. Hopkins had it refurbished in Anglo-Catholic style, installed new punkahs and replaced the choir with a weekly singing practice for the congregation. Regular and solemn (i.e. with incense) worship, with the Mass as the central service, soon drew the men and many of them also made their first confession to him. Community Offices (the Offices are the daily round of services) were said in the private chapel at 17 Garden Reach, now styled 'The Priory', and Anson (writing with information from OSP obtained shortly after Hopkins's death in 1922[8]) claimed a source indicating that at first the Hours of the Church (i.e. the daily offices) followed the nautical system of keeping time by bells. The 1891

Thacker noted Hopkins as sharing The Priory with Brothers John,
Paul, Stephen and James. Together they offered these daily services
in the Seamen's (Temporary) Church that is, The Priory chapel at
7.30 a.m. and 5.30 p.m. (Wednesdays at 7.00 p.m.). On Sundays, the
advertised services were 'Matins and Liturgy (plain) at 9.30 a.m.',
a 'Celebration of the Blessed Sacrament and Sermon' at 10.30 a.m.,
and Evensong and Sermon at 6.30 p.m. It took some time to evolve
a Rule, which was completed on All Saints' Day (1st November)
1893, and closely followed that of St Benedict.

Hopkins made no concessions in religious terms to those among
whom he was working. On the one hand he promised that they
would not have religion thrust down their throats. He had no time for
religious tracts or their distributors ('tract mongers'). Nor were wall
texts, a popular feature of the period, in evidence. On the other hand,
for those who wished, there was a warm welcome at The Priory and
the opportunity to share the life and the table of the brethren. If they
happened to be fasting, as in Lent, the guest would share that too.
Every effort was made to help those coming to the church to be
familiar with the service, which was offered with full ceremonial.
Weekly sheets were produced for the guidance of the congregation.

Hopkins described his methods of work among seamen in
an article for the *Indian Church Quarterly Review* of April 1890,
which suggests, since he was so new in post in Calcutta, that his
reputation had preceded him. The article, entitled 'The Church and
Our Sailors', outlined the general condition of sailors:

> our sailors are neglected by governments, politicians
> and ship-owners alike … their condition today is little
> better in many instances than it was half a century ago.
> And the same may be said for the sailor's spiritual
> condition ….

a statement which he would soon discover had upset his bishop.
The article drew attention briefly to many injustices suffered by
sailors (appropriation of earnings, overloading, undermanning, poor
accommodation, poor food, etc.) to illustrate his point that the Church
needed to be concerned with both the spiritual and the temporal
welfare of the seaman. He denigrated the preaching of uninvited
sermons and the distribution of tracts on board ship, arguing instead
that the men should be approached cautiously, with time to talk
to them and hear of their circumstances. This could best be done

overseas (when men stayed with their ships) rather than in home ports (where the men would have been paid-off) and was being done by The Missions to Seamen and the St Andrew's Waterside Mission. Here, in East Indian and colonial ports, the men would be held up for weeks, sometimes for months, usually working in the boiling sun, often fleeced of their money and sometimes hounded in sickness to the point of deserting ship. In such conditions they would welcome any sign of friendship and thus give the Church its opportunity.

Hopkins thought that opportunity was best seized by treating the sailor, not as something apart, but as a fellow Christian. Port chaplains, according to Hopkins, should not be segregated but parish staffs should be strengthened and the work among seamen firmly based in a parochial context.[9] Their work would fall into two parts: afloat and ashore. Afloat, chaplains could visit ships between 8.00 a.m. and 9.00 a.m. when the men were breakfasting, or after 6.00 p.m. when work was finished for the day. Hopkins stressed the need to visit both officers and men; he did so for two reasons: to avoid the implication that the 'men' were somehow more in need of the Gospel, and to obtain more readily, if desired, the object of holding a service on board. The captain could press the crew to attend but it was, Hopkins thought, much better for their attendance to be obtained freely and willingly. Any service afloat should be simple; ashore they were better sacramental. Services afloat could be supplemented by Bible classes. Ashore, provision for the men should recognise that they had been cooped up, perhaps for months. Many seamen would have signed articles offering 'no liberty abroad', intended to avoid crew members jumping ship in foreign ports, which meant that time ashore could not be claimed as of right. In what liberty they were permitted they sought 'a bright and cheerful Club or Home', preferably furnished with a piano, perhaps frequented by other parishioners willing to make friends and perhaps with access to sleeping accommodation. Sunday, the great liberty day for crews, should not be marked by a strict sabbatarianism; simple board games and amusements would keep many from sin. Given all this, those who did seek Christian ministrations should find a decently and solemnly (the ambiguity is probably deliberate) celebrated Communion service.

Contemporary reports in newspapers and in *The Messenger* and the *Nautical Guildsman* confirm that Hopkins practiced this pattern of ministry. He returned frequently to the theme of Sunday as a

'day of temptation ... when there were plenty of places open ... for
vice and sin' and his references to cricket and swimming caused
one reporter to mistake him for 'an advocate of the "muscular
Christianity" method of missionary labour as contrasted with the
evangelical style.'[10] Different weeknight evenings at The Priory were
set aside to receive the various groups of men (ratings, apprentices,
officers), while Sundays were open to all comers. At special times
of the year, such as Christmas, an extra effort was made. Hopkins
seems to have had a penchant for grand dinners, perhaps inspired by
those he had seen in Jay's parish. His were larger, for he might have
as many as a thousand sitting down, in two sittings, for the dinner
accompanying the New Year Sports (high jump, shot, long jump,
obstacle race, three-legged race, sack race, tug of war) at the Sailors'
Home. Catering was done by the Great Eastern Hotel, the Secretary
of which was a member of Hopkins's management committee.[11]
Donations for these events came from a variety of sources and
Hopkins made sure that it was known that these included the Viceroy,
the Lieutenant Governor of Bengal, and the Commander in Chief.
Police Commissioner Lambert, another committee member, wrote
at the end of 1889 that his men had had nothing to do on the streets
of Calcutta that Christmastide where in previous years sailors had
kept them very busy. He ascribed this happy state of affairs directly
to Hopkins's good work. Similar success began to be found in the
church, and the twenty communicant sailors found on Hopkins's
arrival in 1890 had become 1,450 by 1892, though how this figure
was constituted is not explained.

    To achieve these things Hopkins had the help of his brethren. Two
of these received the salaries intended for his two assistants; other
money came from donations, some of which were raised by Hopkins
on his preaching tours of England. These brethren belonged to the
Society, later Order, of St Paul, which the bishop had insisted must
stand on its own feet financially and must not look to the diocese
for financial assistance. Their good works were supported by and
channelled through SFSSP, the primary aims of which were to defend
the weak against oppression and wrong and to shelter the homeless
and destitute, the aged and infirm.[12] That there was no mistaking
the aims of the SFSSP is evidenced by its contemporary, the secular
American Coast Seamen's Journal of San Francisco, each issue of
which gave its stated aim as 'The Brotherhood of the Sea' and its
motto as 'Justice by organization'. The SFSSP could, and virtually

did, claim the same.[13]

Hopkins was not content to work only in Calcutta. He clearly expected to have founded a society which would eventually provide a network of seamen's homes around the world:

> it is not my wish or intention that we should confine ourselves to this local effort. We desire in addition to organise a body of men to go forth, and undertake the charge and work of Seamen's Missions in other places ....

And so, in India, his work began to spread. Brother Stephen and Chang (an Arakanese apparently adopted by Hopkins, sometimes described as a prince), opened a base in Chittagong, in October 1891. According to *The Messenger* this seasonal (October to February) port welcomed some 800 seamen to its rooms in its first season and Brother Stephen had what appears to have been a Christmas congregation of 150 seamen. There was also work, at first seasonal, undertaken at Budge Budge, which was down-river from Calcutta, where petroleum was unloaded. According to *The Messenger* of October 1891 Budge Budge 'is a village of twenty or thirty huts, and I [Hopkins] firmly believe that more than half of them are immoral houses. Even if you go on shore for a quiet stroll, temptation assails you at every turn'. An 1894 reference to Brother Paul's work at Budge Budge survives in the newspaper reports of Hopkins's court case (below) against Robert Smallman where it is implied that this mission was run from tented accommodation. In 1894, too, Brother Alban began work in Bombay.

In 1893 a British house was opened in Barry, South Wales, carefully chosen as a port where no other society was at work. Hopkins wrote, 'If we are to occupy Foreign Ports in other parts of the world (as we are certainly now called to do) we must establish a Mother House of the whole Society in England.' Barry was a step on the way. As early as May 1892, Hopkins had written in *The Messenger*,

> It may be as well for me here to state the lines on which our Society works in connection with outports. We desire to see each port with its own well organised and firmly established 'Seamen's Mission and Friendly Society', we ourselves constituting a society or community of men ready to go to these different ports to manage and work

these different Missions. We do not seek to absorb into
our own Society existing organisations; but seeing the
past failures of the Missions to Seamen in certain parts
of the world, through the absence of trained, qualified,
and devoted workers in the persons of members of our
own Society....

Apart from Hopkins's adoption of the role of David against the
MtoS's Goliath, and his call for training (a novelty at the time), what
does this article reveal of his intentions? His grant from SAWCM
has already been noted and may explain why Hopkins confined
his criticism to the MtoS. Equally, the differing approaches of
the MtoS and SAWCM may explain the criticism. His emphasis
on his Friendly Society, which clearly has echoes of the friendly
societies that preceded the trade unions, may have a further and
provocative significance when placed alongside the title of the older,
undenominational Protestant, British and Foreign Seamen's Friend
Society and Bethel Union,[14] a society inimical in its beliefs to a High
Church member of the Church of England.

The 'objects' of the SFSSP were fully given in the first issue (July
1891, price 2d.):

1.   To provide Religious Instruction, Worship, and the means
      of Grace[15] at 'the Seamen's Church;
2.   To provide Healthy Recreation and Intercourse for Men
      and Lads at its 'Recreation Rooms';
3.   Offers the Hospitality and Advantages of 'Home' at the
      Priory or Mission House;
4.   Shelters the Homeless and Destitute;
5.   Defends the Weak against imposition and wrong;
6.   Cares for the Sick and Dying on board and on
      shore;
7.   Guards and tends the Graves of the Dead.

Employers would have hesitated at the fifth object. Taken
together, these objects offer a combination of seamen's missionary
work with much of what old-style trade unionism offered. To carry
them out Hopkins needed both men and money. To this end he made
two trips back to Britain. The amount of time he spent away from
Calcutta between the date of his arrival in 1889 and his release by
his bishop in 1894 is revealing. Of the total possible, 59 months,

calculating from the December when he took up his work as full-time River Chaplain, he was away for nearly five months in 1891, and four months in 1893; this represented just about a sixth of his time in Calcutta. The time would have been further eroded by the need to prepare for departure and, on his return, for taking up the reins.

During Hopkins's 1891 visit to England, he left Brother Paul in charge in Calcutta. His visit ran from June to October and coincided with the first issue of *The Messenger*, the community's monthly magazine, which offered these details. His work in the UK was supported from a London office. This 'Home Organisation' was in the hands of a secretary, a Miss Bundy, based initially at 25 Brooke Street, Holborn. The honorary secretary and treasurer was E.I. Charlton Esquire. There were twenty-five district centres with local secretaries (seven men and eighteen women). Hopkins undertook a heavy programme of preaching and speaking engagements the length of England. Donations were received at the office, as were gifts of books. A personal tie was severed whilst he was on this tour when his mother died at Bassein in Burma on 9th October.

The English visit of 1893 was supposed to start with his departure from Calcutta in the February. Hopkins certainly arrived in London in the July. During his absence his Calcutta brethren, lacking a priest of their own, were served by the fathers of the Oxford Mission. Again, he had a hectic preaching programme, supplemented by organ recitals as an additional means of raising money. This visit has a particular significance in that an account of one of his speaking engagements survives not only in a local newspaper but also in the French Jesuit periodical, *Études*, which in February 1894 carried an article entitled *Les Missions Protestantes d'Angleterre en Façeur des Marins* by a Jesuit novice, Eugène Grosjean. Grosjean was taken to hear Hopkins speak at Hastings on 28th August by Fr Francis Goldie SJ, erstwhile Catholic chaplain on Calcutta-bound troopships.[16] Grosjean was in England in the French Jesuit novitiate because the French political situation had forced its removal from France.

Through his work for the Catholic Truth Society (CTS) and its seamen's sub committee Goldie had begun to investigate what was being done by the other churches and what could be done by the Catholic Church for seafarers; his interest was to lead to the establishment of the first Catholic Seamen's Clubs in Montreal and London in 1893.

Goldie was also concerned to extend this work to France, which may explain his choice of Grosjean for company at Hastings. Grosjean's article, in turn, was in part responsible for the founding of the *Œuvres de Mer*. This organisation, founded in 1894 by M. Bernard Bailly in connection with the Augustinians of the Assumption, ran ships to bring the services of priest and doctor to the thousands of French fishers off Newfoundland and Iceland. Bailly had been wondering what to do about these French fishers when Grosjean's article, later to be reprinted as *Et nos Marins?* to recruit interest, brought the British (subsequently Royal National) Mission to Deep Sea Fishermen and Hopkins's OSP to Bailly's attention, a combination reflected in the subsequent structure of the *Œuvres de Mer.* The *Œuvres de Mer* was to play a very important role in the revival of the Catholic organisation, the Apostleship of the Sea, in the 1920s. A clear line thus links Hopkins with this revival.[17]

Grosjean and Goldie were impressed by Hopkins's platform manner at Hastings.[18] They took away some of his literature. Grosjean described him as a High Church minister with 'an animated and lively manner' (*s'ecrie-t-il*), adding that he was *un homme jeune encore, au visage complètement rasé* (a young man, clean-shaven), wearing a soutane and biretta, both bound in crimson (perhaps marking him as Superior of the OSP), and a pectoral cross. Hopkins addressed a large audience which seems to have been drawn by his preaching locally on the preceding Sunday. His subject was his approach to mission, which has been considered earlier in this chapter. This he spiced up with anecdotes and humour but took particular care to dispel the impression that he was against captains and owners 'as being cruel and bad'. He spoke of a number of cases he had successfully taken up to expose cruelty, balancing them with testimony from 'Captains and others' as to the benefits of his 'system'.

Whilst Hopkins was in London, in September his bishop agreed to place the Calcutta work in the hands of his community whereas previously his had been a personal appointment to the River Chaplaincy. For the time this was unusual recognition of a religious order by an Anglican bishop. It may have been influenced by Hopkins's future plans. In 1891 he had hoped to return with a priest, who had had to withdraw on health grounds. This time, he returned with four prospective brethren and a priest committed to three years. By February 1894, however, two of the four had been sent home.

Another priest was clearly an important consideration. Brother

Alban was made deacon in 1894 and subsequently ordained to the priesthood. However, the shortage of recruits and the expansion of work among seamen was obviously a matter of concern for Hopkins. He may also at this time have begun to appreciate the limitation of Colonial Orders. He began to write in *The Messenger* of the pressing need for that Mother House in England. As it turned out, a possibility was to arise in Wales, for in December 1893 he wrote, 'Very soon we must establish our Novice House in England [*sic*]... Mrs Jenner, of Wenvoe Castle, near Cardiff, has given us a piece of land on which to build a small Priory. At Barry...'.

Discussions with the Bishop of Calcutta about the future of his work followed. In spite of what will be seen as his stormy years in Calcutta (below), the bishop was pressing Hopkins to commit himself to a further five years. This seems to have been a confusing period in the River Chaplaincy, too. For reasons of expediency, the work of SFSSP was in the process of being separated from the Seamen's Mission. Since neither of these was technically part of the River Chaplaincy, it is not clear what was afoot, for the three were interlinked. Money may have underlain the problem, especially if Hopkins had alienated the business community which would cause the chaplaincy to suffer a consequent decline in donations. A cash shortage is mentioned in April 1894; the bishop apparently redirected funds and the Port Commissioners withdrew a grant of Rs100 previously used to support the Recreation Rooms. It is odd that this should happen just at the moment when Hopkins should agree to stay on, acquiescing at first to the bishop's request for a further five years (in a letter dated 10th April) before being forced by circumstances to agree to one year only.

The picture painted thus far is of a successful and charismatic ministry among Calcutta's seafarers, despite the initial controversy over ritual. Hopkins had certainly increased his congregations. He had stayed longer in the chaplaincy than any of his predecessors, enhancing it beyond recognition. Yet things are sometimes not as they appear. In this case there had been real problems, especially from his bishop's viewpoint, caused as much by Hopkins's success and dedication as by his temperament. *The Englishman (Weekly Summary)* of 28th September, 1892 (just before the launch of the Seamen's Guild) carried a letter from Constance Bundy, the secretary of the Home Organisation of the SFSSP in response to a complaint carried in the paper in July. She wrote,

The present crowded church and larger Recreation
Rooms that are proving too small to accommodate the
numbers that flock to them, hardly look as tho' the duties
of the River Chaplain are not 'properly performed'.
Cases such as the recent Crofton Hall scandal [below],
and that in which a sailor was charged in Court with
'refusal of duty', and the case was dismissed, because it
was proved that the man had worked twenty-four hours
running in the stokehole, prove, I think, that sailors have
some need of a friend who will dare to speak out for
them.

It is clear from Hopkins's various writings that he considered the
visiting of ships as an important part of his ministry. He found early
on that he was often unwelcome to ship masters who would prevent
his boarding of their ships. At first this seems to have been linked
with the No Popery campaign, for within a fortnight of his arrival
in Calcutta a meeting of masters had demanded that he remove
(unspecified) ornaments from the Seamen's Church. After this
some captains forbade crew members from attending worship there.
Hopkins was caused great displeasure when one of his Confirmation
candidates was among those forbidden to go ashore by a captain but
asked to attend a Methodist service on board ship instead. He was
very careful, however, to make sure that the men did nothing which
might attract the accusation of absence without leave, or desertion,
which attracted severe penalties. Human nature being what it is, it is
not surprising that the men began to seek him out, his unpopularity
with their masters working in his favour. Those associated with
Hopkins also ran the risk of being forbidden to visit ships. In January
1892 Brother Alban wrote of being rudely forbidden access to a
ship when he was discovered to be 'one of Father Hopkins' gang'.
Coincidentally, Hopkins's health problems, at this time manifested
in a persistent eye trouble, which led his doctor to ban him from the
river when the sun was up, meant that he had medical grounds for
no longer visiting ships.
    Problems increased with the foundation of the Seamen's Guild in
October 1892. Hopkins had been involved in parish guilds, groups
of like-minded devotees, in Rangoon. It is possible that he had seen
similar work while in London and may have become interested in
guilds for particular trades; the one for postal workers at St Alban's

Holborn is the best example. It is also possible that the Victorian
fashion for things 'Gothick' had interested him, as it seems to have
done others, in the medieval craft guilds. He was certainly aware of
the temperance movement which organised its members in lodges;
the International Order of Good Templars and the Church of England
Purity Association had reached Calcutta. Membership of these was
surrounded with quasi-Masonic ceremonial. It is also known that
at one time Hopkins hoped to associate his Guild, minus its trade
union aspects, with similar work being organised in the Diocese of
Gibraltar.[19]

Hopkins's Guild had its own magazine, the *Nautical Guildsman*,
renamed *Shipmates* in 1894 and absorbed into *The Messenger* in
November 1896. It was launched in November 1892 at 4 annas a
copy. Unlike *The Messenger*, which was full of articles about the
ill-treatment of seamen, the *Nautical Guildsman* consisted of quite
weighty articles, some about the OSP, some about the Church, but
the largest number about legislation and changes in the shipping
industry. Where this Guild differed from other contemporary guilds
was in its quite specific references to 'a fair day's work for a fair
day's pay' and its condemnation of 'refusal of duty, absence without
leave, and laying up'. We do not know if Hopkins was at this time
aware that Havelock Wilson, founder of the nascent seamen's Union
in England, in his earliest work undertook to recruit men as crews in
North East England committed to honouring these very principles.
Hopkins was described as Superior of the Seamen's Guild. The
bishop was its president. Honorary secretary was J.E. Anderson Esq
(of 17 Garden Reach). The solicitor was Cockerell A.Smith, and
the bankers, Messrs Grindley & Co of Calcutta and London. Three
referees in England were listed, along with Hon Counsel, T.D.Munro,
Barrister at Law, 3 Harcourt Buildings, Temple (London). No other
Church guild advertised a lawyer!

Hopkins had been casting around for a method of organising
seamen. Like Havelock Wilson he seems to have started with the
intention of working with all men of goodwill. The foundation in
1890 of the Shipping Federation replaced what little and disparate
goodwill was to be found amongst most employers with a united
front; employers hardening their united position as unionism gained in
strength. His time in Shoreditch, when he cannot have been unaware
of so much union activity in connection with the 1889 Dock Strike,
may have been what turned his thoughts in the direction of organised

labour. There would have been, too, talk among seamen about the embryonic seamen's Union. The passage time to India would have ensured a delay after the Dock Strike before the seamen's Union became a significant topic of discussion in Indian ports, but arrive it surely did. Havelock Wilson noted in his obituary of Hopkins in *The Seaman* that his first contact with him had been a letter from Hopkins desiring to start a branch of the Union in Calcutta in 1889, and that a considerable correspondence followed, a detail missing from Wilson's autobiography. There is no direct confirmation of this. Union records are seriously incomplete and make mention neither of Hopkins nor of Calcutta for this period. There is, however, a letter to Hopkins from the Bishop of Calcutta which shows that Hopkins contacted him to the effect that he (Hopkins) had been invited to be president of the Calcutta branch of the Union. My opinion is that Hopkins had been the means by which the branch was established and this is confirmed by Hopkins's speech at the Union's annual dinner in October 1916:

> When, in 1889, I found myself in Calcutta, Mr Havelock Wilson had just started his great endeavour to establish a National Union ... I, thousands of miles away, did my little best to co-operate with what he was doing here in the old country ... and the powers that were on the other side of the world called me to task and made it impossible for me to go on with that work ....

It would be natural for the branch to press for his presidency. Mobility of members meant union organisation was always a problem, forcing a heavy dependence on shore-based officers. The bishop's letter is worth quoting in full for the strength of the episcopal response may well indicate how prominent business men, upon whose financial support the diocese depended, felt about Hopkins's activities.

The bishop wrote from Darjeeling on 26th May, 1890,

> My Dear Hopkins,
>   My illness has prevented my writing to you sooner upon the subject of your becoming President of the Calcutta branch of the Sailors' Union. I have considered the matter fully and have talked the matter over with others and have come to the conclusion that it is not

desirable that you should accept the post. You will hardly like my saying it, and it may [be] that you will hardly believe that you have already caused a good deal of irritation amongst the captains and merchants of the city (one firm I am told has withdrawn its subscription of Rs 250) and for you to take so prominent a position as leader in what is simply a trades union would so fix you as a partisan that it could scarcely be expected that men engaged in the shipping trade would support you. I have seen that both the Englishman and the Statesman commenting on your report express their appreciation of your zeal and both regret the attitude you take up towards the employers – I agree with the Statesman it is both unwise and unjust to say as you do in your report that 'Sailors are neglected by the Government, politicians, and shipowners alike' – and to add that their present condition is little better than it was half a century ago.

I am afraid you will not like my saying so, but if you would confine yourself to the spiritual work, assisting and advising sailors, and maintaining such friendly relations with merchants and captains as would enable you to influence them on behalf of the men it would do more good than abusing them.

I feel very strongly that you are assuming too much the position of agitator which only tends to embitter people and make matters worse instead of better for all concerned.

Yours truly

Edward R Calcutta.

The passage, part-quoted earlier, to which the bishop objected, was printed in April 1890, which suggests that Hopkins's letter to which the bishop was replying had been written before the beginning of May, placing the start of Hopkins's union activity firmly in the first half of 1890.

An example of local feeling against Hopkins is illustrated well by a letter of July 1892[20] from 'Observer'. Most letters in the colonial press of the period seemed to favour pennames. Observer wrote,

Sir, If my memory serves me correctly I think about two years ago there was a great outcry from the shipmasters in the port against the Rev Mr Hopkins, for causing seamen to show a mutinous spirit towards those properly placed in authority over them. The ill-feeling grew to such a pitch that the captains in a body refused to have any dealings with the Home until Mr Hopkins was removed from the Committee. This decision… proved so disastrous… that Mr Hopkins had to resign his membership of the Committee. One would have thought that time would have healed the wound, but from what we have been treated to lately the feeling seems as bitter as ever…. Nearly all shipmasters will not allow him on board their vessels. The companion ladder is hoisted up when he is seen coming alongside. Liberty to crews is refused if it is known they are coming to his house….

Unable to make much progress with a Union branch and probably valuing his independence, Hopkins started his Seamen's Guild, the willingness of which to defend its members signalled, no doubt, by the naming of its lawyer on its publications seems to have become the focus for this ill-feeling. The Guild's three stated 'objects' were:

A united and consecrated effort on the part of Seamen, to establish amongst themselves the principles of *Charity*, *Justice* and *Sobriety*.

An earnest and combined effort on the part of Sailors to present, before God and their fellow-men, a body of law-abiding, upright, and sober seamen.

A united effort to defend their privileges and interests, and to obtain for themselves the consideration and respect due to the dignity of the working man.

These objects appeared clearly in the magazine and their references to combination, united effort and the working man would at the time have been capable of no interpretation other than 'trade unionism'. That they were also patent of a less sinister interpretation may have been what allowed the bishop to permit the use of his name as the president, unless he was hoping that his presidency might in some way encourage Hopkins to moderate his position.

Guildsmen had certain obligations: to keep the Golden Rule,[21] to

abide by agreements and to work fairly, to obey all lawful commands
and to give respect where respect was due, to refuse to join any
unlawful act such as a strike, to be sober and honest and 'to attend
religious duties as far as possible in that Denomination to which
they belong...'. They were expected to attend the Friday meeting
when possible and to keep in touch by letter when away. Guild
membership grew rapidly; the thousandth member was enrolled in
1896. The Guild shared the Union's difficulty of the mobility of
its members in collecting subscriptions. There would be a period in
the Union's fortunes when Hopkins's Guild figures on paper almost
matched the number of paid-up members of the Union although the
Union never admitted the sharpness of its decline. This is significant
for it meant that Hopkins could deal with the Union confidently and
on terms of equality.

Hopkins, aged all of thirty, addressed his guildsmen as 'My Dear
Sons'. There is a nice description of him at home in The Priory with
some of his members:

> It astonished me to see sailors comfortably seated in
> big easy chairs and smoking like steam boat funnels.
> 'There's Father', and suddenly the piano sounds and a
> dozen lads rush to it. 'Good evening, Father', I hear
> them say, and 'Good evening to you, you bad boys' is
> the answer given in a merry and hearty tone.

His rule was firm. He would defend members where necessary
unless they were in the wrong; no legal redress could be found for
lads who had deserted, for example, and miscreants would find their
names in the magazine as being expelled if a Friday meeting found
them guilty. Examples of Guild discipline can be given. A member
summoned for insubordinate conduct on board ship was not expelled
because he was willing to apologise. In this case, Hopkins wrote to
the captain concerned, of the *RAHANE*, asking if he would accept
the man's written and public apology but saying that he would
arrange for the man's defense if he would not. The captain declined
to reply. The magistrate agreed with Hopkins that an apology would
be sufficient.

In another case,

> Louis Edwards of the *CASTOR* was called upon...to
> send in his resignation on account of his refusal of duty

and absence without leave. He was on this account
refused the services of the Guild Solicitor when charged
by his Captain ....

But there were benefits beyond legal privileges. Men who died
in membership were given impressive and solemn funerals with
guildsmen and brethren watching at the bier night and day until the
funeral. Hopkins's experience, when a small boy on his voyage to
England, of the funeral of a sailor may have influenced him in the
making of this provision. Funeral rites also provide an echo of the
medieval guilds on the one hand, and on the other, of the earliest
trade unions which were largely benefit and burial societies. That
the guild stood at least in this latter light Hopkins was quite sure:

> The Bishop of Calcutta holds ... very pronounced views
> as to the advisability of the Clergy of the English Church
> having anything to do with Trade Unions. Our Guild is
> not the harmless association usually understood by the
> term 'Guild' in these 'reformed' days of ours, but is of
> the nature of the old world and Catholic Trades Guild
> for the mutual help and protection of its members in
> the temporal relationships and work of this life, as well
> as for mutual help and protection in preparation for the
> life to come ... our Guild undertakes, by the very nature
> of its Constitution, many of the functions of a Trades
> Union ....[22]

In February 1893 Hopkins expressed the hope of being able,
during his trip to England, to organise branches of the guild in
London and Liverpool and to gain for them both the goodwill of
the Shipping Federation and of the seamen's Union. Nothing else
is heard of this plan. He was in London during May and June and
in Liverpool in July. He claimed to have called upon the editor of
Fairplay, which spoke for the ship owners, to take him to task for
referring to Hopkins as a 'sea lawyer' and a 'notoriety hunter', and
to the guild as a 'Unionist agitation'. Hopkins claimed that he was
not given a right of reply. I have failed to find any reference to him
or his guild in *Fairplay* of the period. If what he claimed was true, it
would confirm the opposition of employers, which may be guessed
at anyway from the campaigns Hopkins conducted. His offense in
their eyes would have been in the organisation of his men, which

was most clearly shown in his willingness to use the courts on their behalf and in using his magazine to advise them of the business of the NSFU, the president of which was also to be found in the owners' sights. Not everyone, however, disapproved of Hopkins's work. His 1893 tour yielded some £2,000, much of it in small sums. The meeting at Hastings which the Jesuits attended raised some £20 and there were many such meetings. Friends entertained him at the Holborn Restaurant on the eve of his departure from England, 7th November, 1893.[23]

His various magazines contain a number of references to court cases for which the SFSSP provided legal backing for sailors. Brother Basil later claimed to the COS that during its Indian period the SFSSP took up thirty cases of prosecution, but he gave no details. This silence is frustrating, for he stated that in only one case, unspecified, were they unsuccessful; nor do contemporary newspaper court reports indicate the influence of the SFSSP. He did say that most cases involved bad food, or wages and their payment, or their payment in rupees.[24] Hopkins's own magazines give other cases. For example, in January 1893 a discharge and money owing to a ship's cook were obtained. A first approach to the captain had been rudely rebuffed. Various trips to the magistrate had been unsuccessful. Action from the magistrate and the shipping master was only obtained after an appeal was lodged with the Lieutenant Governor of Bengal, a man sympathetic to Hopkins's work. Hopkins's concern about the exchange rate at which sailors were paid came to fruition at this time. He had discovered that sailors paid off in Indian ports received an exchange rate of Rs10 to the pound when the official rate was Rs15. Hopkins denounced this in the press and from the pulpit and found much support from the community ashore. In 1916 he recalled that this happened at a time when he had been 'turned out' of the Sailors' Home and had nowhere to meet to discuss this question and that of the provisioning of crews. However, the order of events seems slightly askew.

Ship owners and captains were not pleased to lose the profit in such an unfair rate of exchange and this seems to have led to the demand for Hopkins's removal from the committee of the Sailors' Home. Hopkins claimed that Lord William Beresford, then the acting military aide-de-camp to the Viceroy, and Lord Roberts, then Commander-in-Chief of the Indian Army, on hearing of the opposition to his campaign, were persuaded of the justice of his case to the point where the former told him to stick to his guns and 'the officers of the Army in India will supply you with the ammunition you require'. The committee could not expel him as he was a member *ex officio*. Hopkins, typically, demanded a public meeting. In response the committee had the sense to point out to captains that it was the bishop's prerogative to consider his suitability as River Chaplain. It was as River Chaplain that he sat on the Home's committee, for the Home had been separated from the Chaplaincy for some years and was run as a profit-making concern. The captains declared a boycott of the Home, after which the situation was resolved by Hopkins's resignation from the committee. Nevertheless, he did succeed in getting the rate of exchange corrected, and the 1894 Merchant Shipping Act made provision for seamen to be paid-off at the official rate of exchange in foreign ports.

In March 1893 Hopkins noted with satisfaction that there was a decrease in the number of cases concerning seamen being brought by captains to the Police Courts. This was due in large part to the awareness of captains that their men would be defended by Hopkins. Where he could neither prosecute nor defend he would publicise. He wrote to the *Daily Post* complaining of an inadequate sentence (nine months imprisonment) on the Captain and Mate of the *WATCHMAN* for manslaughter. In this most unpleasant affair a sick seamen had died after being cast out of the forecastle and handcuffed to the mizzen mast, a relatively rare method of punishment. In another case, which involved the captain of the *CARMONEY* in the assault of a steward, Hopkins tried very hard to get the captain's certificate withdrawn, sending additional evidence to the President of the Board of Trade. His November 1893 editorial considered the death of an apprentice on the *GARSDALE* and the question of corporal punishment at sea. Naming names was not appreciated by the industry.

In 1894 Hopkins brought to the attention of his readership a most unusual case. Two apprentices had been arrested for travelling on a train without tickets. They had then been charged by their captain with absence without leave, a particularly serious matter for apprentices. Hopkins rescued them and paid their fares. He discovered then that they had been travelling to appear in court after a subpoena on another matter and that their captain had sent them on this train journey without money. This detail, when brought to the attention of the court, led to the court discharging them as having no case to answer. However, as they had been accommodated at The Priory (the captain used the word 'detained') the captain asked the court if he could prosecute Hopkins for their detention! In this, he was unsuccessful. But this was not the end of the story. It transpired subsequently that the captain had been travelling in the next compartment to his apprentices on the train when they had been arrested. The lads continued their apprenticeship in his care, for the conditions of their apprenticeship bound them to this man for four years unless they could be bought out, and the consequence is not recorded.

One of Hopkins's more famous cases came later, when in March 1895 Brother Paul and William Franks (erstwhile brother but now Superintendent of the Scandinavian Mission) engaged counsel to defend four seamen of the *CAIRNIE HILL* on a charge of murderous assault. The story unfolded in a peculiar sequence. The men were so successfully defended that the captain and pilot had to pay Rs2,000 in compensation. The *Sunday Times*[25] was quoted by Hopkins as ascribing the success solely to the OSP. The case provoked much interest. According to *The Messenger* Havelock Wilson of the NSFU and a Member of the British Parliament raised the matter in the House of Commons. Hopkins was sometimes creative in the use he made of texts. I have failed to find in *Hansard*, the official record of parliamentary business, this question put by Havelock Wilson on this subject between 1894 and 1900, but *Hansard* does list a number of questions from Havelock Wilson to which Hopkins may be referring loosely. Hopkins was far from satisfied by the outcome of this case and in June wrote to the President of the Board of Trade asking if some action could be taken regarding the captain's certificate. Captain Faraday had been accused of drunkenness but had found other captains prepared to testify to his sobriety. A further letter from Hopkins went into considerable detail, some of which appears not to have been available to the court: Faraday had refused his seamen's request to see a magistrate, as was their right, they being reluctant to sail with a drunken captain. He had locked them up in an attempt to starve them into submission, illegally putting them in irons. The court had established his being 'worse for liquor', which had been the men's original objection, and Hopkins clearly wanted the man removed from the sea. He failed to get the enquiry he sought but nonetheless achieved a good deal of publicity of the case.

The captains and ship owners, as well as boycotting the Sailors' Home, declined to employ any of Hopkins's known

associates, prevented their men from using The Priory, and withheld
subscriptions. They used the press. Nor did they confine their press
campaign to writing letters, according to *Shipmates* (July 1894),
which gives details of a conspiracy against Hopkins where a boy
said to be aged thirteen apparently threatened to publish in the
aforementioned *Sunday Times* 'a very offensive accusation'. Were
the ship owners trying to play Hopkins at his own game?

The editor of the *Sunday Times* was certainly prosecuted for
obscenity in 1894 for his coverage of a case before the district
magistrate's court involving Hopkins. According to the *Indian Daily
News Overland Summary*,

> The report of the case of the Revd Father Hopkins was
> not a report at all, but was unadulterated filth, revolting
> garbage which had been prepared by putting these
> questions to Father Hopkins in order that all this dirt
> might find its way into the paper....

The *Sunday Times* was a sensational paper and the accusation here
is that it rigged the case so that sensational questions could be asked,
and published, a classic means of providing titillation for readers.
Robert Smallman, the boy, had charged Hopkins with an offence
under Section 511 of the Indian Penal Code. Hopkins retaliated by
pursuing the boy and the subsequent case occupied many columns in
the *Indian Daily News Overland Summary* and the *Englishman*.

The case against the editor of the *Sunday Times* for obscenity was
reported fully in these newspapers alongside Hopkins's case, and in
such a way as to suggest that the accusations to which Hopkins had
responded were already well-known to readers (as might be the case
in what was a relatively small expatriate readership). That there
can have been little doubt in the public mind of the nature of the
accusation is evidenced by reports that followed Hopkins from India
suggesting that he was best kept away from young men and boys.

Section 511 of the Indian Penal Code, under which Hopkins was
charged, applied in cases which would otherwise attract a penalty
of transportation or imprisonment. A footnote in the Code suggests
the sort of situation to which this section might apply, namely
where someone might break open a strong box, not knowing it to
be empty, in pursuit of valuables, and thereby receive up to half the
punishment which the crime would have attracted if the box had
contained valuables. In other words, in the original Hopkins case,

the suggestion is that he was accused of 'trying it on', rather than with successfully achieving his alleged immoral purpose. Hopkins demanded the 'fullest investigation' of what he described as a very serious accusation in order that his name be cleared. The whole affair progressed beyond the magistrates' court in which it had started. Hopkins later claimed it was found that the boy was aged fifteen rather than thirteen, that conspiracy was proven, and Hopkins's name officially cleared, with the editor's appeal being dismissed. There was not, however, any suggestion in the case report that the boy was anything but thirteen; still a complete vindication of Hopkins and his character by the judge is printed. Worse was to follow for the *Sunday Times*.

During the case Hopkins retaliated by pursuing the boy, Robert Smallman, and an older seaman, Arthur Samuels, for criminal intimidation. During the case Samuels alleged that he and the boy had left the *FRANKESTAN* together, the boy at Hopkins's instigation. Encouraging desertion was a very serious offense. The court was told by the prosecution that the boy and the counsel for the defense had met at the *Sunday Times*' office and discussed the questions to be asked, implicitly, the questions which would provide the most salacious copy for the *Sunday Times*. Prosecuting counsel suggested that there existed a conspiracy against Hopkins to 'blast his character'. Hopkins countered the charge of encouraging desertion by producing a letter from Smallman's mother, from Dublin, informing him that the captain of the *FRANKESTAN* had written to her to tell her that her boy had run away from the ship, the captain fearing that 'a sailor had led him astray'. The mother's letter appealed to Hopkins for news of her son's safety. A last minute attempt was made to reintroduce two defense witnesses who were prepared to admit that they had been paid as part of a conspiracy against Hopkins. Although the attempt was unsuccessful, it was nevertheless reported in the newspapers. The boy was indeed convicted of 'criminally intimidating' Hopkins and, in summing up, the court upheld Hopkins's 'excellent character'.

And what of the concurrent and lengthy reports in the Calcutta papers, *The Englishman* and *Indian Daily News* (no particular friends of Hopkins) of the action in which the *Sunday Times* was prosecuted by the Bengal Government for obscenity? Hopkins's action was only part of the case against the *Sunday Times*. As this case unfolded, it was reported that William Franks of the Scandinavian Mission had gone to the paper's editorial office with Mr Christiansen (his name suggests a strong link with the Scandinavian Mission), purchased copies of the paper and later furnished evidence that the offending issues of the *Sunday Times* and its editor were connected. Extracts from the *Sunday Times* for 1st, 8th and 15th July were read out in court and described by the *Englishman* in similar words to the *Indian News* (above) as

> unadulterated filth, revolting garbage, which had been prepared for the purpose of putting certain questions to Fr Hopkins in order that some dirt might be put in the paper. Counsel here read some of the most obscene passages … which he said … would bring a blush even to the cheek of his learned friend on the other side ….

Obscenity was found proven and the editor sentenced to 'rigorous imprisonment and fines' on several counts. In the *Sunday Times*' subsequent appeal, the editor's punishment is described as four months' rigorous imprisonment and a fine of Rs600.[26] Both papers reported that the *Sunday Times*' editor's non-payment of fines led to his paper's press, type, printing materials and furniture being seized, from which the paper seems never to have recovered.

Despite lengthy submissions in court on what might constitute obscenity, and whether what the paper had printed was obscene, nothing appears in what survives to suggest that anyone asked if there was any substance in the boy's allegations or, in other words, that Hopkins propositioned the boy. There was a suggestion that the boy was trying to make some money to pay for his accommodation, which the court rejected. It was asked only whether the boy was the source of the letters which threatened to make the allegations. Apparently at this point an attempt was made by Hopkins's enemies to rake up muck from earlier Rangoon days. The *Indian Daily News* (14th August, 1894) found it necessary, presumably in the face of – at the least – gossip, to publish an article reminding readers that the verdict of the Alipore Court had been 'entirely in favour of Father Hopkins' even though

> unscrupulous persons made strenuous efforts to prove, as they called it, that Father Hopkins had left the work he was engaged in in Rangoon, practically "under a cloud". Needless to say, no right thinking person heeded the cruelly unjustifiable taunt.

Quoting at length from the *Rangoon Times* to the effect that Hopkins had left that port under no cloud at all, it concluded

> We hold no brief for Father Hopkins ... but we do believe that a scandalous and cruel attack has been made on Father Hopkins, who with singleness of aim has worked through evil report and good report according to his lights ... to raise the social, moral and religious standing of the men engaged in carrying our commerce across the seas ... commending his courage and determination.

It is not hard to believe that someone, or several people, had an interest in undermining Hopkins in Calcutta, and his suggestion that this was the work of a section of the shipping community is not implausible. Whoever was responsible, despite failing in court, succeeded in besmirching Hopkins's reputation, and made his bishop's position *vis à vis* Hopkins's future employment more difficult. However, Hopkins was not to be silenced, and it is arguable that this court case was what, in the scheme of things, eventually led to his involvement in the 1911 seamen's strike many years later, after which, who shall say who was the winner?

Hopkins was not only occupied in defensive action, of himself or of sailors. Throughout the period he continued to campaign for their rights. He frequently noted in his magazines cases from around the world where these rights were involved. He printed articles on the current legislation, usually with an appeal for the men to do their duty, and other articles calling for improvements. The first issue of the *Nautical Guildsman* illustrates this approach well. The Superior's (Hopkins's) Letter dealt at length with the folly of 'refusal of duty'. Then followed what was to be the start of a successful campaign on the dangers of making men work in extremes of heat. There was an article on recent legislation concerning ships' stores. A note about recent court cases commented, 'It has been necessary to provide "defence" for sailors in some recent cases, and it would appear this has been resented by some ...'. His editorial line was not solely in one direction, but his concern was always with the careful application of the law. In January 1893, for example, he criticised men for refusing duty on a particular ship. His grounds were interesting. The ship had sailed before the men refused, and had sailed with its load disc submerged. His point was that the men should have refused before the ship sailed or not refused at all. (It happened that in this case the men were prosecuted by the captain for refusal but the magistrate found against the captain for sailing overladen.)

During 1893 a consolidation bill, what was to become the Merchant Shipping Act of 1894, was passing through the British Parliament. Hopkins gave much space to its progress. As he spent much of 1893 in England his cannot have been the only hand writing these articles. His May letter commended the Act being discussed, together with bills recently passed on food scales, seamen's accommodation, transmission of wages, and the extension of the Employers' Liability Act to seamen (which recognised seamen as 'workmen' for the first time). The text of the Merchant Seamen (Accommodation Act) of 1893 is given. This doubled the space to be provided per man from 72 to 140 cubic feet, with a proviso for 18 superficial feet instead of the previous 12 feet on deck or floor. It gives a flavour of the article to know that he mentioned Havelock Wilson's campaign for this space with the detail that, where convicts were allowed 300 cubic feet, paupers 650 cubic feet, and the soldier 680 cubic feet, the sailor had to make do with his 140 cubic feet, and that usually ill-lit (probably with smoky colza oil) and ill-ventilated.

In August 1893 an editorial called for better provision for the sick at sea and for officers to receive training in first aid. A tale was told – probably impossible to source– of a seaman whose symptoms fitted those described for number 11 on the medicine check list or 'paper doctor'. There being no supply of medicine for number 11, the man was given a mixture of medicines suggested for 4 and 7; he died the next day. An increasing awareness of the need for first aid is noticeable throughout this decade, perhaps due to the appearance of the first aid societies (the Red Cross and St John in the UK), and also to the presence among fishing fleets of doctors on hospital ships provided by the National Mission to Deep Sea Fishermen in the North Sea and the *Œuvre de Mer* off Newfoundland. Doctors of the *Œuvre* are known to have given first aid lessons back in France during the fishermen's closed season. English seamen's missions were beginning to offer similar training.

The 1894 editorials dealt, partly topically, but also in connection with the Merchant Shipping Act, with the shipping of incompetents as able seamen, apprentices running away, rights of discharge, under-manning, over-loading, foreign flags, and discipline at sea. The style and content of these editorials contributed to the impression that this was not the magazine of a typical religious guild of the period.

These and other topics on which Hopkins campaigned were also the foundation of the contemporary campaign being mounted by the seamen's Union. Some of them had to wait for subsequent Shipping Acts. Hopkins accompanied his reports on the progress being made in these areas with markedly trenchant comments.

The NSFU, whilst it had no prominent place in his magazines, was referred to regularly. In 1893 he noted that the NSFU in Liverpool was seeking an improvement in sanitary conditions on board ship. In April he offered the Delphic thought that the NSFU's methods were placing it within reach of the law. May brought mention of a struggle at Cardiff and a speech of Havelock Wilson's at a Union meeting. It is significant that these comments on the NSFU were made whilst Hopkins was in England and, one supposes, more likely to be aware of NSFU activity, though his experience of the Union in England remained, apparently, indirect.

Of the NSFU's difficulties at this time Hopkins was certainly aware, but he failed to realise the extreme pressure which the Shipping Federation was bringing to bear upon Havelock Wilson. 'For a long time now I have been fearful of the well-being of the Seamen's and Firemen's Union under its present management...'. He instanced the statements of the receipts and expenditure as being ' not a report and balance sheet', and found in them contradictory figures. (The Federation was making the same point. Ironically, it was a charge which would be leveled against Hopkins and his abbey accounts at a later date.)

> It makes me very angry when I see the affairs of seamen
> so mismanaged; and I long for the time when our Society
> [SFSSP] may be looked upon by seamen as a solution
> to some at any rate of the difficulties which surround
> them.

This is revealing for here is made explicit an implicit rivalry, at this stage, of the Seamen's Guild with the NSFU. Later, as a trustee of the NSFU, Hopkins would be responsible for the proper management of the NSFU's affairs.

In August 1893 the magazine carried an article about Havelock Wilson displaying water and ship's biscuits in the House of Commons in his attempt to obtain the passage of three bills concerning provisions, accommodation, and appropriate rating at sea. The bills were successfully blocked by the shipping lobby which used its

representation in Parliament well. In September Hopkins returned
to the plight of the NSFU. Havelock Wilson had taken out an action
for libel,one of many over the years. 'The revelations which have
come out of Mr J. Havelock Wilson's action for libel against the
editors of the *Evening News & Post* and the *Shipping Gazette* show
the ... Union to be rotten to the core ...'.

A December article touched on Havelock Wilson's impending
bankruptcy, which would deprive him of his parliamentary seat.
It was at this time that Havelock Wilson pre-empted the Shipping
Federation's attempts to have him declared bankrupt by taking
the NSFU into bankruptcy, and so avoiding his own. In May 1894
Hopkins quoted Havelock Wilson in the House of Commons
pressing Mundella, the President of the Board of Trade, for action
over seamen who were killed by their captains. The June issue
carried an editorial mention of Havelock Wilson's success in getting
an official enquiry into under-manning.

There is another indication of OSP's awareness of the NSFU
which also offers a glimpse of the political stance of at least one
brother. In *The Seamen's Chronicle* (10th November, 1894), then the
official Union weekly paper, a letter from Brother Austin at Barry
painted a picture of the many hungry and long-unemployed men at
the door of the Barry Priory. Brother Austin appealed for gifts of food,
books and clothing. Earlier, in the September issue of *The Messenger*
he had written '... men – capitalists if you like – are ready to grow
rich by the labours of poor merchant Jack, but they are, in all but a
few cases, very far from ready to acknowledge any responsibility
to look after Jack's spiritual welfare ...'. His expressed interest was
in the men's welfare but his language suggests a personal political
agenda. It is also implicit that the Union paper was taken at least in
Barry Priory.

There was one figure of the period who loomed larger than
Havelock Wilson in the field of seamen's welfare. This was Samuel
Plimsoll MP. Hopkins's first issue of the *Nautical Guildsman* carried
an article on a government bill recently passed to regulate ships'
stores. His list of horror stories in illustration of the need for such an
Act came mainly from Plimsoll. To these he added his own, of which
probably the worst was that concerning the *CROFTON HALL*, a case
to which he would return over the years, for it had been among his
most dramatic. In his version, the *CROFTON HALL* had returned
to Calcutta shortly after sailing, following the deaths of six crew

members on board. The captain had at first blamed their deaths on under- or over-ripe fruit; it soon became apparent, however, that a cask of pork was at fault, the captain having simply ordered the brine to be changed in a cask which had been open for nearly six months on deck in the tropics. The *Times of India* (Overland Weekly Edition), 24th June, 1892, carried the story with slightly different detail, describing the ship as coming into Budge Budge to unload kerosene oil in January 1892. At this time a new cask of salted beef was opened and put into pickle in the harness cask. There it remained, perhaps because of the proximity of fresh supplies, while the ship was in port, and was issued for the first time on Saturday, 4th June for dinner. All who ate it on the 4th were more or less affected, while those who threw their portions overboard, owing to the bad odour emanating therefrom, were fine. On the next day, Sunday, different rations were issued, but on Tuesday the old cask was reverted to and more men became ill. On the following day two pieces of meat remaining in the cask were transferred to another cask, and those who partook of it were also taken ill. The Calcutta Health Officer, Dr Simpson, and the Port Health Officer, Dr Forsyth, blamed the meat, and the brine was found to contain 'putrefactive organisms', which should have surprised nobody. Hopkins was very careful in the records he kept, especially as he was likely to be challenged, and his version of this story is to be preferred. Either way, it paints a sorry picture. Hopkins worked very hard to get a system for the proper inspection of stores and he made it clear that he believed this captain guilty of a very serious crime. He was quite clear that for the law to be changed satisfactorily it was necessary for the men to combine:

> and the time must come when seamen, united in such an organisation as our own Guild, shall quietly and soberly protest against arrangements which place the carrying into effect of Acts and laws passed for their benefit, where there is not that guarantee of unbiased and independent action which there ought to be.

It would be odd, given these examples of Hopkins's work in Calcutta, if there were not some masters and owners alienated by his action. And an effective way of getting rid of him would be just such as we have seen in the court case involving Smallman; despite his vindication, however, Hopkins was to learn that mud sticks. It

is not hard to see, even without the court case, given his militancy
on behalf of his Guild members and his pursuit of erring owners
and masters, why Calcutta should have become effectively closed
to his ministry and a return to England essential. Nor is it hard to
see why he should convince himself that his ministry depended
upon that return: recruits were required to serve the rapid expansion
of OSP's outreach to seafarers. One can almost hear his bishop's
sigh of relief on hearing Hopkins had made this decision. Hindsight
might suggest that it would have been better had Hopkins stayed in
Calcutta and ridden out the storm before returning to England. As it
was, circumstance dictated otherwise.

6

Meeting Havelock Wilson
1894-1900

In early 1894 Brother James was dispatched from Calcutta to open the new house at Barry, but died suddenly on 29th June. The sending of Brother Austin as his replacement reduced community numbers to the point where it became imperative for Hopkins to return to the UK. His decision to return was ostensibly based upon the need for his presence at what was to be the mother house of OSP. The unpleasantness engendered by the court case for criminal conspiracy must have eased the making of that decision. However, it was in the middle of the case, before there was the hint of a verdict, that the *Indian Daily News* reported that Hopkins's return to England to take over the running of a mother house had been delayed by the necessity of going to court; in other words, his decision to return to the UK predated the action. Nevertheless the court case and the pressure of significant officials in Calcutta's mercantile community explain his bishop's willingness to release him, apparently without reluctance, in September 1894. Hopkins arrived in the UK in late October. By November he was planning to take a larger cottage, apparently with the approval of the Bishop of Llandaff, in whose diocese Barry was situated.

The priory at Barry doubled as mother house and headquarters of OSP's seamen's mission until mid 1895 when Hopkins found and bought, according to his Will in his own name, some land at Medstead, three miles out of the modest Hampshire town of Alton, with the intention of building what was called, even then, The Abbey, though it was to have no abbot until long after Hopkins was dead. Compton MacKenzie, the novelist, who spent much of his boyhood almost next door to what was to be The Abbey, recalled the version told to him by the brethren of how this purchase came about. MacKenzie was clearly fascinated by these monks in their temporary accommodation. He was told that Hopkins had sailed before the mast from Calcutta to Southampton. On the way from Southampton to Barry, Hopkins heard of the Beech Farm Estate, outside Alton, and decided to buy some of Carter's 'Land for the People'. The brethren who settled it walked there from Barry and spent their first night at Alton sleeping rough under trees as their tents had not arrived. Hopkins, perhaps for health reasons, followed by train.

It is a good story, but implies the existence of more brethren than would be guessed from the surviving evidence, though MacKenzie had no reason to exaggerate. Perhaps Hopkins's recruiting methods had been more effective than now appears to have been the case. Certainly, the presence in the United Kingdom of another order for men would have been of interest to many young men who at this time were being touched by the Anglo- Catholic revival. Mackenzie's *The Altar Steps*, though a fictional account of events with the OSP disguised as the Order of St George and its ministry transposed from seamen to soldiers, reads as if numbers were forthcoming, if not retained. For the next five years Hopkins's main work seems to have been getting The Abbey built, first in corrugated iron, then in stone. Its building is an inspiring story but, for the most part, peripheral to Hopkins's maritime ministry.[1]

To function as a priest within the Church of England Hopkins needed Letters Commendatory from the Bishop of Calcutta, which he had, with the countersignature of the Archbishop of Canterbury, which he also had, together, he claimed, with a note of good wishes. He now started to tour the country preaching for funds and recruits. His community continued to work among seamen, opening in 1899 an additional house at Greenwich, handy for the Dreadnought Seamen's Hospital, and but a short walk along or under the River Thames from London's dockland areas. The attraction of a London base is an obvious one. The SFSSP Guild magazine *Shipmates* was merged with the OSP magazine *The Messenger* in November 1896. Hopkins continued to use this as a crusading platform. The Indian work continued, as did the Guild, the thousandth member of which was enrolled in February 1897 in Calcutta. Membership numbering was continuous so that it would be unlikely to discover a thousand members at any one time. There were, however, problems with the Calcutta work. These problems may in part explain why Hopkins's

Former seamen at work with monks on the Alton Abbey grounds
(undated). (Source: Getty Images.)

permission to function publicly as a priest in the UK was not renewed.

In Calcutta, William Franks, once of the OSP and now of the Scandinavian Mission, had been appointed Guild President. He reduced the admission fee of Rs2 to Rs1, which suggests that the Guild had similar problems as the NSFU regarding recruitment and retention. The Guild and the OSP continued to defend seamen in the courts. The continuing problems in Calcutta were probably caused by ship owners bringing pressure to bear upon the bishop, who, anyway, had probably had enough of the publicity associated with the *Sunday Times'* case. Franks would have been beyond the bishop's jurisdiction, at the Scandinavian Mission, but not his influence. In 1896 Hopkins found it necessary to return to Calcutta, sailing from Brindisi aboard the *HIMALAYA*, changing at Aden to the *SUTLEJ* (a rather different journey from his earlier return to Southampton) and arriving in Bombay on 25th July. The reason for his return was explained in a letter in *The Messenger*, dated 31st August, which says that in effect the Bishop of Calcutta wished to take over the work of the OSP, Hopkins seeking the contrary. Having reached an impasse, arbitration was sought from a committee of three, which resolved that the OSP should withdraw from all ports except Bombay (though Bombay was shut by 1900), which was in another diocese. The committee upheld the bishop's position to the extent that this withdrawal should take place, but on the condition that the bishop should take over the OSP's property and pay Rs4,000 for it.

Rumour now began to play its part in Hopkins's difficulties. It was said that Hopkins had got the OSP so heavily into debt (he had a mortgage on the properties in India) that the bishop had had to intervene to the tune of £4,000 (correctly the Rs4,000 mentioned above). To this was coupled more rumour about the court case for criminal conspiracy.

Rumour failed to recall that it had led to the *Sunday Times'* editor being imprisoned, a fine paid, the newspaper discontinued, and Hopkins cleared, but fed on the nature of a case which had been discussed with periphrasis and, at a time when Oscar Wilde's imprisonment was making headlines, had been turned into something quite sinister. This caused problems on two fronts: ecclesiastical and financial. It is necessary to describe these difficulties for, without them, it is unlikely that Hopkins would have found himself in the arms of the NSFU and, some years later, leading an international strike.

The Abbey lay in the diocese of Winchester. Following protocol, in September 1895 Hopkins had written to his diocesan, the Bishop of Winchester, Randall Davidson enclosing a letter of introduction from Dean Hole of Rochester, a well-known figure in the Church, as well as a Freemason, who had raised a lot of Masonic money to restore his cathedral. The Masonic element allows the possibility that Hopkins's link with Hole was through the dean's fellow Mason and Hopkins's friend, Dr John Marks, chaplain for many years of the District Grand Lodge of Burma. But the dean's letter contained nothing of a personal nature, its general terms an example of how one church official can speak to another through what is not said. He noted that Hopkins had visited Rochester twice: 'I believe him to be a very eloquent and impressive preacher. No advocate has had so much financial success at Rochester...'. Hopkins's letter to Randall Davidson said that he hoped to be able to place before him his Letters of Orders, Letters Commendatory from the Metropolitan of India (the Bishop of Calcutta), with licences from the two archbishops (Canterbury and York), and to seek Randall

Randall Thomas Davidson (1848-1930), Archbishop
of Canterbury.

Davidson's approval to establish at Alton 'the Noviciate or Training
College...' at which there would be no public services, on land 'which
has been presented to us'. Permission for Hopkins to celebrate Holy
Communion was requested on the ground that The Abbey was three
miles from Alton Church.

Hopkins's letter appears to have met with no encouragement at
all. He was still waiting to see Davidson in November. He seems to
have been aware of the bishop's disapproval by 1897,[2] and indeed, by
1899, to have come effectively under the ban of Randall Davidson.
This was not helpful. Davidson, later to become Archbishop of
Canterbury, was closely associated with Queen Victoria, bishop of
the third most senior See in the Church of England after London
and Durham, and a man of influence. Davidson may have been
delaying, not because of his claim to be busy, but because *The
English Churchman*, a Protestant journal, was giving Hopkins
extremely poor publicity. Possessing a relatively high profile
because of his preaching tours, and an Anglo-Catholic, Hopkins was
fair game. This paper did not pick up the Calcutta rumours, which
would surface elsewhere (though the supposed sexual activities of
religious usually attracted great interest in such publications) but was
apparently connecting Hopkins's name with that of René Vilatte,[3] a
wandering bishop from whom a number of ecclesiastical outcasts
sought ordination, a connection Hopkins denied. The Vicar of Alton

wrote to Randall Davidson (10th December, 1895) to say that he had
no objection to Hopkins's celebrating in his own chapel for the OSP
'But clergy who take the strong individual line which he does are
apt to be eccentric and are sometimes carried forward into practices
which they did not at first intend'. No grounds were given by the
vicar to justify this opinion but it resonates with every other opinion
of Hopkins so far encountered.

Hopkins's Archbishop's Licence, necessary because of his
Colonial Orders if he was to function as a priest in England, was
dated 22nd December, 1894, valid for two years. Hopkins finally
managed, on 11th December, 1895, to obtain Randall Davidson's
Leave to Officiate, but only within his own community, and the Leave
was to expire concurrently with the Archbishop's Licence, so it was
hardly a major concession. Effectively, this permitted Hopkins to do
whatever he wanted in the privacy of his own community. After its
expiry Hopkins seems to have been punctilious in following correct
procedure for he next wrote to Randall Davidson asking his consent
for the Bishop of Fond du Lac (a friend of other men's communities
in the Church of England having difficulties obtaining Holy Orders
for brethren), and later for a chaplain, to celebrate Holy Communion
whilst at The Abbey. It is not hard to guess Hopkins's interest in
the Bishop of Fond du Lac for it was common knowledge that his
community needed more brethren in priest's orders. As at this time
Randall Davidson had been put on the committee examining religious
communities for the forthcoming Lambeth Conference (a gathering of
bishops from the Anglican Communion), Hopkins had some ground
for hoping that his diocesan would at last visit The Abbey. Plans were
laid for such a visit at the end of August 1897. What remains by way
of documentation implies that this visit never materialised. Had it
done so, Hopkins would surely have mentioned it in *The Messenger*
as it would have bestowed some sort of recognition, which may be
why Randall Davidson was so careful not to visit The Abbey.

By March 1899 Hopkins was writing to Randall Davidson in
confidence begging for the renewal of his licence: 'You can afford
to be generous, and remove the unjustifiable suspicion which hangs
over me that the withdrawal of your licence implies more than it
really did' (Hopkins's emphasis). The bishop played for time by
asking for more information. Hoping to ease his community's
isolation Hopkins stood down from the office of Superior for two
years, but impressed upon the bishop that of seventeen members of

his community, he was the only one in Orders, and that they needed his ministry. In April the Archbishop of Canterbury's chaplain wrote asking Hopkins to obtain a letter from Bishop Davidson, in which Davidson would undertake to renew Hopkins's licence if Canterbury renewed his Permission to Officiate. On 17th April, 1899, Davidson wrote to Hopkins,

> I am afraid it is not possible for me to write such a letter as you desire, undertaking to license you in this diocese in the event of the Archbishop's renewing your Permission to Officiate in England. I write this after fully considering the circumstances of the case.

Randall Davidson's refusal, couched in such terms, left Hopkins in a very difficult position. He replied, asking Bishop Davidson if he could apply to some other bishop, if he would never get Davidson's Leave to Officiate, and how long he might have to wait if Davidson might consider granting it at some future date; a letter marked by patience and an extraordinary loyalty to the Church of his ordination. Randall Davidson replied that to seek permission elsewhere would not be disloyal (quite secure in the knowledge that no other bishop would acquiesce in the absence of his own approval), continuing,

> It is not for me to give you detailed counsel, but my idea would be that you might work under some experienced and trusted parish priest in some great centre of population (perhaps a seaport) if someone can be found who is at once able and willing to accept the responsibility of definite supervision. I do not think there is any suitable opening of that sort in Winchester Diocese.

Hopkins's thinking had been that, if his place of residence was the Greenwich priory, he could approach the surrounding bishops, but he realised that they would need the Bishop of Winchester's approval. To accept the bishop's suggested 'supervision' would imply that he accepted the bishop's doubts about his 'honesty, sobriety, or morality', for what the bishop was asking of him was what would be asked either of a newly ordained priest, or a priest under discipline, or of a priest ordained overseas but seeking an English benefice. Hopkins's situation fitting none of these circumstances. With Southampton in his diocese, Randall Davidson was, at best, being disingenuous when

he claimed to have no suitable opening in his diocese for Hopkins's
ministry.

The nature of Davidson's doubts, which may have been conveyed
privately to Hopkins (a letter from Hopkins to Davidson in 1907
indicates that they had met on at least one occasion), becomes clear
in a copy of a letter which he wrote, dated 31st October, 1899, and in
response to enquiries made to him about Hopkins. It merits quotation
almost in its entirety:

> I was compelled to withdraw from Father Hopkins the
> 'Leave to Officiate' ... not on the grounds of his doctrine
> or ecclesiastical usages, but on account of some grave
> indiscretions which he himself admitted, although he
> regarded them as less serious than I do myself or than
> others in whom I have confidence. I investigated the
> matter to the best of my power. Father Hopkins resigned
> the headship of his little Order, becoming an ordinary
> member under a clergyman [sic] who came from India to
> take the lead. After a few weeks or months this clergyman
> severed his connection with the Order, and I am myself
> unable to say of whom it now consists besides Father
> Hopkins himself. I have no reason whatever to doubt his
> probity in financial matters, but I cannot regard him as
> one entitled to confidence as a worker with young men
> and boys. I say this after very full enquiry both as to his
> work in India and his work in England. Bishop Mylne,
> late of Bombay, who at first supported Father Hopkins,
> has I believe now declined to allow his name to be used
> in connection with the Association.

Careful reading of this letter, apart from revealing a side of Davidson's
character not found in his biography, reveals that the 'indiscretions' are
separate from the reference to 'young men and boys'. It would make
sense if the indiscretions of which Hopkins made light were connected
with his disagreements with the Bishop of Hereford (below), while
the 'young men and boys' reference undoubtedly reflects a garbled
account of the criminal conspiracy case having reached Davidson.

That Randall Davidson had no intention of relenting became
clear when Hopkins wrote to him saying that he had been offered a
position under the Vicar of St John's, Great Marlborough Street in
London ('a very poor and crowded locality'). This gentleman, the

Rev W.E.H. Cotes,writing to Davidson, reminded him of his advice to Hopkins regarding 'some great centre of population', and said that the Bishop of London would not consider allowing Hopkins to serve under him without the Bishop of Winchester's approval. Perhaps the Bishop of London received a copy of the oleaginous but damaging letter quoted above, or received a whispered word from his episcopal brother in the Athenaeum when next they met, for no more is heard of this appointment.

It was Hopkins's misfortune that Randall Davidson became Archbishop of Canterbury in 1903, closing any avenue for appeal which might have remained to him. His last letter to Davidson, now archbishop, in the Lambeth file seems to have been written in 1907 when he sought to marry a niece to a Merchant Navy officer. His letter met with no success. Hopkins wrote:

> I have often felt that I should like to meet Your Grace again face to face; but that is never likely now to be. However, although I have often felt deeply angered at your treatment of me, I realise that perhaps it was all for the best. You were in a difficulty – with a tremendous responsibility on you – and you did at the time what you considered was best. [Hopkins's emphasis]

The significance of all this trouble with his bishop, apart from all the grief it must have caused Hopkins, is that it made his twin tasks of raising money to build his Abbey and recruiting members very difficult. It would be no surprise to discover that it had embittered him against the establishment, for which there is no evidence, making him an increasingly militant figure, but at the ecclesiastical margin. As it was, without a Licence, he could appeal neither for finance nor vocations in any church in England, nor would any potential recruit arriving at The Abbey find the superior recognised either by his own parish priest or the incumbent of the parish in which The Abbey was situated.

It is possible that Hopkins knew of Winchester's reference to 'young men and boys'. What he may not have known at this stage was the way rumour was working against him. The difficulty of raising money is illustrated in the files of the Charity Organisation Society (COS). The COS acted as a clearing house for those wishing to make donations to charities, keeping files which allowed would-be donors to check the probity of the recipients of their intended

donations. Such reports were not made public but would be revealed
to individual donors on request. Private circulation only added to their
potential to damage. In Hopkins's case, the COS investigator started
by tracking down a Canon Mason, named as a referee of the OSP in
The Messenger, the SFSSP treasurer Mr Charlton, and various others.
He concluded that Hopkins distributed funds 'indiscriminately', to
deserving and undeserving alike, a serious failing to the kind of
person seeking advice from the COS, who would wish to hear that
recipients were deserving. Moreover, Hopkins was described as

> a ritualistic Churchman of questionable reputation. He
> committed a crime for which he was tried in the Courts
> of Calcutta, but although acquitted the Bishop dispensed
> with his services…. It is said that his reputation among
> seamen is not good.

It was also noted that the Bishop of Calcutta's Commissary [4]
advised that young people ought to be prevented from coming under
Hopkins's influence. 'He remembers once being told something
prejudicial to his moral character, but what it was he cannot now
remember', a wonderful example of the COS at its worst. The
commissary believed, rightly or wrongly, that Hopkins had threatened
to bring the bishop to court for maliciously injuring his prospects by
not renewing his contract. 'Mr Hopkins is of a litigious disposition'.
The COS agent also approached Canon Gore of Westminster Abbey,
who replied,'I know little about Father Hopkins… I believe him to
be an enthusiastic and good, but not very patient and discreet sort of
man …'. It will be seen from these extracts that COS records were
the repository for innuendo, and particularly nasty innuendo at that.

On at least one occasion, the COS took the initiative in contacting
someone involved in supporting Hopkins rather than simply adding
information to its files until asked for a report. Seeing a report that
Sir Henry Irving and Ellen Terry (their connection was probably
through Compton MacKenzie's aunt, the actress Fay Compton)
were to perform for SFSSP funds, the COS wrote offering that its
agent should call and place his information at the disposal of Mr
Bram Stoker at the Lyceum Theatre. Whether Bram Stoker accepted
the COS offer for its agent to wait upon him is not known. The
COS finally managed to get a reply from the, now retired, Bishop of
Calcutta, who wrote to say, 'Mr Hopkins left me of his own request.
– He did not leave in consequence of any difficulties in regard to

money'. His letter had nothing to say about young men or boys. The COS agent pursued his enquiries for a number of years but came to no substantial conclusion, continuing to record what was little more than gossip, and to disseminate it to enquirers.

A significant item, at least as regards quantity, in the COS file deals with a public skirmish between Hopkins and the Bishop of Hereford. There are tantalising gaps here; it is not clear what was really going on but it is possible to glean an idea, and it seems to be this that lay behind Winchester's accusation of 'grave indiscretions' which Hopkins took less seriously than he. In 1898, the Bishop of Hereford refused to let his clergy chair Hopkins's public meetings, which were intended to publicise his work, raise money, and recruit members – meetings which he was accustomed to hold all over England. This episcopal ban was taken as evidence that the bishop was privy to serious information, though its nature was never disclosed. Hereford seems to have taken this action because his neighbour, the Bishop of Llandaff, had withdrawn his approval of the priory at Barry and its work, again on undisclosed grounds, though it is just possible that Hereford refused because Hopkins lacked the Permission to Officiate, in which case one wonders why the bishop had asked to see Hopkins's audited accounts. Hopkins's meeting in Hereford became a large and controversial item of news in the local paper, the *Hereford Times*, Hopkins having been advertised to speak twice on 14th March, 1898 at the Hereford Corn Exchange.

The Corn Exchange was chosen because the Colonial Clergy Act of 1874 would have prevented Hopkins from preaching in a church without that Permission to Officiate. Any incumbent allowing his church to be used in this circumstance might expect to be fined £10 for each sermon preached, the preacher being fined the same sum. At his afternoon meeting, Hopkins, on the platform in his Benedictine habit, pointed out that a year ago he had preached in Hereford cathedral and several local churches, without objection from the bishop. He had had no communication from the bishop, yet the bishop had asked Mr Treharne, Vicar of All Saints, to withdraw from chairing the present meeting. The bishop refused to countenance Hopkins until he could produce his own bishop's recommendation, together with his published (financial) accounts. Hopkins claimed, presenting the real state of affairs regarding his relationship with the Bishop of Winchester in the best possible light, that Winchester had licensed him (he would initially have given his approval to Hopkins's original Archbishop's Permission to Officiate, now expired) and his church and blessed his work (we may suppose in the sense of a general good wish at the end of a letter). He read an extract from a letter from Winchester (not given). He also quoted his accountants' approval of his book-keeping. He blamed 'another society' in part for his difficulties (probably The Missions to Seamen), and also Mr Mitchell, lately Archdeacon of Calcutta, whose unspecified criticism he rebutted by quoting a letter from the Bishop of Bombay (Bishop Mylne). Hopkins concluded by saying that he would only continue to speak with the approval of the audience and would not (unlike Fr Ignatius[5]) minister in the diocese without the bishop's approval. He continued with a secular lecture and rounded off this hornet's nest by saying that he thought the Bishop of Hereford had behaved neither as a Christian nor as a gentleman.

It is no surprise to discover, after this, that his evening meeting was packed. He conducted it on similar lines, being careful to replace the concluding hymn and prayer with the National Anthem in order not to appear to be defying the Bishop of Hereford's ban. The collection amounted to nine pounds. The newspaper report does not tell whether the audience was treated to the inflammatory performance of the afternoon. The *Hereford Times* (20th March, 1898) quoted Hopkins as explaining his criticism of the bishop thus: a Christian would have told him his fault and a gentleman would have told him to his face. A correspondence ran until the issue of 9th April. The bishop remained silent. His action, however, continued to be used against Hopkins.

The Bishop of Llandaff's disapproval, whatever its basis, and whatever form it took, had done nothing to hinder the work of the OSP at Barry. The temptation is to wonder, remembering the letter of Brother Austin to the Union paper, which painted a picture of the many hungry and long-unemployed men at the door of the Barry Priory and assuming it reflected accurately the views of the brethren at Barry, in the absence of any other reason, if Llandaff's disapproval was on political grounds. The Priory continued to welcome sailors, many of them indigent, in increasing numbers. A small and unspecified number of sisters (only one, Sister Frances, persisted, eventually at Greenwich) aided the charitable work.

On 23rd May 1898, as the Bishop of Winchester's letter indicates, Hopkins had resigned as superior of the OSP in the hope that the antagonism which was attached to him personally should not damage the OSP. He was replaced as superior by Brother Paul. Paul had his own ideas for the future of the OSP, exploring the possibility of it farming in Canada. A number of the brethren hankered for a more cloistered life. The peculiar nature of their life as chronicled by Compton MacKenzie in his novel *The Altar Steps*, implies, *mutatis mutandis*, that some of the brethren had had no connection with the OSP's maritime work, which would certainly be true of those recruited after Hopkins's settlement at Alton. At Alton, brethren farmed in the hope of self-sufficiency, a dream pursued with similar lack of success by Hopkins's contemporary, the founder of the Benedictines of Caldey Island, Aelred Carlyle. A printing press generated a small income, and would later be used to print the Union newspaper. Hopkins returned to the superior's office in 1900 when Paul left the OSP. No public explanation was given for this departure, but it is unlikely that Paul was out of sympathy with the active work of the OSP, for he wrote several campaigning articles about the life at sea and the working of the 1894 Merchant Shipping Act.

Hopkins too continued to campaign for seamen. He wrote in *The Messenger* (March 1900),

> Father Hopkins has been accused of being a dangerous agitator; ecclesiastical circles have been disquieted because he has flung into their midst a wrathful shipowner or two; he has not been asked to preach a second time in certain Churches because he upset the congregation so by his harrowing tales of the sea – people wept, it is said, and remarked 'How awful!' – and what of that? I can, at any rate, look sailors straight in the face today and not feel ashamed…. A Parliamentary Committee has reported, since these days of which I write, that our English ships have been sent to sea undermanned; and steps have been taken to improve matters somewhat; but not yet enough in my opinion…. A Priest must take up such matters if he is to represent, and reproduce the work of Christ, who is the Saviour of the whole man – his body as well as of his soul. [Hopkins's emphasis]

To this end he made sure that he published the working of the 1894 Act and he continued to draw attention regularly to Havelock

Wilson's work in Parliament. By February 1897 his view of the
NSFU, which had been reformed after bankruptcy, had changed and
his knowledge increased:

> All people will, I think, be now convinced that if the lives
> and interests of our seamen are to be safeguarded, they
> must be represented by one of themselves in the House
> of Commons; and until you men have the franchise
> (the voting power) extended to you, we must do all
> we can to make Mr Wilson's seat in Parliament secure
> through the aid of shore friends. But seamen must help
> themselves…. Hence I would advise you to consider
> the advisability of combination, and urge you to join the
> 'Seamen's Union' as the best existing way….

Of that bankruptcy he wrote in the same article:

> With the death of the old S&FA Union I believe a great
> deal of mistaken policy and bad management have
> disappeared, and we have signs that the new Union [the
> NSFU]…will become a real power, and tend to the
> protection of your interests all along the line….

Yet in 1899 Havelock Wilson was forecasting an imminent cash
crisis and collapse of the Union when writing to Thomas Carey in
Glasgow. He wrote again to Carey in 1900: 'I am in a tight fix at
H.O.…As far as the funds of the Union are concerned we have not
got it…'.

Hopkins was no longer directly concerned with his own Guild but
could claim it as a power base when necessary. He seems at this time
to be more convinced of the need for changes effected by legislation
– Plimsoll's position, according to Havelock Wilson – persuasion and
publicity were no longer sufficient. Plimsoll's death was noted in his
magazine. Within three years, a period long enough to see if the new
version of the Union was an improvement, Hopkins was to get directly
involved with it. There are several references in *The Messenger* to his
having written to Havelock Wilson and, subsequently, he actually met
him. There is no date for this meeting nor any hint of explanation for
its delay. If the strange circumstance of their first meeting as recorded
by Havelock Wilson is correct it may indicate in Hopkins a sense
of humour. Havelock Wilson, in Hopkins's obituary in *The Seaman*,

At the TUC conference, 1922.
(Left to right) H. George, J. Havelock Wilson (President, 1894-1929),
Mrs Wilson, James Henson (District Secretary). (Source unknown.)

confirmed that he had indeed had much correspondence with Hopkins
before 1900 but had not yet met him.

Havelock Wilson recalled this meeting in a way suggestive of a
story often retold. 'About the year 1900,' he wrote, 'I was addressing
a meeting of seamen at Well Street, Tower Hill, London'.[6] The venue
makes better sense than the year. References to letters between the
two men in *The Messenger* make 1897 a more reasonable date for
this meeting, and 1897 is not excluded by Wilson's phrase 'about the
year 1900'.[7] Many union leaders, men like Ben Tillett, used Tower
Hill for addressing large gatherings of dock workers. Its proximity
to what were then busy docks was convenient, as it was also close
to the Board of Trade offices where seamen came to draw their pay,
and the large Wells Street Sailors' Home. The setting was therefore
an obvious one for Havelock Wilson to choose. It was Havelock
Wilson's custom to challenge his audience, some of whom would
be voicing a popular opinion that union agitators made a good living
from their talk, by offering to give five shillings to any sailor who
would get up and address the crowd.

> One sailorman in the crowd, to my surprise, accepted
> the challenge; he was dressed in pilot cloth pants, blue

> jersey, and peaked cap: it caused great surprise to the
> crowd, as I had offered this challenge on many occasions
> and could never get anyone to accept it.

The crowd responded with interest, thinking perhaps that Havelock
Wilson had met his match. Havelock Wilson invited the stranger
to occupy the chair which he had recently vacated. 'For over half
an hour, this sailor, in the most polished language and sailor talk,
delivered a most impressive and eloquent address ...'.[8]

Havelock Wilson saw that here was just the sort of man he could
use as an organising delegate. Congratulating him afterwards, he
offered a delegate's job, to which the stranger replied that he was
not looking for a job, but would gladly give a hand in his spare time.
Havelock Wilson failing to recognise him, he revealed himself to be
'Charles P. Hopkins'. 'From that time on he became what we call
one of our "star turns".'

This story, appearing in Hopkins's obituary, also concluded
Havelock Wilson's first volume of autobiography. It would be a
comfort to any biographer to discover at this point, after tracking
Hopkins in newspapers across the globe, that the man with whom
he was to work so closely in his remaining years had chronicled
their partnership well in his autobiography. Unfortunately this is not
the case. Havelock Wilson never wrote the second volume of his
memoirs.

7

Towards a strike
1900-1911

The first decade of the twentieth century has been written about extensively by industrial historians often as a time of rising unemployment. Towards the end of the decade an attempt was made by the government to introduce a limited scheme of payment for those on very low incomes but hardship still abounded. For unions this was also a difficult period as their ability to take industrial action was heavily circumscribed by the Taff Vale Judgment of 1901 and the Osborne Judgment of 1909.

It would be natural for this chapter, as the one preceding the seamen's strike, to describe in some detail the buildup to the strike. This is not easily done as key records are missing. Union records before 1911, where they exist, are extremely patchy. *The Messenger* still very political in content, mentions almost nothing about Hopkins's involvement with the NSFU, though continuing to champion the seaman. The absence of Havelock Wilson's second volume of autobiography compounds the problem. The writings of key members of the trades union movement, such as Tillett, Mann and Bevin, have little to say about the NSFU and nothing about Hopkins. The NSFU could not offer much to those whose natural constituencies lay in shore-based industries. As with Hopkins's time in Shoreditch, we are back in the business of trying to make bricks with little straw. There are, however, some things of which we can be certain.

Hopkins's association with the NSFU was not the only thing to occupy him at this time. The OSP published in 1903 a *Prayer Book for Catholic Seamen*. A copy survives in the British Library. There is no way of knowing how many copies were published or how successful it proved to be. It is a reminder that Hopkins was still very much the seamen's chaplain. Assuming he was spending the bulk of his time at the Greenwich Priory, which was the OSP's main place of contact with seamen after the closure of its Indian houses, the numbers of seamen using Greenwich give an idea of the extent of his chaplaincy work, assisted by Sister Frances. It may be that the attendance figures reflect the amount of time Hopkins was giving to the NSFU as opposed to direct contact with seamen (see p. 154).

The *Prayer Book for Catholic Seamen* bears the date of the Feast of St Michael and All Angels, 1903. It will be remembered that Hopkins's name in religion was Michael, though there is no hint given that these two facts should be connected. It was

> compiled ... mainly for the use of those merchant seamen and firemen who, in seeking either hospitality or shelter in one or other of the Houses of our Brotherhood, are moved by the HOLY SPIRIT through us, with a desire and determination to try to live a Godly, righteous, and sober life; and to look to the Order of St Paul for help and guidance in their spiritual endeavours and duties.

Despite its title the book was clearly from an Anglican stable, and steeped in the *Book of Common Prayer* (whence 'live a Godly, righteous, and sober life'), though it had a Roman Catholic equivalent, called *A Guide to Heaven*, produced in the early 1890s by the Catholic Truth Society and claiming by 1902 to have achieved a circulation of 14,000.[1]

The preface continued:

> Most of you, to whom the Order of St Paul has ministered, have come to us in the first instance, homeless, destitute, miserable. And your desperate state has been the consequence, in most cases, of sins which you have committed against GOD and man. The Order of St Paul has done what it could for you.... In His Name we sheltered you ... we fed you ... ministered to you. Are some of you old and infirm ... we share our earthly home with you....
>
> Moreover, in the Mass, celebrated daily at the Altar of the Abbey Church, remembrance of, and intercession for, the living of you who have wandered afar off, and

for the souls of the dead who have died far away, is
made to GOD ....

At sea, the use of this little book will help you to
lift up your hearts to GOD, and to learn how to avail
yourselves – as opportunities arise – of GOD's means of
grace. On shore it will help you to approach worship, to
prepare for Confession, to make a good Communion.

It was subscribed: Charles P. Hopkins, Priest, Superior General
OSP.

The book outlined the seasons of the Church year, gave a summary
of faith (describing the disunity of the Church as the work of the
devil), including a definition of the terms 'Catholic' and 'Protestant'
(the former having bishops and priests who offer the holy sacrifice of
the Mass and forgive and retain sins in the name of Jesus Christ), and
offering the 'Three- Branch' theory of the Church (that the Catholic
Church is divided between Rome, Constantinople and Canterbury).
Space is given to the Ten Commandments, the 'Chief Precepts
of the Church' (including Mass attendance, confession at Easter,
supporting its pastors), the Seven Spiritual Works of Mercy, the
Seven Deadly Sins, and how to make one's confession; eight pages
are devoted to prayers, including for a dying or drowning shipmate;
instruction is given on how to baptise in emergency. Considerable
detail regarding Mass is given, as also to Catholic church ornaments
and customs. Mass texts are from the *Book of Common Prayer* with
considerable enrichment. Morning and Evening Prayer and Burial
at Sea find a place too. Anyone would find himself better informed
about the duties of a Christian after using this book. If it survived as
our only evidence it would be easy to place Hopkins at the extreme
end of Anglo-Catholicism. Other evidence, however, shows that his
militancy on behalf of the seafarer, consistent though it was with
his religious militancy, increased his remoteness from any Church
party.

So, the question arises: what is known of his other activities at
this time? Until 1910, it is hard to answer this question. In early 1910
Hopkins, writing of his intervention at Southampton, where a strike
was threatened, claimed that he intervened with the parties involved
as one without official union connections. A local history has only
this to say of the strike:

In 1910 the Southampton branch of the S&FU, whose
members had been discontented for some time, struck
for an increase of ten shillings a week, though their strike
was not recognised by the union's central headquarters.
A settlement was soon arrived at, although in the
meantime the White Star liner *ADRIATIC* had had to
sail (slightly late) with the engineers and other members
of the crew stoking and pick up in Southampton Water
a scratch collection of temporary firemen ... eighty-nine
of whom had never been to sea before. [2]

Hopkins's claim is disingenuous. He seems to have been very
involved with the NSFU throughout this period, though lacking
a clearly defined or official role. A reading of the Union records
which survive leaves the impression that Havelock Wilson's most
likely response after meeting Hopkins was to use him as chairman
or president of the Southampton branch. This would have been a
natural step if Hopkins had already presided over the Calcutta branch,
for the Union needed organisers. If Hopkins was indeed one of the
Union's 'star turns', the description suggests public involvement;
backroom officials, however valuable, seldom shine.[3] No doubt he
would make a striking spectacle on a Union platform, sometimes in
his Benedictine-style habit, sometimes, as described by Havelock
Wilson, in peaked cap and blue jersey, where his performance is
consistently described, even by his enemies, as very eloquent.

The evidence for Hopkins's involvement at Southampton beyond
the intervention referred to is oblique: Southampton was the nearest
port to Alton Abbey and the SFSSP worked there at least from 1910,
so by 1911 Hopkins was very familiar with the port. It is also known
that throughout 1910 Hopkins was privy to discussions about what
would in due course become the 1911 strike. In *The Messenger* of
January 1911, referring to December 1910, Hopkins wrote,

> This year, as readers of the MESSENGER are aware,
> The Seamen's Friendly Society of St Paul has branched
> out Southampton-wards, to help distressed seafaring
> men in that Port. Our work is done through the Hon.
> Agency of a local friend and helper.

Details of local social and wider speaking engagements confirm
the amount of his activity. On the one hand the same issue of *The
Messenger* had Hopkins's account of the Christmas parties in

Southampton (below). On the other, we hear of journeys at the turn of the year to speak at meetings of seamen in Cardiff and Newport, both important coal ports.

> The fact is that the 'unrest' among seamen at the refusal of the Shipowners' Federation to consent to the formation of a Conciliation Board for the settlement of disputes has not been allayed; and I cannot escape the responsibility to take counsel with the men as to 'what's best to be done'. All this extra work is teaching me that I am not as young as I was!

It is also known that he had a private room on Union premises in Southampton in October 1911 and that he knew his way round the office sufficiently to remove private documents.[4]

Hopkins's Union involvement is more obvious but less detailed than his links with Southampton, though the two are complementary. Havelock Wilson had great confidence in Hopkins and was not usually a man to place trust in another without taking his measure. Union records show that Hopkins post-1911 was well familiar with Union procedure, this familiarity most probably having been acquired from Union activity pre-1911, and implicit in his speech-making in Newport and Cardiff. There are other explanations, such as experience gained in local politics, or in his community, or his battles with ecclesiastical authority, but all are less plausible.

COS records give an account of a visit made by a COS investigator in 1903 to the Greenwich Priory. Here he interviewed Brother Basil, Hopkins's deputy, and brother-in- charge of the priory, who revealed the OSP at this time as having twelve brethren in life vows, that is, having been at least seven years with the OSP, though the speed of Hopkins's own profession raises a question about this requirement. For seamen, the Greenwich Priory offered fourteen rooms with sixteen beds for the better class of men, the rest being given 'shake downs' (two blankets and a pillow on the floor). No charge was made. The boys were kept apart from the men, an interesting provision in the light of Bishop Davidson's and the COS's suggestion that Hopkins should be kept from boys and young men, and all were excluded from the priory, unless ill, from after breakfast until 5.00 p.m. The convenience of the priory for Union work for Hopkins cannot have been its only attraction. Here he could also be among men still actively pursuing a career at sea, whereas Alton Abbey dealt mainly with 'shell backs' (retired seamen); Greenwich was close to London's busy dockland, and on his doorstep was the Dreadnought Seamen's Hospital. It was also said that the air of Greenwich better suited Hopkins's asthma than the air found in the wooded glades of Alton Abbey.

There is some evidence, slight enough, of early NSFU involvement in the purchase of the Greenwich Priory. There is better evidence for money flowing between the OSP and the NSFU in the early stages of their association.[5] On one occasion Hopkins received a repayment of £50 which was not listed as expenses, but could be explained as a loan previously made to maintain the Union's liquidity. The financial links were much clearer at a later period; a grant of £100 was made from the Union's emergency fund to the SFSSP, 'which society had always been ready to place its houses at the services of the Union in finding shelter and subsistence for members of the Union who were on the rocks', in regard to its charitable work among seamen. After renting rooms in the Greenwich Priory for years, eventually the Union bought the Greenwich property outright, but allowed Frances, the remaining sister, to continue in residence.[6] Given the peculiar state of the Union's finances and the continuing interest of the Shipping Federation in those finances, it does not stretch the imagination to suggest that these loans, rents and purchases were mutually beneficial.

COS records include copies of well-lithographed appeals circulated by the OSP from its own press at Alton. Their quality is so good that they look, at first glance, handwritten. Raising money was a major occupation as it was needed to finance existing work, to feed the brethren, and to build the Abbey. The COS maintained its interest in Hopkins's probity, for example, by writing in 1905 to the editor of the *Church of England Year Book* to see if entries contained in it were an indication of episcopal approval. The editor replied that as he had found Hopkins without either episcopal patronage or licence he would be removed from the next edition. However *Crockford's Clerical Directory* continued to list Hopkins, giving his last appointment as River Chaplain in Calcutta, an entry which would raise questions too. As to the building of The Abbey, COS noted a seaman's complaint which alleged that Hopkins had told him, 'Go to the Devil and be damned to you!' This response, if true, might speak of the man's attitude to work or, perhaps, if Hopkins's temper was shortening, the onset of Bright's disease, a legacy of his malaria. The man added,

> You know, the food and all were much better before they
> began rebuilding [*sic*] the Abbey: now they are restoring
> it by sweeping together broken-down carpenters and
> masons etc. and keeping them without wages to build
> the Abbey.

The tin huts were being replaced by a fine flint-built permanency,
designed on medieval lines, the flints collected by the brethren as they
cleared their own land. If there is more substance to the reference
to broken-down carpenters and masons than simply the pique of a
man thrown out, there may be here evidence of Hopkins's very real
concern at this time, and for some years to come, with the local
workhouse and the need for work to be provided. He had become
a guardian of the poor and took his responsibilities seriously. His
magazine carried constant appeals for comforts for the workhouse
inmates. Each year Hopkins appealed through *The Messenger* for
toys and other gifts which rather suggests that the Father Christmas
who took a generous supply of toys with him to the Alton Union was
Hopkins himself. As to The Abbey food deteriorating after building
began, this may indicate the drain on the OSP's finances made by the
building programme.

Although Hopkins was often away from Alton, principally at
Greenwich and sometimes at Barry, The Abbey and its founder
might be supposed to have been of interest to its neighbours, though
this is not reflected in Hampshire's newspapers. However, local
affairs held an attraction for Hopkins. He stood successfully for the
District Council,[7] according to the COS topping the poll in 1907, but
was forced to withdraw, not in response to pressure from authority,
nor for reasons of scandal, but on grounds of ineligibility: he was
technically still an American citizen by virtue of birth and should
never have been on the Register of Electors, a fact which appears
not to have crossed his mind, but which was brought to official
notice by the local Conservative Party. We can only guess how the
Tories were made aware of this fact. Hopkins himself was under
the impression that he was a British subject, with a British-born
mother, and understood that his father had taken British citizenship
some years earlier. The entry in his naturalisation file in the National
Archive carries a note that as no trace of his father's application had
been found in Home Office records, his application might have been

made, if made at all, in British India.[8] The *Daily Telegraph* of 28th
September, 1907 noted that Hopkins had been on the Register of
Electors for ten years. Now, suddenly, he was ineligible.

The file containing his application for citizenship says only that
at the time of the objection being made, Hopkins was chairman of
the Petersfield Liberal Association. A letter from Herbert Samuel, a
Liberal MP, delivered in person to the Home Office, seems to have
expedited matters. Hopkins himself revealed that he had taken the
Oaths of Allegiance and Supremacy at the time of his ordination
in 1884. His application was checked by the local constabulary,
which found that he was all that he claimed to be, 'a gentleman of
excellent character' evidenced by his [irregular] membership of
Alton District Council and his guardianship of the Alton Union, and
intending permanent residence in the United Kingdom. Hopkins
now took the necessary oath before a local Justice of the Peace at
the end of August 1907, with citizenship being granted one month
later. A letter from the Home Counties Liberal Association[9] replied
to a query from Hopkins: 'I am told that an alien who had become
naturalised is eligible for Membership of the House of Commons'.
It added that Holy Orders, even if colonial, could be resigned,
to remove the final obstacle to a seat in the House of Commons.
Hopkins never stood for Parliament, but it is revealing to discover
that he was in correspondence about this possibility. Havelock
Wilson was a Liberal MP and it may have been his encouragement
that led Hopkins to consider standing. Contemporary issues of his
magazine show that at this time Hopkins was giving much thought
to political issues. Adding this to his other various involvements one
can only wonder at his taste for activity, for his health continued
to trouble him. On doctor's orders he had taken a cruise in August
and September 1904 and numerous references to ill health appear in
succeeding years.

His association with the Alton Union as a guardian and his
growing awareness of the problem of unemployment in 1906
seems to have provoked a period of intense political thought.
There was rising unemployment among seamen too. Contemporary
newspapers reveal that people were beginning to worry about the
import of cheap labour, at first in the South African gold fields, later
into the Merchant Navy. It became known as the Chinese Problem,
for Chinese were the cheap labour. In later years Hopkins would
make many speeches about this problem on behalf of the NSFU. The

smack of racism would not have been apparent to the contemporary listener; the issue was low-paid employment. His response was more measured than that of Tupper, a Union official, who would claim to have liberated girls from enslavement by Cardiff's Chinese community during the strike and, later, sailors from the opium dens of London's East End, and who, particularly during war time, spoke virulently about perceived cowardice on the part of Chinese crews on British ships. Careful reading of Tupper confirms that the real objection was that owners, who were making huge profits during wartime, were cutting labour costs by 40% every time a Chinese crew was employed.

Another issue in 1906 was the revision of the Plimsoll line, a subject on which Hopkins had become an authority. The carrying capacity of a ship could be altered at a stroke if the Plimsoll line was allowed to be adjusted in the owner's favour. Hopkins believed such a revision was being dictated by the desire for greater profitability rather than increased safety. His work on the Plimsoll line was to extend over the next seven or so years, certainly until he published his book *Altering Plimsoll's Mark* in 1913, which will be considered in its chronological position in some detail. Suffice it to say, this was an issue which found space in *The Messenger* at this time.

In the November 1906 *Messenger*, he wrote:

> I am myself no believer in the Socialism of Keir Hardie[10], and others.... But if... labour finds itself treated as the mere instrument of capital for turning out profits, then Socialism – unless something else intervenes – will pervert labour and the forces behind it, and then – chaos!

He returned to the subject of Socialism in 1907, commending it in detail in August, where he made clearer what he meant by Socialism. He appealed to a number of contemporary Anglican writers (Fr Healy CR, Fr William SDC, Fr Waggett SSJE), all members of religious orders, and commended an article which criticised people who received incomes for which they did not work. This was a reprint of an article by Fr William SDC, then living an austere Franciscan life among the very poor in Plaistow, in London's East End. Hopkins noted that some of the forms of Socialism horrified him whereas the spirit, or substance, did not. He defined Socialism by quoting Genesis (3:19), 'In the sweat of

thy face thou shalt eat bread, till thou return unto the ground', and
2 Thessalonians (3:.10) 'If any would not work neither should he
eat'. It was his view that some forms of Socialism would crush out
individuality, energy and enterprise, which he believed was not a
tendency of its substance, using theological (specifically Thomistic)
language to make the distinction. In contrast, the present political
system was fast breeding a nation of industrial slaves and paupers,
side by side 'with a dependent, even idle, aristocracy'. Whereas in
1895 and 1896 his fund raising platforms had been shared by such
establishment figures as the Earl of Meath now, in 1907, such people
were seldom to be seen at his side. With his experience of the Alton
Union and the pauperism he had seen he was moved to say, though
these (the paupers and, by extension, his seamen) had laboured, their
profits had gone elsewhere.

He returned to this theme in November 1907, when, in an article
which seemed to be a defence of his own community, he wrote of the
need to improve social and economic conditions:

> Just and wise legislation alone can bring it to pass.
> Man has to work out his social and economical, as
> well as his own religious and spiritual salvation. The
> OSP is ... well out of the storm and stress of tackling
> Governments and political questions. But, individually,
> I feel that a Priest or Brother who is given work to do,
> must be allowed to do it in his own way so long as he
> remains loyal to the principles of his State and to the
> rule ... of his Community.

In December he added that he had, from time to time, indicated
the need to grapple with the causes which underlay such problems.
He hoped for legislation for social and industrial reform: I have
not hesitated to let it be known that I accept the responsibility of
identifying myself personally with active practical endeavours
to secure such legislation ... I am now warned against..a seeming
tendency in the direction of Materialistic Socialism ...

Much of his Christmas message was typically Catholic and
incarnational. However, in his development of it, those readers who
kept abreast of current thought within the Christian community
would have spotted the influence of Christian Socialism:

> The human family has become social and industrial –
> Interdependent (none are now independent really) and
> Productive (by the sweat of his brow man labours, or
> should labour, to live). What shall be the type of this
> Social and Industrial Community? Shall it be of the
> Christ or of the anti-Christ type ...?

The complete text is suggestive of wide and recent reading in the field of social theory and cannot have endeared Hopkins to those members of the Church establishment whom he had previously had dealings with and who were, at least in part, responsible for his increasingly isolated position.

In February 1909 Hopkins related this theme to unemployment, arguing for a 'Christ consciousness' which would reorganise society 'upon the divine foundation of Justice ... a possible universal brotherhood'. Ben Tillett and Tom Mann, who had risen from the ranks of Protestant nonconformity, would have recognised some of their early thoughts in his text. Hopkins focussed particularly on unemployment among seamen and firemen. He referred back to an article by Brother John[11] in the previous issue of *The Messenger*. Here John had written about his work in Barry, blaming the poverty there upon 'the profit- hunger of the local ship-owning concerns'. So long as goods were produced for profit rather than use, the miserable conditions would persist. Hopkins was moved to words which combine politics and religion to achieve a prophetic quality:

> I see already a pretty nearly worn out and utterly undone
> multitude of disinherited children of God waking up
> to the fact of what and where they ought to be – and
> might be. I see them at last reaching out after the
> political power which will, I believe, enable them to so
> help reorganise things that the necessaries of life will
> be no longer produced primarily for profit but for use,
> so that all who will might have life and have it more
> abundantly, and that unemployment and destitution
> may be obliterated, instead of being only inadequately
> relieved by philanthropy and pauperism – but I must
> also be with these men in their movement towards the
> 'Good time' coming, in which I most sincerely believe.

If Hopkins spoke as he wrote it is possible that here may be glimpsed what others described as his powers of oratory. His

Messenger letter was supplemented with many accounts of individual unemployment and its causes. A further clue to the sources of his political thinking is given in his appeal for the gift of a copy of a new book by Canon and Mrs Barnett, *Towards Social Reform*, though the contents of this particular book relate to his connection with the Alton workhouse. Barnett was a noted social thinker of the time and Warden of Toynbee Hall in London's East End. It is still not possible to link Hopkins directly with the Christian Socialist movement but enough evidence has now accumulated to say with confidence that he was clearly aware of its thinking. It is significant that this is the year in which his thoughts were of standing for Parliament.

In *The Messenger* of April 1909 he wrote of a 'constitutional uprising of the people – the workers – brain workers – roused into movement by the voice and example of Priests and Prophets'. In May he detailed questions on maritime issues asked in Parliament 'by the one solitary member who directly represents them in that assembly', Havelock Wilson. The July issue listed the objectives of the NSFU and gave the text of an address which had been given by Havelock Wilson at a big demonstration in Canning Town, part of London's dockland, in May. Succeeding issues dealt with wealth and usury, demonstrating that the Church had a tradition of long involvement in such matters. He wrote of the need for more MPs to represent seamen. Havelock Wilson was a Liberal, which may explain Hopkins's correspondence with that party. Rising trade unionists were more likely to favour the Labour cause, but Havelock Wilson's generation, and therefore Hopkins's, was more interested in achieving results than in being united in theory. Whilst Liberals had the ascendancy, bills had more chance of being passed with government (Liberal) support. Perhaps Hopkins's unique position as a Religious led him to believe that, vowed to poverty, he would be less restricted after the Osborne Judgment, and its turning off of the tap which paid those who spoke in Parliament in the interests of organised labour, if he was a MP. Had he been a successful candidate he would have been the first religious to sit in Parliament since the Reformation. Clergy of the Church of England are barred from sitting in Parliament; despite the Liberal Party letter advising his resignation of his Orders, Colonial Orders then would have been no obstacle to his becoming a MP.

In January and February 1910 Hopkins was writing in *The Messenger* to commend the new scale of seamen's rations and the extension of workmen's compensation, seamen having but recently become 'workmen' in law. This suggests, more strongly than much of the social thinking which has been considered, that *The Messenger* was still circulated among seamen. It is not known whether there were still guildsmen among them.

His vision of some sort of popular uprising, which may have more significance for those who can read of it now with the benefit of hindsight may well have been encouraged by the foundation in September 1909 of the International Committee of Seamen's Unions (ICOSU). ICOSU seems to have been a response to the Shipping Federation's initiative in establishing the International Shipping Federation (ISF).[12] Membership of both organisations came from Belgium, Denmark, Germany, Holland, Sweden and the United Kingdom, which must be more than coincidental. With ICOSU behind it, the NSFU was able to demand with rather more confidence in July 1910 a national negotiating and wages board to consider, among other things,

1.   a uniform sliding scale of wages for all ports and with a minimum wage;
2.   a scale of manning;
3.   the right of a union representative to be present at signing on;
4.   the abolition of all Shipping Federation offices, with ships' officers only being empowered to engage crews;
5.   the abolition of all Federation medical tests. [13]

On 7th July, 1910, the NSFU addressed a circular to British shipowners asking for a conciliation board. The ICOSU unions of Belgium, Denmark, Holland and Norway did the same in their respective countries. This was a well-trodden path and one which led to refusal. In Britain it was a route which had been taken also by the railway workers, with as little success and for the same reason: that any concession was tantamount to union recognition. British shipowners had tried hard to discredit Havelock Wilson over the years and saw no reason to truckle with him now. The principal excuses given were that the Union was neither representative of the profession nor a registered union.[14]

With regard to the Union being representative it is true that its membership had sunk considerably to a Federation estimate of some 2,000 real members. Registration would have required access to records and betrayed to the owners the Union's true strength. It would also have required publication of the Union's accounts which might not have born too close an examination. Initially the owners ignored Havelock Wilson's letter demanding a conciliation board. Their refusal came after he and a delegation had addressed the President of the Board of Trade on 28th July. Replying to a letter from the Shipping Federation dated 18th November[5] (the wheels were turning slowly) which said that the Federation was unanimously agreed that it could not entertain proposals for a national conciliation board, Sir Walter Howell, for the Board of Trade, replied to the Federation on 25th November, 'I regret the decision at which your Council have arrived, but I recognise that in these circumstances no useful purposes would be served by carrying the matter further at present'. Writing to Havelock Wilson on the same day, Howell said that the Federation was unwilling to entertain his (Havelock Wilson's) request, the Federation arguing that 'questions arising between shipowners and seamen, which might contain the germs of general dispute, are dealt with finally and satisfactorily at their very earliest stages' as grounds for its unwillingness. This refusal led to a conference of the Central Council of the International Transport Workers Federation (ITWF) and seamen's representatives in Antwerp where it was resolved that patience should be maintained at least until the spring of 1911, when according to *The Seaman* it was resolved to meet again.

It is known that Hopkins sent Brother John to Antwerp in 1910, but not whether he was there specifically in connection with this ICOSU activity. In the March 1911 *Messenger* Hopkins wrote that Brother John was 'still' in Antwerp 'helping to fight the crimps and the sharks'. In the February issue he had written:

> It was pointed out to me, a little while back, that Antwerp was much in need of a reliable man – one calculated to secure the confidence and respect of seamen to look after the interests of British ships' crews in that port; especially members of the men's Union. Brother John volunteered to go; and I sent him … I forgot to say that the cost of Brother John's presence in Antwerp does not fall on us. The men's Union sees to that.

This provides a clear and early link between Hopkins and the ICOSU action of 1911. Brother John seems to have kept Hopkins in touch with events as Hopkins quotes from his letters. It is also probable that Havelock Wilson kept Hopkins informed. It is known that by December 1910 Hopkins had provided Havelock Wilson with a donation of £50 towards a special fund in connection with the ICOSU and that Wilson was banking on him as one his three key speakers at rallies during this period.[16] Hopkins's exact status at this time is impossible to determine from Union records but he does seem to be some sort of Union official as Herman Jochade of the ITWF suggested in a letter that he believed Hopkins had 'seen the paperwork'. Whatever the exact nature of the situation, Hopkins was sufficiently in touch with the ICOSU to be invited in 1911 to be its secretary. ICOSU meetings seem to have been held in February (Copenhagen) and November (Antwerp) 1910, and in March (Antwerp)1911. A further meeting took place at the Greenwich Priory on 1st May, 1911, at which Hopkins was certainly present. A record of this meeting has Hopkins drawing the attention of those present to the refusal of the ISF to establish conciliation boards on the grounds that the demand was not made by representative persons and that there were no grievances requiring adjustment by the means suggested. He proposed a letter to the ISF asking if it would be willing to meet with the ICOSU. He

> stated that the International Strike Committee ought to be kept distinct from the permanent International Committee of Seafarers Unions. He hoped that an International Strike Committee would be formed

and this was agreed. He suggested that Chris Damm of the NSFU should be the secretary of the Strike Committee, which was also agreed.[17] This is a curious point because at the Antwerp meeting of 14th March, 1911 it was agreed that Hopkins would take up this position.

The Messenger of January 1911 refers to the SFSSP starting a branch of its work in Southampton to relieve hardship among liner crews and others, strengthening the link between Hopkins and that port. The OSP had already given a Christmas concert and supper in 1910 for 150 seamen and their wives and sweethearts, and a party for 200 sailors' children, so Hopkins was well in touch with the affairs of the industry in Southampton. The same *Messenger* reveals that Hopkins had visited a number of ports, in addition to Southampton, to speak and listen to seamen: Cardiff, Newport, Shields, Middlesbrough, Manchester, Liverpool, Glasgow and Leith.

Nor was Hopkins the only person addressing seamen at this time. At the beginning of February Havelock Wilson wrote to Hermann Jochade of the ITWF, 'During the past two weeks I have addressed over 150 meetings'.

Throughout this period the shipping unions of Europe and America had been improving their organisation. Havelock Wilson had been a founder member of the ITWF and had argued for closer unity of action at a number of international conferences. It was essential for seamen's unions to act together to prevent shipowners from circumventing any strike action by crewing abroad, often at a lower rate, for rates differed from port to port. In London as early as 1902 Havelock Wilson had argued for a uniformity of organisation with a tightly centralised base and this had been confirmed at subsequent conferences. Writing about it, Jochade had deplored (as a German where German seamen had formed a single solid union with allied workers) the 'egotistic rigidity of organisation combined with wide fragmentation which in England – for example – has gone so far that there are almost 1200 units there.'[18] A result of this was that in an increasingly international situation, unions were too diffuse to help their brethren in other countries, as Havelock Wilson's friend Charles Lindley discovered when he sought assistance in England for a general strike in Sweden.[19] The 1908 Vienna Congress had brought seamen together to discuss their problems of organisation, a topic confronted again at Copenhagen in 1910, which created, as Jochade put it, 'something through which it will be possible for the seamen's union to win inner strength and increase their clout' or, in short, the ICOSU.[20]

That there was 'clout' was recognised by the Federation and lies behind an urgent letter from Jochade to Hopkins (18th May, 1911) requesting details concerning an article he had seen in *Hansa* where Federation-sourced allegations were made against Havelock Wilson regarding finances, a familiar subject.[21] Havelock Wilson was the Federation's key target. Jochade believed the allegations of financial irregularity to be true on the basis of his own information and confirmed in his view by the normally litigious Havelock Wilson's failure to proceed for slander against the English source of the paper's information. Jochade appealed to Hopkins for detailed information 'as it is known to us that you went through the books and must know what is true in the statements of the shipowners'. Hopkins replied that Havelock Wilson had been incautious but not dishonest ('much mismanagement and consequent compromising complications, but no dishonesty'). Two significant points emerge: that Hopkins had been through the books and must at this stage, therefore, have been deeply involved in Union affairs and that the Federation was aware that the Union was serious in its intentions and must be stopped at any price. The capacity in which Hopkins was involved is revealed in a letter from his secretary, Anderson, to Jochade in May 1911, where it is stated that Hopkins has been elected to the NSFU Executive Committee and is co-trustee elect.[22] It is possible that he was the member for Southampton.

A search of the relevant literature reveals nothing to clarify the level of Hopkins's involvement. L. H. Powell, historian of the Shipping Federation, says only in his single mention of Hopkins in connection with the strike, 'Father Hopkins, who had been a seamen's padre in Calcutta, and who had espoused the men's cause, was also playing a leading part...'. Phillips in his study of the NTWF fails to mention Hopkins.[23] Ryan and Marsh in their official history of the Union describe him as Havelock Wilson's 'kind of trusted managing lieutenant... the equivalent of the union's research officer and national organiser... honorary treasurer, member of the executive and trustee', all of which offices would follow the strike. Their index entries for Hopkins are fewer than either for Captain Tupper, recruited to lead the strike in Cardiff and subsequently the NSFU's national organiser for twenty-six years, or the Union's secretary, Cathery, which may indicate the sources most readily available to them. Tupper, particularly, was a self-publicist who amplified his role in the strike in his autobiography, *Seamen's Torch*, the style of which is sensational in the extreme. Its principal value is in indicating the continuing struggle between seamen and employers beyond 1911. Chatham associated Hopkins with the NSFU only from 1911, giving Tupper the pre-eminent role, claiming that Tupper had been 'left in charge of union apparatus' during the period of Havelock Wilson's incapacity, and that he was a trustee of the Union from 1911 to 1929 and Havelock Wilson's substitute.[24] In fact Tupper, as his autobiography makes plain, was none of these. It was Hopkins who was the trustee from 1911 to 1922. As to which man was Havelock Wilson's substitute, if Tupper is correct in portraying Havelock Wilson as a pain-ridden and crutched cripple (arthritis seems the ailment), the position of each man is better explained by placing Hopkins at the centre guiding in matters of policy and Tupper in the field as the man of action. The *Dictionary of Labour Biography* (volume IV) gives Hopkins no attention even in its entry on Havelock Wilson. Lindop has five textual and seven footnote references to Hopkins, mostly relating to Hopkins's book, *The National Service of British Seamen 1914-18*, but almost nothing of his significance, making him chairman of the International Strike Committee. Wailey's thesis follows Lindop.[25] To discover Hopkins's true role on the strike committee and his actions during the strike it is necessary to go to original documents.

The ICOSU held a further conference in Antwerp (12th-14th March, 1911) when action was agreed upon. Representatives from Belgium, Britain, Denmark, Holland and Norway at once formed themselves into an International Strike Committee with Hopkins as its secretary.[26] It would be naive to think that Hopkins had gone to Antwerp simply to be initiated into ICOSU business: in the Messenger of March 1911, as this meeting was taking place, Hopkins had written, apparently with foreknowledge, 'probably the seafarers themselves will before long take the matter of their liberation and just treatment into their own hands'. Present at the Antwerp meeting were Havelock Wilson (NSFU president), E. Cathery (NSFU secretary), Hopkins (role undefined), C. Damm (Cardiff branch secretary, NSFU), Th.A. Markham (secretary, Dutch Seamen), Niels Emil Aal (Norwegian Seamen), C. Mahlman (Belgian Seamen), Chr. Jepeld (Danish Firemen), Charles Lindley (Swedish Seamen), Mme Sorgue (French – observing), and Willem Schenkeren (president of the Belgian Seamen). Hopkins's secretaryship was proposed by Mr Markham (Holland) and carried unanimously. His presence must have been with this appointment in mind. His precise status, alongside the other NSFU representatives, is given as 'Executive Council', on which his seat could well have been as delegate for Southampton, but that is not said.

Hopkins accepted the position of international secretary on condition that he should have such assistance as might be necessary, which would be paid for, whilst his own position should be an honorary one. Together with Havelock Wilson and Cathery, Hopkins was appointed to a subcommittee which would act for the ICOSU on this and other matters which might arise. Hopkins was to have full voting rights. He was to be an *ex officio* member of the International Strike Committee. It was further agreed that, whilst the press might be allowed to attend public meetings, no official statements would be made to the press on behalf of the International Strike Committee unless signed by the international secretary, Hopkins. *Minutes* would be sent to the ITWF. In the meantime each union would send the secretary £2 to cover initial expenses.[27] In his role as international secretary, Hopkins would correspond with Jochade.

Initially Hopkins had as his secretary Lewis J. Anderson,[28] who described himself in all letters as 'the Revd Father's Secretary'. Writing on behalf of Hopkins to Jochade (10th May, 1911) he said that Hopkins had been elected to the NSFU's Executive Council (which Jochade must have known from the *Minutes* of the earliest meeting of the ICOSU) and was co-trustee elect 'but it would be most ill-advised to enter upon any reorganising scheme until the present situation has been dealt with'.[29] The reader may wonder if it was Hopkins's role to clean up the NSFU. This letter also reveals that the NSFU had demanded a conciliation board of the Federation on 3rd May, 1911 (this was clearly a new round of correspondence over the issue) and that the NSFU had failed to reply.

It is hard to discover the exact sequence of events from this point as documentation is lacking, but a further letter from Hopkins to Jochade (17th May, 1911) mentioned a report in *The Times* declaring that a strike had been decided upon, and confirming that preparations for it were now being carried forward. His letter of 30th May dealt with the *Hansa* article and considered the likelihood of the Federation using it to discredit Havelock Wilson.

By June Hopkins's letters were being signed by A.M. Weavin. His letter to Jochade (10th June) said,

> In accordance with the arrangements agreed upon at the
> last meeting of the Committee on 1st May last, Holland,
> Belgium, and Great Britain will commence a strike
> on the date there appointed. Your organisation will of
> course use every endeavour to prevent blacklegs being
> sent to any of the countries involved in the struggle.[30]

(Most of the correspondence was conducted in English at Hopkins's request.) Having been relaunched the Union's newspaper, *The Seaman* kept up the pressure for action against the Federation. Hopkins is likely to have been the pseudonymous 'Sky Pilot' who contributed a regular article at this time. Slowly the momentum for the strike was beginning to build.

Year	Seamen Visiting
1900	589
1901	1243
1902	1421
1903	1548
1904	1715
1905	816
1906	457

Numbers of seamen using Greenwich Priory. Source: Hopkins's *Altering Plimsoll's Mark*.

8

The Strike

The Greenwich Priory, 38 Hyde Vale, Hopkins's base during the strike.
(Courtesy of the Dominican Sisters of Zimbabwe.)

The seamen's strike of 1911 could so easily have sunk without trace.
No relevant NSFU papers seem to have survived, there is little in
the Shipping Federation records and I am aware of nothing kept
at Alton Abbey. Fortunately it survives in newspaper reports but
these have their limitations; the angles from which they report are
sometimes dictated by other factors. Examples of these are easily
given in the instance of this strike which took place during a period
of exceptionally hot weather. This undoubtedly contributed to its
success but the heat wave also coloured the way it was reported.
Also, it took place around the time of the Coronation of King George
V. Newspapers were concerned with Coronation questions. It was
pondered whether the strike, for example, would hinder the Review

of the Fleet, rather than whether it was justified. There was also a controversial Budget from Lloyd George in May to replace the strike on the front pages.

Lord Askwith saw the seamen's strike as part of a wave of strikes for which it had been the starting point.[1] Dockers and transport workers followed the seamen out, to be followed in turn by carters, railwaymen and others. Towards the end of the actual strike by seamen, therefore, a complicated picture had emerged, involving very large numbers of people, and costing the country a considerable sum of money, not least from the number of police and troops required to be kept on stand-by. The other associated groups who chose to strike with or in support of the seamen are not part of Hopkins's story, but it is indicative of the industrial mood of the time to know that, for example, on 10th August – well after the end of the seamen's strike – there were still 77,000 men on strike in the Port of London alone, a figure illustrating the labour-intensive nature of the port industry before the advent of the container. This was a year in which there were 872 industrial stoppages.

For the NSFU the strike was a venture into the dark. It had last had direct experience of anything other than a local strike in 1889 when seamen had joined the great Dock Strike. Now it was facing its first international strike. Viewed retrospectively, it became a landmark in the NSFU's history, not to be repeated until 1966. The difficulty in discovering when the date of the strike was actually decided is lost in the periphrasis recorded towards the end of chapter seven. It seems odd that there should be conflicting accounts of something so important. One otherwise reliable source says that the date of the strike, namely 14th June was decided at the Antwerp ICOSU meeting of 13th March, 1911. Another version[2] in the ITWF records notes

> At a meeting of the ICOSU held at the Priory, Greenwich, on May 1st, 1911, a resolution fixing the date for the International Strike of Merchant Seafarers was passed. The date was kept secret up to the moment of the declaration, *viz* on the night of June 17th at Southampton by myself [Hopkins] as Secretary of the International Committee in the presence of Mr Havelock Wilson and Mr Lewis [the Southampton branch leader].[3]

Whenever the decision was taken, the date of the announcement itself is not hard to find. In the meantime, there was much work to be done. In April it was announced that Havelock Wilson and Hopkins would tour Norwegian ports from 18th to 24th April. *The Seaman* reported them as speaking at Christiana (Oslo), Bergen and Stavanger. London received a visit from Jochade (leader of the ITWF) who had arrived from Berlin for discussions. He declined an invitation to stay at the Greenwich Priory on the ground of not wishing to cause inconvenience. Perhaps it was too spartan for him.

The Seaman (April) announced

> Every man of the sea, regardless of whether or not he is a Union man, hates the Federation like poison, because he recognises it stands for oppression. Seamen of all countries feel the same pinch, are subject to the same Tyranny. For that reason the feeling has been expressed in unmistakable terms throughout the world that the time has arrived when seafarers of all countries, on the same day and at the same hour, must withhold their labour until their Unions receive proper recognition and have established the right of collective bargaining, in order that they may get something like uniform rates of wages and uniform conditions of labour on all ships.

On 17th May the text of Hopkins's letter of the 3rd, written in his capacity as ICOSU secretary to the Shipping Federation regarding a conciliation board, was published in *The Times*.

> I am instructed by the International Committee of Seafarers' Unions … to ask if the Central Council of the International Shipping Federation (Limited), or any committee appointed by that organization, would be prepared to meet the members of my committee to discuss the situation created by the refusal of the Shipping Federation to agree to the establishment of a Conciliation Board on the grounds that the request for the formation of such a board was made by non-representative persons and that there are no grievances on the part of seamen which require adjustment by the means suggested. In the event of the Shipping Federation being unable to arrange for a meeting on the lines suggested above, I am directed to enquire if it would be possible

for the Central Committee of the Shipping Federation
to authorize its National Associations, or, if necessary,
its individual members, to meet representatives of the
National Organizations of the Seafarers.

... [L]et me have a reply on or before the 15th inst.

On 4th May the *Journal of Commerce*, a paper in the Federation
pocket, published an interview with Cuthbert Laws, General Manager
of the Federation, in which Laws submitted that the whole thing
had been 'got up' to replenish Union coffers.[4] It was not made clear
how a strike might replenish those coffers but the Federation never
missed an opportunity to attack NSFU finances, knowing that this
was its weakest point. Laws declared that a conciliation board would
be pointless since, he claimed, only 1% of 150,000 seamen belonged
to the NSFU. The *Journal of Commerce* published on succeeding
days a letter to the effect that the strike would gain little support, then
a leader describing a strike as impractical. Further letters accused
Havelock Wilson of an undemocratic style of leadership.

By 12th May talk of a strike had percolated the system sufficiently
to leave the confines of the shipping papers and reach *The Times*,
which carried a report that Captain Tupper of the NSFU had gone
to Cardiff, apparently to begin a major recruitment drive in that
busy port. Whoever controlled the ports of South Wales controlled
the supply of coal which fuelled the shipping industry. Writing later,
Tupper described in typical fashion (his autobiography consistently
enhancing his role, here with some justification) how his visit 'was to
begin the campaign which was to end in the big strike of 1911.[5] Tupper
began a round of speeches and meetings and arranged for access to
fields, christened Neptune Park, which would host a gala and tented
accommodation to hold his men together. The *Journal of Commerce*
was moved to call on 15th May for talks before 'it is too late'.

Hopkins at this time was office-bound in Maritime Hall in
London, still described as trustee-elect (though by whom elected
is never stated) of the NSFU. The nature of his business is not
hard to discover; on 17th May *The Times* reported that a strike had
been decided upon and reported Hopkins's letter to the Shipping
Federation. Hopkins's secretary, Anderson, wrote on his behalf to
Jochade that, 'Here in England preparations for a strike are being
hurried forward'.[6] The preparations included speeches from the
French labour leader Mme Sorgue. Mme Sorgue represented French

dockers and was a welcome observer at the ICOSU, where her role was to report back to French seamen's leaders. Hopkins seems on occasions to have shared her platform.[7] Mme Sorgue declared that the suggested strike dates were all inaccurate. While most shipowners were now said to believe that a strike would fail, the *Journal of Commerce* (19th May) reported, without explanation, that shipping circles believed the strike date would be 19th May. Strangely *The Times* of the next day confirmed this and again reported Hopkins's attempts to persuade the Federation to agree to a conciliation board. A letter from Cathery, NSFU secretary, spoke of men taking a 'holiday', which could become a strike. The confusion about dates was obviously tactical.

In the next week letters from Havelock Wilson repeated the call for a conciliation board. His letters were probably written to maintain the support of moderate opinion rather than with any real hope of achieving their stated object. On 23rd May, posters were issued at South Shields warning men to watch for a strike[8] and, over the next few days, various papers reported posters appearing around the country. A further development was the arrival of Tom Mann, the well-known activist, at Hull.[9] *Lloyd's Weekly Shipping Index* suggested that a strike was imminent and that the leaders were being put in place. Havelock Wilson joined Mann at Hull on 28th May to address large crowds of men. On the following day *The Times* drew attention to the strike's international dimension by reporting that Danish seamen had reached an early agreement with their owners, but noted the likelihood of a simultaneous strike at Antwerp.[10]

Hopkins's secretary wrote to Jochade that Hopkins was all over the country and that this was delaying his replies. *The Messenger* (July) reported that

> Owing to the trouble in connection with the sailors and
> the present unrest in the shipping world the Rev. Father
> has been using his influence with both masters and men
> to bring about a settlement of the difficulty. Under these
> circumstances our readers will this month … understand
> why the Superior-General has not written.

Hopkins was now becoming increasingly busy as the dispute began to take shape. On the one hand he was having to speak in defense of Havelock Wilson, particularly in the face of attacks aimed at Wilson's financial probity, a ploy which the Federation had used with success in the past and which derived mainly from the Federation's campaign to discredit the NSFU. On the other, seamen in Hull and Cardiff were becoming increasingly active.

At Cardiff, Tupper had organised sports and accommodation for 3,000 strikers (Cathery's 'holiday') but was facing a strike-breaking threat which was believed to involve the importation at Barry of 2,000 Chinese, the 'Yellow Peril' becoming blacklegs. In fact, at no time was anything like that number of strike-breakers brought in to these important ports or, indeed, to anywhere else. But rumour was rife. With the passage of time trains of blacklegs would be turned back, and there would be riots, especially aimed at the Chinese community, with troops also being brought in by the train-load. In the middle of all this, on 31st May, newspaper attention was diverted by the launch of the *TITANIC*.

Support for the Union came from unexpected quarters. The *Journal of Commerce* (3rd June, 1911) printed a letter in defence of Havelock Wilson and the Union from the Rotterdam Chaplain of the British Sailors' Society, the letter prompted by a visit that the chaplain had made to see Hopkins at Maritime Hall in May. The BSS normally kept well clear of anything resembling an industrial disagreement. Another letter (the correspondence dealt with an alleged incident at Maritime Hall, which probably explains its presence in the *Journal of Commerce*), sent by Hopkins's secretary, Anderson, maintained the interesting position that '[Hopkins] holds no office in the NSFU ...'. It is implicit in this disingenuous statement that Hopkins had still to be confirmed in his trusteeship, which he would be after the strike, and that he was acting as ICOSU secretary. Perhaps by chance, the first real sign of trouble at this time, albeit unofficial, appeared in Southampton when coal trimmers walked off the White Star liner *OLYMPIC*,[11] an action which, should there be any doubt in the matter, reinforced awareness of the dependence of the industry on coal.

On 5th June *The Times* reported that the ICOSU had begun a three-day conference from which Hopkins issued this statement:

> My committee desire me publicly to express their regret
> that, having exhausted all possible means of averting or
> limiting the extent of a general strike of seafarers, no
> alternative is left but to stand aside and allow events to
> take their course.

It seems that the conference finished early, with the strike date still kept very much a secret.

In the week following this statement, attention returned to the *OLYMPIC*. The White Star Line cannot have been happy that the publicity surrounding the *OLYMPIC*'s maiden voyage should be associated with the coal trimmers' dispute. The men were asking for six pounds a month, according to *The Times*, or the same rate as the crews of the *MAURETANIA* and the *LUSITANIA*. The unrest prompted *The Times* (10th June) to suggest that Waterloo Day, 18th June, would be the date when the strike would start, a date denied by Havelock Wilson, while John Bell at Hull announced that the date would be given on the evening of 14th June at a mass meeting at Paragon Square, Hull. *Justice* (17th June) published an interview with a crew member listing a series of problems on the *OLYMPIC*. When other trimmers were imported to replace those in dispute, by the next day twelve other ships were without coal. The imported trimmers came from Sheffield and probably knew little, if anything, of the situation to which they were being brought.[12]

On 12th June, while ships at Southampton were being coaled by six hundred men under police protection, *The Times* and the *Journal of Commerce* quoted Havelock Wilson's letter to the owners making a last appeal. The *Cardiff Journal of Commerce* declared that the fall-off in shipping was 'solely attributable to the intervention of the Whitsuntide holiday'. The Whitsuntide holiday was marked by fine weather, to the relief of Tupper at Cardiff, who had his sports arranged. Most of the papers forecast an imminent strike, despite the Federation view that this was 'absolutely ridiculous'. The *Journal of Commerce* began a daily series entitled MR J H WILSON'S LAST STRUGGLE and quoted Cuthbert Laws as saying, 'There will be no international strike although there may be a little trouble here and there'.

On Tuesday, 13th June, according to the *Daily Graphic*, Tom Mann moved to Liverpool to be ready to act as the local organiser when the strike started, while Hopkins addressed a large evening meeting at Southampton, accompanied by Havelock Wilson. The Southampton meeting took place in Kingsland Square, with Councillor T. Lewis presiding. Wilson spoke first, saying that he had come to Southampton as the men had insisted on a strike.[13] But Hopkins had the star role. The only detailed report of his speech seems to have been that in the *Liverpool Echo*:

> At the big mass meeting of seamen in Southampton last night the men threw down the gauntlet ... Father Hopkins made an impassioned speech. He drew on his experience as chaplain to missions to seamen in India and elsewhere, described his efforts to better the lot of sailormen, and gave the history of the movement to internationalise the cause of seafarers. He complained bitterly that although he represented the seamen of many nations as secretary of the International Strike Committee, the Shipping Federation had treated his representation with indifference. 'The time,' he continued, ' has come to draw the sword and use it to obtain for seamen the just conditions of life to which they are entitled.' He then read an official notice declaring the international strike.

Hopkins announced that the strike would begin on the following day (14th June).

The report in the *Liverpool Echo* can be supplemented by the *Southampton Times and Hampshire Express* (17th June), which remarked that 'It is not clear why Southampton was brought into especial prominence by having the first announcement of the strike ...'. It confirmed that the venue had been Kingsland Square, the meeting chaired by Cllr Lewis, and that Havelock Wilson had also spoken. Wilson had claimed not to have expected to be in Southampton that evening but had come when the men had insisted on striking.

This leaves open the possibility that the strike began, through local pressure, a little earlier than had been planned. The build-up to Hopkins announcing the strike, apart from smacking of stage management, is explained by his secretaryship of the ICOSU. Southampton was the venue because of the attention attracted by the trouble surrounding the *OLYMPIC*, her maiden voyage an ideal target. It is tempting to wonder, however, whether Hopkins, who was well-known in the port, and had been working there through the SFSSP since the end of 1910, had not engineered, or at least capitalised on, the OLYMPIC walk-out. The local paper included in its report the sort of detail beloved by Hopkins, perhaps from his speech, that the White Star Line had made £1,000,000 profit in the year preceding.

Of the five countries originally in the ICOSU, the British strike was the most important, partly because of the size of the British fleet and partly because first Denmark and then Belgium settled early. (British seamen in Antwerp continued to strike when the Belgians returned to work.) Ironically, the White Star Line also settled quickly, the next day, in the interest of its reputation and regular passenger service, as other passenger companies were to do. Throughout 15th June the strike was being declared in ports throughout the country, though in some ports the effect was not immediate because of the nature of the men's contracts. Mme Sorgue had by this time reached Cardiff where she spoke, after the strike had been declared by the firing of rockets, in Neptune Park. The strongest responses came at first from Liverpool, Hull (though here was a peculiar case as members of a local union continued to work), Glasgow, the North East of England, and Cardiff. In fact *The Times* was reporting strike action in twenty ports, noting as it did so, that for all that had been said about a conciliation board, the main and immediate concern of the men was an increase in wages. This was to remain a feature of local agreements.

The Federation, meanwhile, was trying to forestall the strikers by arranging for depot ships to accommodate blackleg crews for its members' ships. The government sent two companies of soldiers to Newport in South Wales where the action was at its liveliest, described in one newspaper headline as TONYPANDYMONIUM. The sailing of the *OLYMPIC* beguiled some of the more popular papers into thinking, as did the *Daily Graphic* (15th June), 'The great strike ... has come and gone, even if it can be said to have come at all'. Several non-Federation companies began to make concessions, especially on weekly ships at the regional ports. In the *Minutes* of the Shipping Federation's Humber District committee meeting of 14th June, Mr Sanderson recorded a lightning strike by deck hands of the SS *AARO*, apparently the first cargo vessel to be struck, and suggested that members 'should decide on preparations being made for any eventuality that might occur'. [14]

The Shipping Federation's General Purposes' Committee, meeting on 16th June, made its first formal reference to the strike:

> Seamen's Agitation. The General Manager reported
> the steps that had been taken or were in contemplation
> at the various Districts affected, for dealing with the

seamen's strike, and the intimidatory picketing by which it was accompanied. It was <u>resolved</u>: "That the steps be confirmed and the District Committees have the power to take such further measures as may in their opinion be necessary whether by way of the hire of depot ships or otherwise, for the purpose of obtaining and protecting men willing to work".[15]

On the same day the Humber District agreed to hire tugs at £5 a day, to telegraph for a supply of Fleet Reserve men, to approve the secretary's action in ordering a supply of men from Liverpool and Newcastle and to send an agent to Yarmouth for men. Further, it was agreed to order from the 'Continental Ports' a supply of up to 100 men from each port. A meeting reconvened there later in the day was to discover that there were no men available from Newcastle, Cardiff, Liverpool, Antwerp, Hamburg, Amsterdam or Rotterdam, or from the Navy Employment Agency, and that their depot ship had on board about twenty men. After this revelation, their next meeting was to be with the police authorities. It was agreed that no concessions would be made.

There were some heartening signs of support for the Union, for example the handing in of seamen's discharge books by the hundred in Cardiff, but Havelock Wilson, writing to Jochade on 17th June, offered a slightly different picture. He noted that many were not on strike because they had been signed-on ahead of time and his advice to them had been to honour their contracts. He wrote, 'we have practically won our battle'. He listed some substantial pay rises granted, especially on 'the Scotch boats'. At the same time he added,

> Our only difficulty has been one of finance, as the Shipping Federation has kept us all spending our money for years. We were compelled to go into this fight without any funds whatever. Now if anything can be done in Germany in the way of giving us a little financial help, it will be very acceptable to us…. This fight will have to continue for another 4 months, if we slacken our efforts in the slightest….
>
> We have not abandoned our idea of a Conciliation Board, and the points that we put forth in our programme, but we thought by dealing with the wages

> and obtaining a few victories it would give the men some
> encouragement, as to tell you the truth, very few seamen
> understand the importance of joint bargaining... [16]

The shortage of cash that Havelock Wilson mentions was confirmed in a later statement made by Tupper that the NSFU started the strike with £6..13s in hand. His friends would have described his second point as realistic, his enemies, as paternalistic. *The Times* of the same day reported that Wilson had sent a telegram to Mr Buxton, President of the Board of Trade, objecting to crews being recruited at South Shields for Southampton. His further objection concerned the signing on of Chinese crews at Poplar and elsewhere: 'Request that language test be properly applied'.

Two days later Havelock Wilson wrote to Jochade giving a port-by-port picture. On some 200 'coasting boats' the owners had conceded 35 shillings a week, an increase on 28 shillings. He mentioned ten ships sailing with 'blackleg crews', short-handed and with men who were neither firemen nor sailors, instancing the Royal Mail steamer *BRITON*, which sailed from Southampton crewed by 110 locomotive firemen from Leeds in Yorkshire, men who had never been to sea before, while the stewards were German waiters from London's West End. He mentioned particularly the desire of the Hull men for him to come and speak in person so that the local union might be shown for what it was by Havelock Wilson's claim, a tool of the Federation. He was particularly encouraged by the dockers who were beginning to come out in support of the seamen in a number of ports. In turn, he would discover they were to be followed by the carters, and later the railwaymen, in pursuit of their own claims. This procession of striking unions was to continue for some time after the seamen had settled. Had Wilson written this letter a day later (19th June), he would have been able to add that 2,000 Glasgow dockers had joined the strike, while Hull was blocked and the local Hull union (obviously not a tool of the Federation) had also joined the strike; Goole and Southampton were similarly blocked and 1,000 dockers were on strike in Liverpool. He concluded this letter also by referring to finance, which was 'the only thing that is likely to interfere with us'.

The Times of the 19th June calculated the cost of a two-month strike to be equivalent to £10 a year off a seaman's annual wage, and an increase in cost per annum to British shipping of at least

£1,375,000. These figures were most probably from a Federation source, and prompt the question of how events appeared, not from the view of the NSFU, but of the employers. The answer is not easy to find. Mention has been made of Powell's book on the Federation and its minimal reference to the strike, perhaps because it was something not happily recalled, and his one brief reference to Hopkins in connection with another matter.[17] Shipping Federation *Minutes* are also silent on such particulars. It is not only for details of the NSFU's role, therefore, that one is forced to depend, almost exclusively, upon contemporary press reports. Yet for news of the Federation's reaction the papers are less than helpful, quoting Cuthbert Laws almost exclusively, speaking as the Federation's general manager, a role requiring him to play down the sequence of events. Newspapers with a shipping interest followed the Federation line and the shipping interest found the Board of Trade sufficiently amenable to pressure to prevent it from becoming seriously involved at this stage.

The interest at this point of most public figures concerned the effect a strike might have upon the Review of the Fleet. As early as 14th June a *Times* leader had condemned the NSFU for choosing the week of the Royal Review for a strike, adding

> The public may have to endure inconvenience for a time here and there, and some of the weaker shipping companies may suffer more or less injury, which a little later will fall upon the men themselves... there is no organisation strong enough either to control the general body of seamen or to offer shipowners the opportunity for collective bargaining....

As tension mounted and the NSFU seemed to be succeeding, a Press Association report appeared in the *Journal of Commerce* on 22nd June to the effect that Havelock Wilson had announced that the Review of the Fleet would be unaffected. Not everyone was bothered about the Review. Glasier, a labour journalist, wrote in his diary, 'This is the day of days, the apex of all the vast rubbish heap of toil, vanity and falsehood which has been diligently piled up for a whole year'.[18] On the same day it was announced that the National Transport Workers' Federation, a body in whose foundation Havelock Wilson had been involved, had written to the President of the Board of Trade (Buxton) asking him to intervene with the shipowners.

And there were uglier reports, almost lost in the Review's shadow, including one that a picket had been fired on at Hull from aboard the SS *LADYWOOD*.[19]

From 22nd June, Coronation Day, news began to improve. This despite the Humber District of the Shipping Federation recording that all work in the docks had ceased on Friday, 23rd June. *The Times* published a list of vessels cancelled for the Royal Review, though the *Cardiff Journal of Commerce* reported a temporary truce, perhaps misunderstanding a Press Association report, or finding encouragement in several settlements announced by liner companies, for by the 23rd, a settlement had been reached at Southampton. The liner companies at Liverpool had also conceded, but they were not Federation members. Next day, *The Times* announced a proposed conference of owners meeting 'today'. *The Times* report seems to have been premature in its 'today' and Cuthbert Laws was quoted, on the 26th, to have described this as a joint meeting of local associations of the Federation, to be of 'all shipping interests in the UK'. He failed to mention that it did not include the NSFU. In fact the meeting was scheduled for the 28th June, until which time the Humber District, after an approach by the Mayor to Mr Sanderson offering to bring the two sides together, resolved to do nothing.[20]

The NTWF received a reply to its letter addressed to the President of the Board of Trade wherein Buxton opined that the time for his intervention with the Federation was not yet opportune. The Transport Workers were dissatisfied with this, as they had asked him to approach the shipowners rather than the Federation, a fine distinction but one offering room for manoeuvre. They too agreed to confer on the 28th about their next step.[21]

Perhaps it was this news that prompted John Bruce Glasier to write in his diary (26th June):

> This seems to be turning out a big affair – which I almost regret as it will rehabilitate Havelock Wilson who is a scamp, and Tom Mann who is hardly less so. The latter must need have some new jumping off ground to afford him a fresh start as an agitator. Since returning from Australia he has been unable to 'catch on' either in the Socialist or Trade Union movement and this strike is just the thing for him.

Against this background, Hopkins, Tupper and Havelock Wilson were about the country speaking where they could.

With news of two conferences, Union and Federation, pending, the rest of the day's news gave a confusing picture. *The Times* reported that ten Glasgow firms had agreed to new rates of pay, to recognise the NSFU, and to abolish the medical examination required before signing-on. Only one of the ten firms belonged to the Federation. For his part, Havelock Wilson was reported as threatening to resign if his men failed to honour their new agreements. He also expressed displeasure that some ships chartered for the Royal Review were to be crewed by Lascars.

Generally the strike was beginning to bite. In the Hull area, where 10,000 men were reported to be idle because of the strike, Mr Bell had asked the railwaymen to postpone their sympathy strike. At Leith thirty-seven ships were without crews. *The Times* gave Southampton's estimate of the cost of the strike to date as £100,000, as against the *Cardiff Journal of Commerce*, under the headline THE SHIPPING WAR, which gave a figure of £10,000. In Cardiff, taxis carrying a Chinese crew were said to have been stopped, with one arrest being made. And so on, round the country. The *Journal of Commerce* quoted the owners: 'It is pleasing to note that, with a few exceptions, the Shipping Federation firms are standing solidly together.' However many those 'few exceptions', press reports indicate that where increased and uniform wages were conceded a truce was called.[22] However, the Board of Trade replied to the NTWF that it saw no room for improvement. Hopkins wrote to Jochade that a possible outcome of the morrow's (28th) special meeting of Transport Workers was that 'we may hear surprising developments'.[23]

What of the meetings on the 28th June? Was it still 'War' or was it nearly all over? The Federation meeting predictably deplored the behaviour of pickets. It agreed that in certain ports a rise might be conceded, as had already been the case, though it claimed that British rates, which were not uniform, were higher than many on the Continent. It recommended standard rates of pay. It refused unanimously to recognise the NSFU though it considered how it might extend its scope to cover such things as wage disputes. Conversely, the NTWF meeting, with delegates representing 100,000 workers, announced its regret at the inability of the Board of Trade to arrange a meeting between shipowners and Union, and threatened to meet again on Monday, 3rd July, to consider drastic action if no settlement had been reached by 1st July. Between these two extremes fell a range of actions in individual ports. For example, in Liverpool, where most firms, liner companies in particular, had conceded the men's pay demands, the dockers declined to return to work until the NSFU had obtained recognition. Glasier noted in his diary on 1st July seeing on the Mersey 'three big liners – *CARMANIA*, *CEDRIC* and *EMPRESS OF IRELAND* – all out in mid stream ready to start, but, so it is said, without crews. They probably will not sail.' On the 3rd he recorded that they had sailed 'with the consent of the strike committee'.

At Hull, however, it was rumoured that the owners were prepared to meet the men and, accordingly, a truce was declared pending the outcome of this meeting.[24] Lord Runciman had chaired the Federation meeting and had taken a firm line, but as in many disputes, there appears to have been movement behind the scenes. At this stage the Federation declined to recognise publicly the action being taken by some of its members. From the Board of Trade, Mr Askwith, a very senior official, a King's Counsel, and an experienced mediator, was meeting with the North of England Shipowners Conference in Hull at the invitation of Sanderson.[25] He arrived with Mr Mitchell of the Board of Trade 'with a view to settling this dispute'. According to the press, this first meeting on 29th June took eight hours before proposing terms to the seamen, who later rejected them at a mass meeting at which, according to Askwith, there were some 15,000 men present. Indeed, serious riots took place.[26]

The Humber District committee *Minutes* give a slightly different picture, in which the shipowners agreed to meet a delegation of the men drawn from the NSFU, the dockers, the lightermen, and the coal porters. Hopkins was not listed as present, nor was there anyone from the local union (nicknamed 'Butcher's men', Butcher being their leader, whose withdrawal of labour at Hull had confirmed local owners in the view that this was a serious strike). Askwith asked what the men were seeking and J.R. Bell of the NSFU named three demands: the first, the abolition of the Federation ticket, was an absolute; the second, the presence of a man's doctor at the medical examination; and the third, an increase in wages. The terms agreed at this meeting to be put to the subsequent mass meeting included the Federation ticket being voluntary, the men to have their own doctor with each side paying its own medical expenses and further discussions on wages to follow. The large meeting, which Askwith suggested was attended by 15,000 men, at which these terms were rejected, recorded a vote of five for, and 4,000 against, according to the contemporary Humber District *Minutes*; Askwith's figure was a late one.

The same day (29th June), according to the NSFU historian Borlase, Hopkins was in Manchester at a conference, the nature of which is unclear but from which, Borlase maintained, an agreement emerged.[27] It is likely that Hopkins was privy to the North of England Steam Shipowners' Association (NESSOA) meeting with Askwith in Hull and that, if Hopkins was in Manchester rather than Hull, the two meetings were somehow related. However, it is more likely that he went straight to Hull when Askwith went there and that Borlase is mistaken. *The Times* (1st July) and the *Journal of Commerce* (4th July) both report him as being in Hull, where he seems to have gone direct from Southampton. It appears that when the NESSOA proposals were presented to a mass meeting of the seamen at the Hull City Hall, the men refused to give a hearing to Mr Oswald Sanderson, Managing Director of Messrs Wilson's, the principal Hull shipowner, who was loudly booed. The newspaper reports suggest a fairly lively encounter between the two sides, following an earlier meeting of the men's leaders which had lasted an hour and a half. Now outside the City Hall were five hundred policemen, some from London according to the *Daily Graphic*, with two squadrons of the Scots Greys, and some companies of the 'Green Howards', being held in readiness at York, where special trains waited at York station to convey them at a given signal.[28]

Whilst all this was happening at Hull, the *Journal of Commerce* reported that Federation members were expected to start laying up ships soon, being recompensed from an indemnity scheme put together specially for the purpose, but the reporter wrote

> It was pointed out to me that it was ridiculous to connect J Havelock Wilson and his union in any way with the success of the men in getting a rise in wages at the present time. For years past the Shipping Federation had been warning ship owners that a shortage of sailors and firemen might be expected....

In fact, apart from liner companies already mentioned, at Hull a rise had been conceded, as it had in Glasgow, but in neither case with Union recognition being granted. The *Labour Leader* (30th

June) commented, 'The most notable feature of the strike, so far as the men are concerned, is undoubtedly the cooperation of the shore hands with the seamen.' The rises in pay conceded, and the support of other unions, together with a sudden increase in NSFU membership, meant that the Union could fairly feel at this stage that it was in a very strong position. *The Times* (1st July) reported that about half of the shipowners nationally had reached an agreement giving a rise of about ten shillings a month, and that in London, the local shipowners' meeting had agreed to meet the NTWF, but not the NSFU, not later than 4th July. The Federation had every reason to be worried; the government more so if the continuing riots in Hull spread to other ports. The *Daily Mirror* (1st July) hardly exaggerated in its headline: BLACK OUTLOOK IN SHIPPING STRIKE. But this was the weekend, during which little progress could be expected.

On Monday, 3rd July, Hopkins and others had a further meeting with Askwith in Hull, while troops remained on stand-by, as they did also in Liverpool. According to the Humber District *Minutes* this was the first meeting at which Hopkins was present, and he was there as one of fourteen delegates. The meeting was to consider the men's revised proposals and it was agreed to resume negotiations. The men offered to return to work if an increase could be added to the dockers' wages. The final agreement was much as before: no charge for the Federation ticket, which would be voluntary; the presence of their own doctor; wage increases. The wage increases were to be considered at a series of further, more detailed meetings at Hull. Over such fine details can agreements be made and faces saved.

At Hull 150 ships now stood idle. The *Daily Mirror* mentioned the continuing presence of 500 Metropolitan Policemen, presumably based in York, remaining after the weekend. If the figure of 500 is not an exaggeration, it suggests the amount of trouble anticipated by the authorities. *The Times* offered another indicator of the strike's effect, reporting that flour, which had been 1s..5d a stone on the Thursday, was fetching 2s..11d by the Sunday evening.

Following his meeting with Askwith, Hopkins addressed a mass meeting of the men in Hull on the Monday evening. Between 10,000 and 12,000 men were present. The meeting was presided over by Councillor P FLanagan, assisted by Hopkins, Mr J.R. Bell, Mr O'Connor Kessack, Mr Burn and others, all of the NSFU.

Hopkins was the last to speak. He told the men that agreement had been reached for the time being, based on an offer of more money for seamen and dockers, and the agreement of the owners to further discussions. The importance of the latter point cannot be over stressed: the more discussion, the more, at least *de facto*, recognition of the Union. The mass meeting agreed, presumably on Hopkins's proposal, that the details could be worked out at sectional meetings the following morning, where the dockers were also likely to be offered a farthing an hour. According to the *Hull Daily News* (4th July)

> Father Hopkins, who had a cordial reception, agreed that
> the men had obtained a great victory, and he said he also
> wanted to congratulate the shipowners of Hull for having
> manifested such a generous spirit of conciliation ....

He repeated Mr Kessack's regrets over the booing on the previous Friday evening of Messrs Wilson's Mr Sanderson. He could afford to be gracious. He had managed to repeat the key word, 'conciliation'. He also knew that behind him stood the dockers, carters, even the flour millers, while the railwaymen were threatening to follow if they should be asked to handle blacked cargo. And such support was not limited to Hull. Next morning a fairly conciliatory letter from Runciman to Havelock Wilson appeared in the *Journal of Commerce*.

This mass meeting in Hull seems to have been a turning point. More details appear in various sources. We glean that Hopkins had been involved in all the Hull meetings and that he seems to have been able to exercise considerable control over men who were ready to riot. According to the *Journal of Commerce,* at the meeting's conclusion their feelings had been expressed with a bonfire of 500 Federation tickets. When Hopkins had asked the men to approve his expression of deep regret to Mr Sanderson for his impolite reception at the meeting of 29th June, they had responded unanimously in favour. The July issue of *The Messenger* printed a report of Hopkins's speech to the men from the *Hull Daily News* of 4th July. His words clearly struck a chord:

> Now, boys, go back to work and do your duty by the
> settlement, and God give you His blessing. For a moment
> a hush fell upon the crowd, and then a cheer burst forth

from each one of those twenty thousand throats, whilst
instinctively each man turned to his neighbour and said,
'He's a grand man,' or words to that effect.

The Messenger confirmed Hopkins's request to the men to express
their deep regret to Sanderson for his reception at the Friday meeting,
after which 'Father Hopkins was carried shoulder high all round the
field'. It is worth remembering *The Messenger*'s source here was the
local paper and not Hopkins. According to Humber District *Minutes*
in a summary of the strike, 220 vessels had sailed during the dispute,
187 seamen had been supplied to thirty vessels from the Depot Ship
(a Federation vessel used to hold waiting men willing to crew ships),
and 300 had passed through the Depot Ship. Detention money paid
to these men totalled nearly £400. Hopkins's reception by the men
suggests where they felt that success really lay.

From Hull, Hopkins was to move to Manchester, as confirmed
by the *Manchester Courier* (6th July), where the atmosphere was
equally febrile. *The Times* mentioned baton charges. Glasier recorded
of Manchester in his diary on 5th July:

> Carriers ceased work yesterday and have completely
> paralysed traffic, riotous incidents, police charges,
> military in readiness. This is a sudden infection of the
> Seamen's Strike. Shows how epidemic is the feeling
> of battle. Here we see the Manchester carriers suddenly
> cease work and become transformed into barricadiers
> all because of the reverberation of the Seamen's struggle
> and supposed victory, whereas a thousand speeches and
> appeals to their reason and sense of justice would not
> have induced them to strike and risk their jobs.

Hopkins was to hold further discussions with Askwith in Manchester
that evening (5th).

Despite the excitement in Manchester, *Lloyd's Weekly Shipping
Index* (6th July) commented:

> Generally speaking there are signs of calm following the
> storm. But it cannot be anticipated that there will be no
> more trouble, seeing that in some cases the concessions
> which have been made are quite incompatible with the
> successful conduct of business. It is on the Mersey
> more especially that the future is uncertain.

It was on the Mersey that Tom Mann was busy organising for the NSFU and where the dockers were so supportive. The suggestion that settlements were too high ('incompatible with the successful conduct of business') would have been meat and drink to Hopkins who would readily have defended his position with statistics for owners' profits.[29] The NSFU had to seek gains where possible. Hull had fallen, Manchester was ready to talk.

Askwith, arriving in Manchester on the evening of 5th July at 8.15 p.m., was met by the Lord Mayor and taken to the Town Hall, despite the hour, to meet the representatives of men and employers. Hopkins took the Union lead in the four hours of discussion which followed. The meeting continued the following morning. During the evening of the 6th July Hopkins told a reporter from the *Manchester Courier* that he thought the conference would not be over by the evening of the following day. That was at 7.00 p.m. The reporter added, 'Discussing the situation ... at midnight, Fr Hopkins, the seamen's chaplain, said the hopes of a settlement were being maintained.' On the 7th July, Askwith sat from 9.00 a.m. until 8.00 p.m., with Hopkins and the local NSFU secretary (a Mr Carpener) in attendance. It may be assumed that Askwith spent an equal amount of time with employers, for Hopkins was able to escape from the meeting to join a procession of wives and strikers at Broadway in nearby Salford, marching with them through the principal street to the Albert Street Police Station Yard where a meeting was held. Just as in Cardiff the weather was helping the 'sports' and demonstrations, so here in Salford hot days were facilitating open air events.[30]

The hope of a settlement was beginning to spread. *The West of England Observer*, the *Bristol Guardian*, and other regional papers announced that the seamen's strike was to end on 8th July. It had certainly ended in some ports, for example, Southampton; and the Hull agreement was still holding. *Justice* (8th July) quoted a Southampton source as saying, 'I should like particularly to mention the splendid work done during the campaign by Father Hopkins and Mrs Palmer, the Socialist Member of the Board of Guardians'. But in Hull, and now in Manchester, there were no colleagues from the Board of Guardians to help him, and the conditions to be negotiated differed from those of Southampton's liner trade, with its peculiar imperatives. The details of his negotiations, of which few remain, would be important if trouble was to be avoided in other militant

centres such as Cardiff, where the *Cardiff Citizen* (8th July) reported
Chinese boarding houses being stormed, the Chinese being feared,
largely unfairly, as ready and cheap crew substitutes. In the *Journal
of Commerce* Runciman was rejecting the idea that the Chamber of
Shipping should have any mediatory role.

Settlement in Manchester came on 10th July after another very
late meeting. The *Manchester Courier* reported 'at 1.15 this morning
Mr Askwith made the following announcement ... "all sections have
now agreed"'. Hopkins was a signatory on behalf of the NSFU (in
which officially he still held no office). The hours, late or early,
spent in negotiations as revealed by the *Courier* and other papers are
not those usually associated with the sick man we know Hopkins to
have been.

As if to increase the pressure on the men, by raising the spectre
of unemployment at a time when agreements seemed to be the trend,
the *Journal of Commerce*, whilst giving the Manchester agreement
in detail, reported that ships were being laid up under the recently
agreed indemnity scheme, and commented that seamen might yet be
unaware that their action would surely lead to the loss of jobs in the
industry. Each agreement was locally made because of Federation
refusal to recognise the Union. The Manchester agreement, which still
avoided NSFU recognition and the establishment of a conciliation
board, so largely concerned wages and hours, was extended to
Liverpool where the seamen who had not already agreed with liner
companies could return to work; there the spotlight switched to the
dockers. Three days later another agreement was reported, from
Rotterdam, though not Amsterdam, where the owners had declined
government mediation.[31] In South Wales a settlement had still to
be reached. There, Tupper was finding himself on the wrong side
of the law in the dispute over the transport of blacklegs by local
tugmen.

It is possible that Hopkins had needed to return to Hull from
Manchester to tie up loose ends. Whatever the case, he arrived
in South Shields on the 11.15 a.m. train from Hull on Monday,
17th July to a big reception.[32] Here, he was following in the
wake of Havelock Wilson who had spent the weekend in this, his
home area, having arrived on the Friday. On Saturday 15th July
Havelock Wilson had made a significant speech, on the Mill Dam,
in which he had referred to the Federation refusal to treat with
an unregistered union. He had said that if he thought there was

any likelihood of the Federation recognising the Union, he would advise his Union to register forthwith. In fact, registration would involve a delay of some weeks, but the Union was feeling the financial pressures of the strike as much as its opponents, as well as its inconvenience. The government too was involved in no small expense through the army units it was having to send to the ports to keep the peace. At Cardiff, for example, incendiarism and looting were now being reported, while throughout South Wales, where there was a complete stoppage in the docks (including flour mill workers, trimmers, the women who worked on the potato boats, the laundry women, and just about everyone else), 500 men of the Lancashire Fusiliers and fifty men of the Devon Regiment were sent.[33] To avoid the delay in recognition, Havelock Wilson made a suggestion which took account of the more reasonable attitude of the northern shipowners, many of whom had settled, many of whom he knew of old, and some of whom had so recently been negotiating with Hopkins.

The *Journal of Commerce* (22nd July)[34] reported Wilson's suggestion:

> The Tyne and Blyth District of the Shipping Federation, having recommended the Executive Committee of the Federation to take action with reference to the following proposals contained in a speech by Mr Havelock Wilson, at Newcastle, on July 15th, 1911,'He was prepared to advise his Executive Committee to register the NSFU forthwith, but as that would take some weeks if the Newcastle shipowners could within the next four days appoint any three North Country shipowners they liked, to proceed to Maritime Hall, where he would place at their disposal all the books and documents of the union relating to the membership and finance ...' this Council requests the North of England Steamship Owners' Association to appoint three of their members to make the examination, and that if the report of this examination be satisfactory the NSFU shall be recognised provisionally depending on its registration under the Trades Union Acts provided a proper undertaking be given ... that the application for such registration shall be made not later than 31 July....

It was in the shadow of Havelock Wilson's speech that Hopkins's arrival in South Shields took place. That may have been no coincidence. At the station he was met by some 500 men who carried him in a chair shoulder-high, escorted by the police, to Mill Dam. Here, the local official, Mr R.F. Bell, introduced him to a mass meeting where 'he had a reception which he is not likely to forget'. 'Father Hopkins said he was very anxious to be among the chaps on Tyneside, but, as they all knew, he had been busy elsewhere'. He listed the victories achieved by the strike so far, and hoped the same could be achieved on Tyneside. The *Shields Daily Gazette* noted that Hopkins was going to take charge of the strike committee. 'Father Hopkins stated ... that his mission to Tyneside was not to widen the breach ... but to heal it.'

Talks continued. On the morning of 20th July Hopkins told the press that the NESSOA had given no intimation on the question of conciliation. He was joined during the day by Cathery, the NSFU national secretary, probably in recognition of the seriousness with which the NSFU was taking these talks with the NESSOA. In the evening Hopkins attended a private meeting of the seamen and firemen at Sunderland and told those assembled that during the day he had heard from the Board of Trade to the effect that Askwith was ready to proceed to South Shields at any moment to preside over any conference which might be arranged. With a conference in view, Hopkins had contacted Runciman of the Federation. Hopkins had also attended the meeting of the Central Joint Strike Committee in South Shields in the afternoon, apparently drawing up terms for the proposed conference. The same evening he spoke at a public meeting on the aims of the strike.[35] At this point the weekend intervened.

During the weekend, interest shifted to Cardiff. Here, too, a meeting had taken place between representatives of the owners and Chris Damm and Tupper of the NSFU, with the Mayor in the chair. The rise sought by the men was conceded on condition that it indicated no recognition of the Union, a condition Tupper was not prepared to accept. He insisted on adding a clause to the agreement stating that the signing of it would constitute recognition by the Federation of the NSFU. The owners capitulated and a further round of negotiation started on behalf of the dockers, who were represented by Ernest Bevin.[36] Tupper, on horseback, led a mass demonstration to reinforce the Union's position. He did so, he says in his autobiography, only with the reluctant agreement of the police for he was still only at

liberty on the strength of £800 bail for various charges in connection
with his strike organising.

The news of the owners' agreement in Cardiff, it may be
presumed, would have been sent by telegram to Havelock Wilson.
With this agreement behind him, no doubt Havelock Wilson, arriving
in South Shields on Saturday 22nd July, at midnight, was able to feel
more confident of the strike's outcome.[37] Hopkins, we may guess,
spent the Sunday afternoon briefing him on the agreed terms, which
had so far not been made public. According to the *Cardiff Journal
of Commerce* (24th July) the Cardiff settlement terms concerned
wages, the bypassing of the Federation offices for recruitment,
the end of the Federation medical, recognition of the NSFU, and
arbitration. A search for these conditions in some detail managed
only to find them, apparently printed in full, in the October issue of
The Messenger. In the absence of better information it is necessary
to assume that the Cardiff agreement formed the bones of the final
settlement. Briefly put, the Federation ticket was not withdrawn but
became optional, the Federation doctor who conducted the medical
was to be replaced by one from the Board of Trade, with the medical
taking place in a room set apart for the purpose, the Union was to be
recognised and 'in the event of any dispute the award of an arbitrator
mutually agreed upon shall be final and binding'. The strike was to
be suspended pending further discussion with the owners. There
was also some adjustment of wages.

The meeting between Hopkins and the NESSOA would be a
delicate one concerning full recognition by the Federation of the
Union. The Cardiff settlement had been reached at a time when
riots threatened and, although it represented the thin end of a wedge,
full agreement there had yet to be accepted. Initially The NESSOA
met alone, on Monday 24th July, to consider Hopkins's proposal that
a conference should be held. It must have been aware that at such a
meeting it would speak for the Federation, and that it could not be
construed as representing a single port, as had the meeting in Hull,
but in public it maintained the fiction that this was a local meeting.
The NESSOA members met under the chairmanship of John Coull
in the Mayor's Chambers in Newcastle Town Hall before replying to
a telegram from Hopkins:

> In response to the telegram received from Father Hopkins,
> the North of England Steamship Owners Association

> are prepared to meet a local committee of seafarers in
> conference, and suggest ... Wednesday 26th Inst at 3.45
> p.m. at the Central Station Hotel, Newcastle.

The NESSOA telegram was worded carefully to avoid later use as evidence
of Union recognition. However, 'local' was to include Hopkins.

According to the *Shields Daily Gazette* the proposed meeting
took place with six representatives from each side, presided over by
the Mayor or his Deputy. Hopkins's presence was as President of the
Joint Strike Committee, on which he was described as representing
the Mercantile Marine Service Association, a new title for him, and
probably a gesture to maintain the self respect of the NESSOA. He
would be accompanied by C. Bellem, H. Johnson, E. Hudson, C.
Fredrickson, and J. MacDonald, several of whom appear in NSFU
Minutes as NSFU members from the North East. By the 27th July
provisional agreement had been reached. Hopkins did not return to
South Shields until late at night after interviewing several shipowners
in Hartlepool and on the Tees.

Lloyd's Weekly Shipping Index reported on the same day a rather
ragged picture:

> Another conference between shipowners and seamen
> was held at Newcastle and a provisional agreement
> drafted. There is now no dislocation of trade or traffic
> on the Tyne .... Negotiations took place at Cardiff and
> many of the points of dispute were settled this morning,
> and it is hoped that a complete resumption of work will
> be brought about in the course of a few days.... At
> Glasgow, matters look more hopeful .... At Port Talbot,
> where there are about 1,200 men on strike, a number
> of ... vessels are held up in the docks ....

The *Journal of Commerce*, which was closer to the Federation,
noted that in addition to Alderman John Coull (Chairman of the
NESSOA), the owners were represented by James E Tully (Vice
Chairman of the NESSOA), Arthur Scholefield, W.J. Noble, G.P.
Cutting, and George Lunn. Hopkins went from this meeting to
address a mass meeting of the men in the King's Hall of the Golden
Lion Hotel. He explained the terms of the provisional agreement.
The men declined (at his prompting, one wonders) to act upon them
until they had been agreed to by the shipowners of Middlesbrough,

Sunderland and the Hartlepools. Hopkins went to Hartlepool and
Middlesbrough in the afternoon, as mentioned above, returning
late. He interviewed the Sunderland owners on Friday, 28th July,
and obtained their agreement to all the provisional terms except
a paragraph on overtime.[38] Effectively, from this point, the North
East strike came to an end and Hopkins's negotiating skills were no
longer required. A note in the ITWF records 28th July as the date of
the final agreement.[39]

    What actually happened at the end of the seamen's strike is hard
to discover. A number of newspapers were wise after the event.
Regional ones, like the *West of England Observer*, tended to count
the cost of policing when strikers could simply have been driven
from the streets at the point of a bayonet. For the public the end
must have been hard to distinguish, for many groups other than the
seamen remained on strike, including the dockers and the carters.
According to *Lloyd's Weekly* South Wales was not back to normal
until 3rd August. By 7th August there were still 20,000 men on
strike in London, the docks were still blocked, but it was no longer
a NSFU problem. As late as 11th August, Glasier's diary referred
to a revival of the dockers' strike in London and Liverpool, with
riots and military charges, though on 14th August he ascribed this
to a blunder on the part of the police. NSFU officials had to rally
round Havelock Wilson when he had some kind of breakdown and
departed to Droitwich to recover, though he was fit enough to make
the annual meeting. Hopkins had loose ends to tie up, which he did
on his return to Greenwich. At the end of August he was writing
to Jochade to apologise for the Union's long overdue cheque, its
affiliation fee to the ITWF,[40] so we may guess that he was acting as
trustee-designate, though still described by Havelock Wilson at the
AGM as 'outside our movement'.

    What had the Union achieved? The provisional agreement has
been given above. It became firm as the Cardiff agreement, effective
from an unknown date, but before the end of September, as witnessed
by its publication in the October issue of *The Messenger*. Hopkins
wrote that he believed the men and the Federation were truly entering
a 'new era'. A review of the initial aims of the strikers agreed on 14th
March at Antwerp is revealing. The first requirement, for a conciliation
board, had not been achieved. Indeed, it would have to wait until
the pressure of war made such a board imperative. Wages had been
increased and rationalised, though they were to drop somewhat in

Local transport workers gather in Liverpool on 'Red Sunday', 13th August 1911.

1912 and 1913, and Tupper would be kept busy trying to make sense of the different rates of pay. A manning scale was not achieved, but the abolition of the Federation medical was. Seamen were no longer obliged to sign on at Federation offices but the presence of a Union official at signing-on was not clarified. A Board of Arbitration over wage disputes, with three representatives from each side, was agreed. So the Union had made some progress, and in the process had matured. The requirements of Union registration meant that its record keeping of Minutes and accounts would be greatly improved. The Humber District (NESSOA) committee reported to the Shipping Federation's General Purposes Committee as late as 15th September that the Union had still to complete its registration, the delay in some way connected with its financial position (perhaps to be understood as trying to get its accounts in order).[41] As to its recognition, the Shipping Federation record has Mr Coull moving that the NESSOA report be adopted, but amended to base recognition of the NSFU 'upon freedom of contract and the employment of Union and/or Non-Union seamen, free from interference of one with the other'.[42]

Tribute to Hopkins's role was paid at the annual dinner which followed the NSFU's AGM. Present was Walter Runciman, according to *The* Messenger, seated on Havelock Wilson's right, making the first attendance by a shipowner, and one about whom Hopkins had been scathing in Calcutta days. Hopkins was on

Havelock Wilson's left, with Mr Devitt, Chairman of the Shipping
Federation on his left. Runciman reflected on recent events in his
speech, saying:

> We have emerged from one of the most bitter fights that
> has taken place during my time. I never suspected six
> weeks ago that to-night I should be a guest at your festive
> board .... I venture to say that there is not an owner at
> this table who is not pleased you have got [10s. a week
> more] .... [M]any of the shipowners had been converted
> to the view that it was the proper thing to recognize the
> men's union ....

Havelock Wilson said,

> In every port those responsible for the conduct of the
> campaign did splendidly. There are, however, a few
> conspicuous figures whom I must mention, as they are
> to some extent outside our movement. First I shall refer
> to Tom Mann, who did for our cause magnificent work
> in Liverpool.... Then our good friend Father Hopkins
> rendered yeoman service – first at Southampton, then
> at Hull – afterwards Manchester – finally at the North
> East coast. Without his help victory would have been
> uncertain ....[43]

If Hopkins had wondered at any stage what might be said about
his efforts in the Church press, he would have looked in vain.
Throughout the strike the *Church Times* maintained its silence. In
his own paper in October 1911 he wrote,

> Twenty-two years ago I was urged – commanded in fact
> – by my Ecclesiastical Superiors not to identify myself
> with the Labour Movement and Trade Unionism; I
> obeyed for a time; but was soon constrained by 'a voice
> within' to readjust relationships so as to enable me to
> become free to do what conviction told me I ought to
> do in the matter. Although my persistence lost me the
> help of some friends and has plunged me from time to
> time in much 'hot water', I do not regret my persistence.
> I much appreciate that title 'Banner-bearer' [bestowed
> on him by the *Frankfurter Zeitung*]. If I am a Banner-

bearer today in the great Labour Movement of the people they know that on that banner is blazoned the Cross of my Master Christ, with the words written large beneath it '*in hoc vinces*'. That has been and always will be my justification.

9

After the Strike

After the strike, Hopkins largely disappeared from the wider press. Instead, with the improvement of the Union's record keeping, probably the result of registration, he appears in NSFU papers, and in the Union weekly, *The Seaman*. *The Seaman*'s editorial address was given on headed notepaper as Alton Abbey, its secretariat as the Abbey Gatehouse. His community's *The Messenger* is also helpful but not easy of access.

At the AGM on 25th September 1911 Hopkins was appointed a trustee of the Union. He remained a trustee until his death in 1922. His co-trustee was Richard McGhee MP, son of an Ulster Orangemen, who, with Edward McHugh, had founded the National Union of Dock Labourers in 1889. McGhee's Orange background made him an unlikely partner for an Anglo-Catholic monk, but they shared a common cause. The role of a trustee involved oversight of the Union's finances and good practice. Hopkins's letters to Jochade show that before the strike he had assumed something of this role and was expected to understand Union finances. Trustees were expected to attend the Executive, and the Finance and General Purposes, Committee meetings. Indeed, the latter could not meet without a trustee present, and one of the trustees' functions would appear to have been approval of expenditure. Perhaps because of Hopkins's declining health, or pressure of parliamentary work on McGhee, in 1916 a third trustee, Councillor Wright from South Wales, was appointed.

Hopkins appears to have been a conscientious trustee. The Executive Committee met several times a year without a clear pattern and often for more than a single day. In addition there were occasional special meetings. In all, in the years which remained to him, Hopkins could have attended sixty-two Executive

Committee meetings (including AGMs), totaling seventy-four days, of which he was present for all but eight days; at least three of these absences were due to illness and a further two through attendance at other meetings on Union business. It was not unusual for him to take the chair in the absence of Havelock Wilson. The Finance and General Purposes Sub Committee met more frequently. Hopkins could have attended 229 of its meetings, of which he missed fifty-seven, again through a mixture of illness and other commitments. The total attended of meetings of these two committees is 238 in ten years. It will be noted below that he was occupied by the Union in a number of other ways, including producing various of its publications, doing necessary research, speaking at public meetings, attending AGMs, and being about various items of Union business. The total time spent on Union-related matters must have been considerable.

In 1912 and 1913 much of his time was occupied in campaigning for a National Wages Board, but including in that campaign improvements to the load line, seamen's accommodation, and their working hours.[1] This involved letters to the press, visits to the Board of Trade, and speeches to men in various ports. He wrote to Jochade in early 1912 suggesting that the International Committee of Seafarers' Unions, which had been formed on 11th March, 1911 might be convened to consider its dissolution or its continuance as the Marine Section of the ITWF.[2] Later in the year he was to tell him, 'although not much sought after or consulted in normal times – I am nearly always at once called to the front & given responsible work to do when labour <u>trouble</u> is being experienced' (Hopkins's emphasis). As an example, he represented the NSFU before the NTWF for refusing the affiliation of the BSU, a small breakaway union which had left the NSFU in mid strike (6th July).[3] A typical day might be 13th December, 1912, a Friday, when he spent the day with Havelock Wilson meeting owners and men of the North East before being the principal speaker at Unity Hall in South Shields in the evening.[4] When they visited the Board of Trade in March 1913, it was Hopkins and Wilson again, with Hopkins making most of the submission.[5] It was Hopkins who gave the main speech at the 1913 AGM, again with complicated and comprehensive facts and figures. Some of these speeches give an idea of his thoughts at this time. He was apt to make the point that

> He did not think he had ever been prouder in his life of any office he had held in Church or State, or anything else, than he did of being Trustee and an elected delegate on the supreme authority of one of the finest organisations as to numbers and efficiency that he thought trade unionism had ever known.

That particular speech concluded with the comment, 'God help the shipowners'.[6]

Addressing a packed Hippodrome at Yarmouth (9th November, 1913) on conditions of pay and food he tackled the issue as a religious one

> because it affected their daily bread, and the churches which taught them to pray for it should see they had the opportunity not only to get it, but plenty of it, here and now.... It was contrary to the laws of nature and to the will of God that the man who worked hardest got the least money.... It was the God-given responsibility of workers to get what was their due, and this was the religion which should be preached from our pulpits.... They were acting upon the doctrines of religion in seeking to improve their lot, because God had filled this world with His bounty, and the key to unlock it was human labour.[7]

He returned to this theme, again at Yarmouth, on Sunday evening, 22nd March, 1914:

> he did not preach to them destruction or spoliation, but the gospel of holy discontent with the share that came their way of the wealth which they were the main factors in creating.... As his Master before him had asked, whose image and superscription was upon all this wealth? And in the name of religion he said, render to the toiler what was the toiler's due.... In the name of God, he said there was need for a revolution to alter it all. That need not be a bloody revolution.[8]

This speech was apparently rounded off with some very emotional words about living in pig styes with starving children. It is not surprising to discover that his words were received with great enthusiasm. This style of speech seemed to make palatable the rather dry facts and figures which demonstrated that pay and conditions were not keeping pace with profits. He repeated this sort of speech all over the country. One of interest was at the Town Hall, Falmouth in July 1914, where he mentioned that he had arrived as a boy of eight to be educated at the Grammar School.[9] 'He was the son of a Master Mariner, and had qualified himself as a seafaring man...'.[10] The Union valued his work to the extent of making him secretary of its Manning Campaign, and asked him in February 1912[11] to give two days a week for the next four weeks to the subject; this, in addition to the time he was already giving as trustee.

If Edward Tupper can be believed, it was Tupper, in his many years as National Organiser and, by his own claim, Havelock Wilson's right hand man, who travelled the country dealing with issues over pay following the strike. His book, *Seamen's Torch*, chronicles a number of injustices which it was his task to remedy. He confirmed that the increase in pay which had been agreed in 1911 was not maintained in 1912 and 1913 and was, if anything, more complicated. In 1913 a Union handbook, *Official Wages – Agreements*, was issued, embodying all the agreements made in 1911, 1912 and 1913. It is strange that he makes no mention of Hopkins in connection with this handbook, especially as thus far in the Union's history such statistics had usually featured large in Hopkins's writing and in his speeches, and would in his *Seafarers'Annual*. The handbook listed agreements made in ports around the globe.

> It must be understood that in those days we had won no Maritime Board with its national wages scale and agreement. There were dozens and dozens of different agreements. In some places like London there were even different agreements for different docks.The rates of pay for different ratings and different departments, on different classes of ships, varied everywhere; only overtime, at 9d per hour, appears as a figure almost universal.... Some of these agreements are quoted as made, not with a port, but with individual shipowners. There are even some in which rates and conditions vary in different ships belonging to the same owner! Agreement had to be reached not only on the question of Monthly and Weekly Pay, Sabbath and Overtime Pay, but on Tides Work, Boating and Running Lines, and Shore

Work. For some ports half a dozen technical movements
to do with shifting ships in harbour are itemed with rates
of remuneration under Tides Work – and another half
dozen to do with tying up, kedging, and letting go, etc.,
under Boating and Running Lines.[12]

The Minutes of the Finance and General Purposes Committee
(F&GP) reveal that at this time Hopkins was being used for a variety
of tasks. Mention has been made elsewhere of his encounter with
Emmanuel Shinwell when sorting out the breakaway BSU, which took
him to Glasgow, Southampton, and probably Liverpool. Disputes, for
example between the crew and owners of the *HOLMWOOD* (12th
February, 1913), came his way for resolution. The same meeting
asked him to obtain the services of a full-time agent in Fowey, the
small china clay port in Cornwall. Later in the year irregularities in
the NSFU office in Leith in Scotland required his attention. For all
these activities, some of which would require a considerable amount
of time travelling, he received his expenses.

Occasionally, too, he was involved in the various property
deals of the Union, but these were really McGhee's special area of
responsibility.

Similarly delicate was Hopkins's role in a threatened strike of
1912. Havelock Wilson had left for America, mainly to convalesce,
leaving in the air the threat of a strike if the Federation would not
agree to a conference on wages. On his return he found a stoppage
in the Port of London of all transport workers called by the NTWF,
which required the NSFU to pay some 4,000 of its members strike
pay, about £1,000 a week, a large sum for a union with a modest and
irregular income, and one for which no contingency fund existed.
With the likelihood of a national stoppage being declared by the
NTWF, Hopkins, in Wilson's stead, called an emergency meeting of
the NSFU Executive Committee for 7th June, to which he indicated
the huge financial implication if such a strike was called and the
jeopardy in which the NSFU's provincial settlements, won at such a
cost in the previous year, might be placed. The Executive decided to
tell the NTWF that a strike would benefit nobody and that, if called,
the NSFU would have to ballot its members, a delaying tactic, for
it was no easy process balloting scattered members. In the event,
NSFU members voted against a strike. Havelock Wilson's view was
that the NTWF strike call was hopeless and advised strikers to return

to work. Askwith was brought in by the Port of London Authority's chairman, Lord Devonport, and everyone was back at work by the end of July. Havelock Wilson's speaking out, with Hopkins behind him, undoubtedly made the pair very unpopular in some trade union circles,[13] with repercussions in years to come. The NSFU resented the control that the NTWF wished to exercise and wished not for a triple alliance but for a quadruple alliance: railwaymen, miners, transport workers and seamen. The continuing relationship of these groups and Havelock Wilson's strained membership of the various labour groups fall beyond the scope of this book but are worth remembering when labour historians criticise Havelock Wilson. What is significant at this point is Hopkins's role in the decision not to strike. In 1916, when pressing for a quadruple alliance, the Executive took its decision not to support the proposed strike after a presentation by Hopkins on the history of the present situation.[14]

Against this background of multiple calls upon his time, Hopkins was working on his book, *Altering Plimsoll's Mark*, published in 1913, financed largely through the Union buying enough copies for distribution to all its officials, and published by Simpkin, Marshall and Co at one shilling; clearly the fruit of many years' labour and campaigning. It will be recalled that Hopkins had first become involved with the load line issue in his first chaplaincy at Rangoon, over the affair of the *CALLIOPE* and at a time when legislation allowed the load- line to be placed at the discretion of the ship's master. Hopkins had heard the master in this instance tell the mate to alter the load line to accommodate an increased cargo. Subsequently the ship had been lost with all hands. The offence had been to move the line, once placed. It was not until 1890 that the line's position became prescribed permanently, a situation considered to be of benefit by all seagoing men. Unfortunately in 1906 the Board of Trade began to make changes, perhaps under pressure from owners. To fight these changes required evidence, and the accumulation of evidence was Hopkins's strength. His campaign is revealed in his book. Its prefatory note is headed 'St Mawes Priory, October 1913', which dates publication with some precision; the St Mawes Priory was a cottage purchased by the OSP in the hope that Hopkins could use it for respite as his health deteriorated. It had the advantage of being near some members of his family. The book is not easy to find today.

The Introduction to *Altering Plimsoll's Mark* deals with Samuel

Plimsoll and his legislation generally. The first chapter is a polemic of the kind we have come to expect from its author, who is sanguine about neither the Board of Trade nor the owners: 'while Capital remains avaricious, while self-interest is on the grasp for more, while officialism hates the trouble and the added responsibility of reform, the natural tendency will be ever backward'.

Chapter Two explains the origin of the load line which had been made voluntary by the Act of 1876. A committee chaired by Sir Edward Reed had reported in 1885 in favour of its compulsory positioning and this had been the effect of the Load Line Act of 1890 after agitation by Samuel Plimsoll MP, Havelock Wilson MP, and George Howell MP, who had promoted a private member's bill in Parliament. From this point the book gets more technical. Chapter Three deals with the alteration of the North Atlantic freeboard in 1899. The Board of Trade apparently had reduced the margin of the Winter North Atlantic (WNA) line in vessels of less than 330 feet in length and abolished it in longer vessels. (Readers unfamiliar with the load line need to be aware that there is a different buoyancy between salt and fresh water, and further differences are recognised between Winter and Summer, and the North Atlantic and Tropical waters.) The North Atlantic was a profitable route and the reduction in the line meant an increased cargo could be carried, giving greater profit for the owners, but greater risk for crews.

Chapter Four records consideration of the WNA line by a Board of Trade committee in 1906. This committee had made its recommendations without the benefit of representation on it of any practical seaman. Chapter Five explains that the committee had been set up in 1905 by Lord Salisbury, then President of the Board of Trade. Careful consideration was made of the impact a reduced WNA line would have: on the one hand, ships could carry more at a greater depth, with the consequence of more coal being consumed, and more damage to each ship, while on the other, the trade would require fewer ships. Havelock Wilson had been able to establish that the committee had comprised Sir Alfred Chambers (Principal Nautical Adviser to the Board of Trade) and a few shipowners. In February 1906 the Report was ready for the signature of the new President of the Board of Trade, Lloyd George. On 31st October, 1906, Lloyd George, in answer to a Member's question, stated in the House that the new assignment of freeboarding would only be sanctioned in 'certain classes of vessels of modern construction

and approved strength, but older vessels...are allowed no deeper
loading'. Hopkins demonstrates that the new freeboard was given
virtually on request. Chapters Six and Seven deal with specific
cases; the former with the loss of the *NORTH BRITON* off Ushant on
4th March, 1912 (the Mercantile Marine Service Association and the
Imperial Merchant Service Guild, under the aegis of which Hopkins
had earlier presented himself, had both written to the Board of Trade
for a reconsideration in this case), and the latter with the case of the
DUCHESS OF CORNWALL which had been badly damaged after
loss of freeboard. The book contains photographs illustrating this
damage.

The book's Chapter Eight deals with Parliamentary Questions
about the changes. Hopkins notes that in 1906 the President of the
Board of Trade had by the stroke of a pen added a million tons to
the carrying capacity of British ships. Now, even in 1913, the Load
Line Committee still lacked among its members a merchant seaman,
a lack ascribed to its 'highly technical character', and its meetings
were held in private. Hopkins's fellow NSFU trustee, McGhee,
had asked in the House of Commons in 1913 why seamen should
be excluded from the committee, which was revealed to consist of
builders, surveyors and naval architects. Hopkins prints the Questions
concerning this 1913 Committee. In his view the 1906 WNA line
abolition had been a *quid pro quo* between the Board of Trade and
the owners, the latter having by 1906 legislation been required to
supply crews with improved (and thus more expensive) provisions.
Chapter Nine reports a meeting of what is called the National Union
of Masters and Mates, and notes other pressure being brought against
the change.

Chapter Ten is vintage Hopkins. Sets of figures show numbers
of ships, lives lost, and similar details. Some correspondence is
quoted. Hopkins had received a letter dated 19th September, 1913
from Thomas H. Sanders, secretary of the Load Line Committee,
inviting him to its meeting of 15th October, just when Hopkins's
book must have been ready for the printers. Hopkins replied that he
would attend despite being asked by seamen to decline the invitation
in protest at the absence of seamen from the committee, but that he
would do so, not as a representative of the NSFU, but on behalf of
the SFSSP 'of which I have been the head for 25 years'. 'My whole
life has been passed, from birth to the present day, amongst ships and
sailors at home and abroad', and in supporting evidence he cites the

statistics of numbers of sailors using the Greenwich Priory. It is at
this point that he comments on those ships from his earlier life, the
GEOLOGIST and the *CASSIOPE*. Both form part of his evidence.
Of the *GEOLOGIST* he writes, 'The sailors called her a "death trap"
and she all but drowned me on the main deck', this on the occasion
of his return to England to school 'in or about' 1870. This seems
to be his first allusion to this incident. While it seems unlikely that
he would embroider his evidence for a committee of record, its
implication, that his father, an experienced pilot, would consign his
son to a dangerous ship, is odd.

The book is slight and of a campaigning nature. But he was
not alone in his campaign against freeboarding. H. M. Hyndman,
the President of the Social Democratic Federation, a well-known
Socialist in his day whose influence had begun to wane as Labour
Members won seats in Parliament, had also joined the campaign. A
fiery speech of Hyndman's survives in his *The Murdering of British
Seamen (by Mr Lloyd George, the Liberal Cabinet and the Board
of Trade)*, which he published in April 1913, some months before
Hopkins published his own book. His preface says that Hopkins had
sent him a congratulatory letter on behalf of the NSFU regarding
his campaign to save lives at sea. The title page of the fourth and
enlarged edition of Hyndman's work, which suggests wide circulation
as it was still dated 1913, adds 'With a Statement and two Returns
prepared by Father Hopkins ...'. He describes Hopkins inaccurately
as the President of the NSFU, despite Hopkins's letter being signed
as 'Trustee NS&FU, Chaplain MM ...'. The second letter from
Hopkins introduces the statistics he has supplied and shows that,
as a result of the 1908 WNA line decision, whilst the number of
vessels lost had decreased, a greater tonnage and more lives had
been lost. The outbreak of the Great War in 1914 effectively silenced
this campaign while the creation of the NMB later gave seamen the
voice that had previously been lacking.

A very different area of continuing concern was the question of
foreign sailors on British ships. The issue was not new, for fears of
Chinese crews being used as strike-breakers were voiced in Cardiff
in 1911 and, indeed, by Havelock Wilson in the 1890s. The rising
problem was the mass recruitment of Chinese and Lascar crews.
Their presence on ships which traded in the tropics could be defended
by the need for local crews, for example by P & O for its Gulf-India
run, and there was also a belief that such crews could better stand

the heat in the boiler rooms of the increasing number of coal-fired ships.[15] Where many individual members of British crews were and had been for many years either Indian or Chinese, paid at standard rates, now there was wholesale recruitment of such crews, and the purpose was to undercut the British-by-birth seaman. From 1911 onwards this was a subject in which Hopkins was heavily involved. He spoke widely and wrote extensively about it. Havelock Wilson argued that such crews should be accorded all the benefits of British crews on British ships in British waters which he knew well would make them no cheaper for British shipowners to employ. There was no final solution to this problem in Hopkins's time.[16]

The outbreak of the Great War in 1914 changed everything. Disputes fell into abeyance in the interest of national unity. The Greenwich Priory became a receiving centre for alien seamen and Alton Abbey took a further 200 aliens. Most of the brethren were called up so that the 'staff' was severely limited. Guards were refused at The Abbey, leaving the two hundred men to be cared for by three brethren. Two more at the Greenwich Priory supervised sixty men. When the aliens' camp closed, all the remaining brethren who were eligible joined the army, of whom four died subsequently.[17] The closure of the camps followed the sinking of the *LUSITANIA* and was not because of lack of security. Seamen generally were appalled by the submarine war which destroyed forever the idea of the brotherhood of the sea; the Union withdrew from staffing the aliens' camps in its care and those associated with Hopkins's community went the same way.

During 1917 Hopkins was contributing a regular column to *The Seaman* entitled, 'Extracts from the Reports of Admiralty Cases'. This series was densely written. It consisted of court judgments in connection with wages and other, especially manning, agreements. There is no indication that Hopkins had help with these and every likelihood that he was trawling one of his many files of collected information. Agreements in wartime could easily become muddied, one of the reasons for establishing the NMB, and this series clearly indicated the rights of the seaman. His readers would be better equipped to defend their rights, as had been his intention when publishing similar material for his Guild members during his time in Calcutta. The series may also reflect the Union's pressure on management and government to come together to negotiate conditions.

The Union sought to work in harmony with the shipowners but not to the point where it was blind to the massive profits which wartime brought them. Figures relating to these profits were part of Hopkins's stock in trade. The Union continued to build up its strike fund with an eye to the years which would succeed the war. For its part, the Federation continued to demand that all seamen carry a Federation ticket. In mid 1916, when the Union was becoming increasingly aware of crewing problems, it extended a hand to the Federation, but without a response.[18] It was not until August 1917 that industrial discontent led the government to establish joint meetings between the Ministry of Shipping (a wartime creation), the Union and the Federation. From this evolved a National Maritime Marine Board, soon abbreviated to National Maritime Board (NMB).[19] Speaking in 1921, Jim Cotter, a militant, and member of the BSU, said, 'the National Maritime Board was formed in 1917 during the War because the government and the original Maritime Board could not carry on themselves as far as the working of the seamen were concerned'.[20] The Munitions of War Act of July 1915 had allowed the government to impose arbitrated settlements upon unwilling employers. Unrest among seamen was not only caused by owners' excessive profits but also by the threat of conscription. There was also the issue of wage differentials between British and American ships which meant that large numbers of British crews were to be found sailing under the Stars and Stripes, exacerbating the difficulty in crewing British ships. By the end of November 1917 the NMB had agreed to a standard wage for seamen, firemen and officers; that for catering staff followed shortly.

Hopkins later dated the first proper sign of movement towards a conciliation board to June 1917 when the Union and the Federation met informally and the Union had suggested district committees be set up to resolve overtime issues on weekly vessels (always a special category). This would involve a Standing Joint Central Committee. This suggestion of the Union was passed back by representatives of each side to their respective main body for formal consideration. Events were overtaken when Lloyd George's newly established Ministry of Shipping invited both parties to confer with government representatives on the supply of seamen, wages, and delays. These were potentially sensitive areas: some delays were caused by seamen joining ships late and this led to calls for conscription which the Union opposed vigorously, likening it to the press gang, against which legislation existed.

The Union agreed with the idea of a national wage for seafarers determined by a joint committee but proposed that it – the Union – should supply labour, a proposal to which the Federation objected. A solution was devised by the Ministry of Shipping through the independent Liverpool Shipowners. The process is described in detail elsewhere.[21] The solution was to have a body drawn from both sides which would recruit and supply. This led to the formation of the NMB, which was formally announced on 23rd November, 1917.[22] All appropriate organisations representing the men found a place, with the exception of the BSU, which was given local representation. The NMB had four main panels: deck officers, engineers, sailors and firemen, and cooks and stewards.[23] Hopkins's panel involvement was primarily with the sailors and firemen, but an examination of the minutes of this panel reveals that most of the time he fielded a substitute, as would be expected from his health and his other commitments. A network of port offices was established. Hopkins and Cuthbert Laws (of the Federation) were appointed joint secretaries. By 1918 the Shipping Federation had accepted the need to work with the NSFU sufficiently to resist attempts by the Ministry of Reconstruction to form a single National Council rather than something distinct to deal with seamen and questions affecting dock labour and to argue that it should consist of an equal number of shipowners and seamen.[24] The structure was not a perfect one. In 1920 Hopkins wrote to a Mr Brett, apparently about some of his own Union members:

> The patience (& forbearance) of Shipowners & officers & officials with some of these men surprises me. So 'sick' am I, at the moment, with the majority of the seamen's representation on the N.M.B. that it would be a relief to resign my Joint Secretaryship. But I doubt if it would do any good. Possibly Borlase or Mr Vey [?] might be appointed in my place.[25]

Until his death, Hopkins's signature was appended with that of Laws to every official document which went out to the entire Merchant Navy. Indeed, the last such circular, on accommodation, was issued on 22nd March, 1922, the day of his death.[26] A conciliation board had finally been achieved and Hopkins was its joint secretary. It had taken many years to reach this goal.

Father Charles Plomer Hopkins in later life. Source: unknown.

At the end of the Great War Hopkins put together a comprehensive account of the role of the Merchant Navy, published in 1920, entitled *The National Service of British Seamen 1914-1918*. Its sales were helped by Union purchases. The book is a well-documented guide to the prejudice and discrimination against the men then to be found in the Merchant Navy, and to the profits made by the owners during the War. Once that was published, he started another project, a *Seafarer's Annual*, which came out in 1921 with the promise of further volumes dependent on demand. This was a departure from his campaigning works and, priced at 6d, intended for the popular market. It was obtainable from the SFSSP. Its annual nature is emphasised by Hopkins recording the events of the preceding year as they concerned the seaman. His chronology of 1920 dealt with the reduction of wages, the new engine-room union, and the new union for cooks and stewards. A chapter on organisation explains the Seafarers Joint Council (of which Hopkins was the treasurer), and which union to join, according to rank and profession. Another explained the structure of the NMB with its panels for masters, officers, engineers, sailors and firemen, and catering personnel. All pay scales and entitlements to leave are listed. Further chapters deal, some heavily, with Union history, and others, usefully, with such issues as rates of exchange. The final chapter, on revolution, takes an anti-Bolshevist line, which reflects the concerns of the time.

His friends had been accustomed to Hopkins's recurring ill-health. The Priory at Greenwich was supposed to provide him with better air than the woods of Alton Abbey. In addition a cottage had been bought for him by OSP at St Mawes, near Falmouth. Sister Frances, last of the sisters, remained at Greenwich, welcoming the few seamen who came, dealing with queries and orders to the SFSSP. At Alton, departures of brethren in protest at Hopkins's part in the 1911 strike,[27] and losses among those called up to serve in the war, left but two brethren at The Abbey to care for the shellbacks (retired seamen) there. In March 1922 Hopkins, at St Mawes, was taken seriously ill. Sister Frances wrote to Cathery explaining that Hopkins would not be able to attend the next finance meeting because 'he is dangerously ill and the doctor holds out little hope of his recovery'. On 24th March, five days after her letter was written, he was dead. He died at the Priory Cottage. The nephritis which had plagued him for so many years does not appear on his death certificate; instead the primary cause of death is listed as a cerebral haemorrhage of fourteen days earlier, and the second, cardiac failure, by Dr John Llewellyn, who must have been the attending doctor. His occupation is given as 'Priest'. The person registering the death was A.E.Tiddy, of nearby Manor Cottage, described as present at the death (Mrs Tiddy later sent a wreath). His body was taken to Alton.

The local newspaper, the *Hampshire Express*, of Saturday, 8th April, carried a full report of the funeral, which took place 'on Thursday afternoon last week in the beautiful little cemetery at The Abbey'. His sister, Mrs Baker, led the mourners, with Brothers Aidan and George of the OSP, Sister Francis (sic) Magdalene, and Associate Brother Wilfred. Other relatives were prevented from being present by illness or residence abroad. There were representatives from the NMB, the NSFU, the Shipping Federation, the Hull Seamen's Union, the Marine Engineers' Association, the Seafarers' Joint Council, the Imperial Merchant Service Guild, the International Seafarers' Federation, the Thames District Maritime Board, the Gravesend Sea

Alton Abbey (date unknown). Source: photograph taken by Brother David Williams OSB.

School, the Alton Union, the local council, and many more, together with local residents and 'many typical British seamen, weather-worn and stern-visaged, who had come to pay their last tribute to a man who had done so much for their betterment'.

Hopkins's coffin was covered with the Union Jack and surrounded by a wealth of floral tributes. On it were also placed his cross as Superior General of the OSP and his insignia as a Commander of the Order of the British Empire. It was placed in the Abbey chapel 'with the head, as is customary with Priests of the Church of England, facing the altar'. His brethren kept vigil through the night. The Rev C.E. Bond, Vicar of All Saints, Alton, said an early and solemn Requiem Mass for relatives and close friends, later conducting the funeral service, which was also solemn (i.e. with incense). The service started with the hymn, 'Jesus Christ, Eternal God'. Later, at the graveside, two hymns were sung: 'Eternal Father, strong to save' (the so-called Sailors' Hymn) and 'On the resurrection morning' before the grave was sprinkled with holy water and censed.

While he was in Calcutta, Hopkins printed in his community magazine an extra verse for the hymn, 'Eternal Father', which he may well have written, and which seems to have been used at the funerals of seafarers which he conducted there. Perhaps it was among the verses sung at his own burial, for it makes an appropriate conclusion to an account of his life:

> And for our brethren called away
> by death's swift summons, Lord, we pray;
> O grant them rest and peace and light,
> their sin-stained souls make pure and white;
> so at Thy Coming they may be
> raised up triumphant from the sea.

Some business remained to be done after the funeral. Probate on his Will was granted in June 1922. His executors were 'Ernest Hall of the Abbey and Frances Isabel Lawrence of the Priory', the two senior members remaining of the OSP. The gross value of his estate was given as £8,754..14s..2d, and the net value, £4,197..15s..9d. This included the Abbey, which had been purchased in his name. His Will had gone through several phases. A version was made in January 1917, replacing an original of 1899, and prompts one to wonder if this indicates a time when his health was of particular concern. It left everything at Alton Abbey, and the leasehold of the Greenwich Priory (the property of the NSFU), plus the money in various bank accounts, to his executors. All his nautical books were to go to the Union. A trust fund was set up for his niece Ivy Hopkins, the money, should she die before her twenty-fifth birthday, to be divided between his sister Mary Ann Baker and his brothers Freeman and Frank Hopkins. A codicil was added in 1919 revoking his gift to the NSFU, instead giving the Union the option of buying his books and papers. A further codicil was added in February 1921, making provision for his godson, Frederick Charles Hopkins Emmett, provided he 'shall be in my service at the time of my decease', suggesting the executors allow him to purchase a cottage and parcel of land in the vicinity of St Mawes or elsewhere after reaching the age of twenty-one, a provision to be forfeit if his godson troubled his trustees for money for other purposes before reaching the age of twenty-five. The most significant point arising from his Will is that he had remained in touch with his family, scattered though they were, over the years.

Conclusion

Is it possible to place a man like Hopkins? In many respects he
was a product of the period. The British Merchant Navy was at
its peak, the transition from sail to steam was in process and the
British Empire was growing and confident. The Church of England,
and by extension its daughters overseas, was recovering its Catholic
heritage and those caught up in the process, like those extending the
Empire, were imbued with a sense of purpose; Church confidence
would peak around 1920. There was a general rise in trade unionism
and successive governments showed an increasing willingness to get
involved in industrial practice.

At the same time, Hopkins's personal career seemed to move in
two different directions. He was increasingly involved in the affairs of
the sea, a ministry to an essentially invisible group of men. However,
the further his journey down the road of industrial action, the more
he became isolated from his church, ostracised by the authorities
of the Church of England and of diminishing interest to its Anglo-
Catholics. Although this Church party was to produce its handful of
prophets (Basil Jellicoe, Bishop Frank Weston, and a few East End
of London clergy spring to mind) who found Christ in the highways
and byways, a good many of its members got lost in ritual and the
accompanying Church furnishings. Today he is numbered among the
very few Anglicans who founded religious communities for men,
rather than as a visionary in the maritime apostolate. As to whether
his treatment by his church was shabby or merited, at first reading,
it was unquestionably shabby. Yet he proved to be a man capable of
marked indiscretion, and given the spirit of the times, the surprise
would have been to find his bishop treating him any differently;
few of his bishop's contemporaries in the establishment would have
questioned that treatment. The wonder is that Hopkins continued

faithful both in the church of his baptism and in his vocation.

Hopkins's relationship with the NSFU ought to be obvious, as it is in most respects, but he still occasionally flew the flag of his own quasi-union, the SFSSP, or the colours of, for example, the Mercantile Marine Service Association and the Imperial Merchant Service Guild, as occasion required. His early ministry to individual seafarers evolved into a less personal one to the industry. Some of his functions within the Union are clearly shown: the statistics, the trouble-shooting, the speeches, the wise counsel, all the duties of a trustee, and more, but there is a feeling which remains after examining all the available evidence that Hopkins, rather than being a shadow cast by Havelock Wilson, was in fact the Union's Grey Eminence. Which was the puppet and which the master, or were they equals working in tandem? More than forty years in Hopkins's company inclines me to the view that Hopkins's influence over Havelock Wilson was at the very least substantial. If that is the case, why is he such a neglected figure in Union history? Part of the answer lies in the changed spirit of the Union, in its youth subject to the patriarchal control of Havelock Wilson, not until the 1960s a satisfactorily democratic body and now absorbed into a much larger amalgamation of transport unions. Suffice it to say, that a union searching for a democratic present can very easily slough off its paternalistic past, forgetting its debt to its founders in the process. Personality held together the Union in its early years and the personality, the figurehead, for whom there is only ever room for one, was Havelock Wilson, and it is his name, rather than that of Hopkins, which survives.

Conciliation is a characteristic which emerges from few of these pages (so many of which chronicle a fight for the disadvantaged) despite its being a theme to which Hopkins frequently returned. He shared this wish with Havelock Wilson in a way in which Tupper and other late recruits to the seamen's cause could not. As far back as Rangoon he had tried to bring men and employers together. His failure often stemmed from the very publicity necessary to obtain justice for the wrongs he sought to right. The establishment of the NMB went a long way towards this goal. Wailey[1] described the formation of the NMB as a 'conquest ... of the union leadership by the Federation', a view which Hopkins would strongly have rejected and which is hard to demonstrate from the evidence.

After Hopkins's lengthy exposure to the injustices of sea life in

Burma, to encounter real power amongst a group of workers must have been a heady experience. It would accord with the evidence to ascribe Hopkins's great turning point, not as he does to the encounter with drunken apprentices in Rangoon, but rather to his proximity to the 1889 Dock Strike and its consequences and, equally, to Plimsoll's campaigns. A master's contemporary experience was that 'At this time every ship had much trouble with the crew. Plimsoll's agitation had caused much unrest and given rise to absurd expectations'.[2] The same source noted in 1889 that

> Havelock Wilson was coming into prominence as a seamen's agitator. His methods were some fifteen or twenty years before their time, for his policy was to force all members of the crew excepting the officers to become members of his Union and pay an immediate levy...

and gave an instance of the problems caused by the insistence of the Union that crew members belong to some union. If this was the experience even of a fair-minded master, as this one seems to have been, then a port chaplain must have seen in it a chance to improve the lot of the men for whom he cared. It is possible that Hopkins's use of the cover provided by the Mercantile Marine Service Association and the Imperial Merchant Service Guild was to give him links with officers as well as crew.

What of the Strike? Despite the extraordinarily brief reference by Havelock Wilson at the NSFU annual dinner to Hopkins's role in the 1911 strike, Hopkins was clearly in at the beginning. Then he seems to have been responsible for much of the stage management, the announcement of the strike, a major role in encouraging strikers, and most of the negotiations which led to the strike's conclusion. If something looks like a dog, barks like a dog, and chases sticks, there is a very fair chance that it is a dog. On the same principle, it seems fair to suggest that Hopkins's role in the strike was the key one.

A recurring question concerns Hopkins's sexual orientation. In one sense this question is an anachronism prompted by the obsessions of our own time. Asked of a man who had chosen celibacy it can also be seen as impertinent or irrelevant. Yet the records show that it was also a contemporary question which stemmed from the Calcutta court case. In Calcutta Hopkins was cleared, though it seems nobody was required to testify to his character in the matter, which was taken for granted. Homosexuality was topical in the 1890s, the decade of the Oscar Wilde trial, and an easy means of smearing the new and unfamiliar religious communities of the Church of England, where in fairness, one has to say, charges were sometimes substantiated, as in the case of some members of Joseph Leycester Lyne's circle. Had there been any real evidence against Hopkins neither the Shipping Federation nor the COS would have hesitated to use it. It is unlikely also that Union leaders would have tolerated his company for long. Seamen know a good deal about mankind and its sexual preferences. They also have a nose for hypocrisy in a clergyman, yet were happy to cheer, in their thousands, Hopkins to the rafters as he fought their cause. In short, homosexuality does not seem likely; active homosexuality even less so.

To end this biography with a discussion of Hopkins's sexuality might perpetuate the blight cast on his life post-Calcutta. Yet it has a place here, for Christians believe all kinds of people and circumstances can be vehicles for God's purposes. It is tempting to imagine Hopkins, perhaps in a Calcutta court room, perhaps being chaired by 20,000 north country seamen or perhaps when signing NMB documents, stopping to reflect on the route which had brought him there. Vocations are seldom obvious from the outset. Only afterwards do they make sense, and, in between, the question must be pondered, whether this is what God wants of this particular person. The prophet Elijah discovered that he could not see God's face; God's presence was only detected in his passing. Discernment is achieved as much by discovering which doors are closed, as by which remain open. Where circumstances seem odd, it is necessary to remember that the God of Christians, who was to be revealed in a stable and on a cross, is the God of every situation. Perhaps Hopkins reflected, that if certain rather strange events had not happened, he would be somewhere else. Only in retrospect would the closing of doors by bishops (Rangoon, Calcutta, Hereford, Winchester), by rumour (the COS), by his health, have made sense. Conversely, the opening doors (seamen's welfare, the Union, the strike) would begin to emerge as a vocation.

In Scripture and throughout the history of the Church many powerful figures have come and gone, largely forgotten. Conversely many who are remembered now were, in their day, neither well known nor powerful. Religious authorities have a poor record when it comes to recognising prophets. Many early Christians chose a hidden life in the desert to serve God and fight the demons. Later Christians find their desert in the social housing and high-rise flats of our own time, among the dying, the mentally handicapped, the marginalised, and in other equally unlikely settings; their heroism is usually recognised afterwards. For Hopkins, his desert, the place where he would carry the name of Christ and fight his demons, proved to be among the seamen of the largest merchant fleet in the world, in their Union, and in all those mountains of meticulously compiled statistics which he used to ameliorate their working conditions.

Notes

Preface

1. R.W.H. Miller, *Charles Plomer Hopkins*, unpublished MA thesis, 1993.

Introduction

1. R.W.H. Miller, *Ship of Peter*, unpublished MPhil thesis, 1995.
2. Roald Kverndal, *The Way of the Sea*, 2008.
3. P.G. Parkhurst, *Ships of Peace*, vol. 1, 1962. It covers the period to 1885, giving an inside picture of the Board of Trade.
4. British Parliamentary Papers, 1873, XXXVI and 1874, XXXIV. See also P.G. Parkhurst, *op. cit.*, p. 216.
5. P.G. Parkhurst, *op. cit.*, pp. 208-226 gives the Board of Trade's view of Plimsoll and notes some of his inexactitudes.
6. George Peters, *The Plimsoll Line*, 1975, pp. 121ff.
7. George Peters, *ibid.*, pp. 97ff gives the progress of Plimsoll's bill in Parliament and describes in great detail Plimsoll's passionate appeal to the House and his expulsion for unparliamentary behaviour. His campaign greatly affected his health.
8. J.H. Wilson, *My Stormy Voyage Through Life*, vol. 1, 1925, p. 91.
9. P.G. Parkhurst, *op. cit.*, p. 223.
10. J.H. Wilson, *op. cit.*, p. 33.
11. *Ibid.*, pp. 162ff.
12. D.G. Bovill, *Education of Mercantile Mariners in the N.E. Ports (1840-1902)*, unpublished DPhil thesis, 1987, p. 16. *Report of the Committee of the Society for Improving the Condition of Merchant Seamen*, 1867. George Budd, *Remarks on the Cause of Scurvy*, 1843.
13. Alston Kennerley, *British Seamen's Missions and Sailors' Homes 1815-1970*, unpublished PhD thesis, 1989, pp. 112ff.
14. See P.G. Parkhurst, *op. cit.*, p. 406 where fatalities are given for 1867-82.
15. Alston Kennerley, 'Ratings for the Mercantile Marine: The Roles of Charity, the State and Industry in the Pre-Service Education and Training of Ratings for the Mercantile Marine, 1879-1939', 1999, pp. 31-51.
16. D.R. MacGregor, *The China Bird*, 1961, p. 85. See also P.G. Parkhurst, *op. cit.*, pp. 180, 187, 235. See also V.C. Burton, 'Apprenticeship Regulation and Maritime Labour in the Nineteenth Century British Merchant Marine', 1989, pp. 29ff.

17. H. Falkus, *Master of Cape Horn*, 1982, p. 66.
18. Alston Kennerley, 'The Shore Management of British Seafarers in the Twentieth Century', 2007.
19. V. Marsh & A. Ryan, *The Seamen*, 1989, pp. 17f.
20. Mss 175/1/1/1, NSFU Minutes.
21. K. Hawkins, *Trade Unions*, 1981, p. 40.
22. Cited in A. Flanders, *Trade Unions*, 1968, p. 13.
23. G.D.H. Cole, *Introduction to Trade Unionism*, 1953, p. 26.
24. S.& B. Webb, *The History of Trade Unionism*, 1973, pp. 405f. V. Marsh & A. Ryan, *op. cit.*, p. 32.
25. J. Schneer, *Ben Tillett*, 1982, pp. 33f. V. Marsh & A. Ryan, *op. cit.*, p. 25.
26. H.A. Clegg, Fox & Thompson, *History of Trade Unionism*, vol. 1, pp. 55f.
27. Mss 175/3/4/3, NSFU Correspondence with SFSSP. A letter on the subject from the Bishop of Calcutta, 2nd May, 1890 survives in the archive of Alton Abbey. See also Hopkins's speech to the 1916 NSFU AGM, p. 35 (Mss 126 S&FU/4/1, AGM Reports 1912-16).
28. See Mss 367/TSF/1/4/1, GP Committee Minutes, 12th June, 1891. Mss 367/TSF/1/1/1, Minutes of the SF, 26th October, 1906.
29. V. Marsh & A. Ryan, *op. cit.*, pp. 30f.
30. A. Bullock, *Life and Times of Ernest Bevin*, vol. 1, 1960, pp. 24f.
31. Mss 159/1/5/1 ITF, Report of the Seafarers' Conference 1910.
32. Tom Mann, *Memoirs*, 1923, p. 225. Mann has nothing to say of Hopkins.
33. E. Tupper, *Seamen's Torch*, 1938, p. 19.
34. *The Seaman*, January 1912, pp. 205, 207.
35. A. Bullock, *op. cit.*, pp. 24-25.
36. Mss 367/TSF/1/4/1, GP Committee Minutes, 6th March, 1891.
37. A passage from one of Wilson's court appearances is printed in the *Nautical Guildsman* of 15th September, 1893.
38. R.W.H. Miller, *From Shore to Shore*, 1989, pp. 125f.
39. P.F. Anson, *Call of the Cloister*, 1964.

Chapter One

1. P.F. Anson, *Call of the Cloister*, 1964, p. 106. V. Marsh & A. Ryan, *The Seamen*, 1989, p. 260 note 40, where there are inaccuracies.
2. *The Messenger*, 1899-1904 has a series of reminiscences. See esp. Dec 1899.
3. I am indebted to Dom Andrew Johnson of Alton Abbey for making available to me his notes on the ships' logs.
4. *The Magazine* of Falmouth Grammar School, April 1922, contains a brief notice of his death.
5. *The Messenger* of Nov 1891 refers to 'a younger son who has decided to go to sea...'. CPH's funeral reports mention a third sister. Anglican baptismal registers from Bassein list five more children. Mrs Janet Rees, a grand niece of CPH, has traced 11 children (not counting Mary Ann), of which CPH was the eldest.
6. Mary Elizabeth Pauline, according to family records, was born 1866.
7. I am grateful to Dom Andrew Johnson OSB for this summary.
8. I am grateful to his grand niece Mrs Rees for this piece of family lore.
9. I am grateful to Mrs Rees for this information.

Chapter Two

1. *Indian Churchman*, 12th Feb, 1881. *Proceedings*, June 1881.
2. *Indian Churchman*, 29th July, 1882.
3. The 76% may refer to the percentage of men using the chaplaincy but is far from clear.
4. See N. Chevers, *A Manual of Medical Jurisprudence for India*, 1870, which details drinks available in the bazaar.
5. John Ebenezer Marks, *Forty Years in Burma*, 1917, a book cobbled together from Marks' letters and journals by W.C.B. Purser, makes no mention of CPH. Abp Randall Davidson's foreword described Marks as a man of 'remarkable personal powers' who 'had opportunities of an extraordinary sort, and he used them extraordinarily well'. He went to teach in Burma as a SPG missionary 1859; was ordained 1863 after attending Bishops' College, Calcutta; Principal of St John's from 1876; Hon DD 1879. He was fluent in Burmese and translated the Prayer Book from English, plus part of the Gospels, which would have featured in the petition for his award of the DD. He obtained royal Burmese patronage for his school and fell out with Bishop Strachan over political protest about King Thibaw's atrocities in Upper Burma. Apparently a very active Freemason.
6. Bodleian USPG CLS47, Archdeacon Blyth, 4th Jan, 1892.
7. H.W. Tucker (ed.), *Records of the S.P.G., 1701-1892*, 1893.
8. See *Hastings & St Leonard's News*, 1st Sept, 1893.
9. The ship is likely to have been the *CALLIOPE*. See C.P. Hopkins, *Altering Plimsoll's Mark*, 1913, p. 66. Lloyd's *Register of Shipping*, 1884 says that the vessel belonged to the Australian Shipping Company of Limerick, registered Liverpool, Master: W. Withers, and records it as 'missing'.
10. I am grateful to Dom Andrew Johnson for this information, most of which comes from Hopkins's own writing in *The Messenger.*
11. *The Messenger*, October 1899, August 1900. This is Hopkins's own account. In November 1899 Hopkins recalled his committee was so unhelpful that, with the bishop's approval (perhaps one of his positive glosses), he started his own mission at Phayre Street, which the Committee (a diocesan one) declined to take on for pressure of work.

Chapter Three

1. P.F. Anson, in *Call of the Cloister*, 1964, p. 109 further explained the move to Akyab as offering 'more time for prayer and meditation' and few ships – apparently Anson's attempt to cast Hopkins in a mould to suit a book on the religious life in the Church of England rather than to describe the life of the chaplain of Akyab in the 1880s.
2. R. Grant Brown, *Burma as I saw it, 1889-1917*, 1926, p. 4.

Chapter Four

1. Sarah Wise, *The Blackest Streets*, 2008, p. 193.
2. I am grateful to Dom Andrew Johnson for some of this information.
3. A.O. Jay, *Life in Darkest London*, 1891; *The Social Problem: Its Possible Solution*, 1893; *A Story of Shoreditch*, 1896. All further details about Jay come from these books unless otherwise indicated. At no point does Jay

mention Hopkins, though Hopkins must have been his one successful recruit.

4. Jay's own words need to be accepted with caution. The fullest account of his life and work in Shoreditch is in Sarah Wise, *The Blackest Streets*, 2008. She shows him at loggerheads with his bishop and with local clergy. The book's illustrations show well the horrors of this slum parish. There is a picture of Jay taken in 1895 on p. 193.

5. H. Walker, *East London – Sketches of Christian Work and Workers*, 1896, pp. 71f. A picture of Holy Trinity is given on p. 97. The accompanying description of a service there suggests that it was 'bright' rather than 'High'.

6. J.H. Wilson, *My Stormy Voyage Through Life*, vol. 1, 1925, p. 150.

7. *Indian Churchman*, 17th May, 1884.

8. By a strange circuity, SVP was to begin its work among seamen in 1893, also indirectly because of Hopkins's speech at Hastings in that year. See R.W.H. Miller, *Ship of Peter*, unpublished MPhil thesis, 1995, pp. 59ff.

9. Alston Kennerley, *British Seamen's Missions and Sailors' Homes*, unpublished PhD thesis, 1989. Alston Kennerley, 'Joseph Conrad at the London Sailors' Home', 2008, pp. 83ff.

Chapter Five

1. *The Indian Daily News* described Franks in court reports as coming to India as cook on board the *KHYBER*, from which he deserted to look after carriage and horses of a Mr P. Tusant. He then joined 'Fr Hopkins' Mission' for two and a half years, leaving for the Scandinavian Mission, supported by Danish money. (7th and 14th August, 1894).

2. Unless otherwise stated, all references in this chapter are from *The Messenger*, *Shipmates*, or *The Nautical Guildsman*, all produced by Hopkins.

3. Norman Chevers, *On the Preservation of the Health of Seamen, especially of those frequenting Calcutta*, 1864. The Clewer Sisters were responsible for nurse training at the hospital from 1881, and during Hopkins's period. V. Bonham, *A Joyous Service*, 1989, p. 68.

4. *Proceedings*, 1882.

5. Letter from R.A. Horn (3rd Feb, 1892), Ipswich County Records Office, HB1/5A/1/18.

6. *Hastings & St Leonard's News*, 1st Sept, 1893.

7. Shalimar, *Ships and Men*, 1946, p. 340. Hendry sailed in the Merchant Navy before joining the Rangoon Pilot Service (1908-1923 including a wartime interlude in the Indian Army Reserve). This means that he would, in addition to meeting Hopkins in Calcutta, have overlapped with Hopkins's father and brother who were also river pilots.

8. A pinch of salt might be helpful here as Anson's article managed to get a number of details wrong, including Hopkins's name.

9. Working in a parochial context was what distinguished the High Church SAWCM, with its grants for missionary assistant curates, from the MtoS, which pursued a policy of appointing port chaplains usually unattached to parishes. Hopkins received a SAWCM grant for some years.

10. *Hastings & St Leonards News*, 1st Sept, 1893.

11. See *The Englishman (Weekly Summary)*, 11th Jan, 1893.
12. C.P. Hopkins, *Altering Plimsoll's Mark*, 1913, pp. 65f.
13. For an earlier American labour use of the title 'Seamen's Friend Society' see Paul A. Gilje, *Liberty on the Waterfront*, 2004, p. 256.
14. The BFSFSBU may well have been the parent body of the original Calcutta Seamen's Home.
15. The means of Grace would be the administration of the Sacraments.
16. There is no evidence to link Goldie's Calcutta visits with Hopkins.
17. R.W.H. Miller, 'An Anglican Contribution to the Catholic Maritime Apost-olate', 1996. R.W.H. Miller, *Ship of Peter*, unpublished MPhil thesis, 1995, esp. chapters 5, 7, 10, 11.
18. *Hastings & St Leonards News*, 1st Sept, 1893. *Hastings & St Leonards Times*, 2nd Sept, 1893.
19. SAWCM Reports 1894-5. *Nautical Guildsman*, 15th Oct, 1893.
20. *The Englishman (Weekly Summary)*, 26th July, 1892.
21. Do unto others as you would have them do to you.
22. *The Messenger*, Jan 1897.
23. COS Archives: A/FWA/C/D251/1, at the Greater London Records Office. I am grateful to the FWA for permission to see the file.
24. *The Messenger*, 9th Nov, 1903.
25. Copies of this scurrilous and ephemeral paper seem not to have survived, probably destroyed as a result of its conviction for obscenity in August 1894, which raises a question about the date of this case. It may be that Hopkins confuses his papers for, as what follows suggests, the *Sunday Times* was no friend to Hopkins, nor one which one would want to cite as a witness of character.
26. *Indian Daily News*, 16th August, 1894.

Chapter Six

1. Material in this chapter comes from two main sources: *The Messenger*, various issues, and the Family Welfare Association (Charity Organisation Society) files kept in the Greater London Records Office. I am indebted to Dr Stephen Friend for drawing my attention to the FWA files. In addition the *Hereford Times* has been consulted at obvious points. Contemporary descriptions of The Abbey show it to have been influenced by its Indian origins. The Anglo-Catholic response to it can be found in Compton MacKenzie, *My Life and Times: Octave Two*, 1963, pp. 190f, 203f, 219f. MacKenzie spent holidays with OSP and his theatrical aunt, who lived nearby, was a great supporter of the OSP.
2. Most of the Davidson material comes from the Davidson papers in Lambeth Palace Library. It is fully referenced in R.W.H. Miller, *Charles Plomer Hopkins*, unpublished MA thesis, 1993.
3. Joseph René Vilatte, 1854-1929, *episcopus vagans*, joined the Roman Catholic Church several times, each time leaving it for a different Protestant denomination. He obtained Antiochene episcopal orders by dubious means in Colombo in 1892 and proceeded to ordain a large number of bishops and priests who were recognised by nobody but himself. In 1898 he ordained Fr Ignatius OSB of Llanthony, a friend of Hopkins, to the priesthood, a step denied him by the Church of England, rendering Ignatius finally beyond the

pale. See P.F. Anson, *Bishops at Large*, 1964, pp. 91ff.

4. A local clergyman who represents a bishop in another country, in this case handling the bishop's UK business in his absence.

5. Joseph Leycester Lyne (1837-1908), in religion Fr Ignatius, deacon and founder of a quasi-Benedictine monastery at Llanthony, in 1898 accepted ordination to the priesthood, which the Church of England had refused him, from the *episcopus vagans* Vilatte. Hopkins was known to be a friend of Ignatius, which did not help Hopkins's reputation.

6. J.H. Wilson's obituary of Hopkins in *The Seaman*, 31st March, 1922, p.3.

7. Mss 367/TSF/3/2/1 includes a number of letters of Havelock Wilson to a NSFU official, Thomas Carey, around the turn of the century, wherein he details available manpower, but makes no mention of Hopkins.

8. When Hopkins adopted the style of dress described here is not clear. On other occasions he would wear his habit on platforms. The difference probably depended upon the impression he wished to make.

Chapter Seven

1. R.W.H. Miller, *Ship of Peter*, unpublished MPhil thesis, 1995, p. 67.

2. A. Temple Patterson, *A History of Southampton 1700-1914*, vol. 3, 1975, pp. 126f. I have failed to find further details. Patterson seems to be using as his source a local newspaper. Nowhere is Hopkins referred to. Did this event prompt Hopkins to start work in Southampton, and provide his link with ICOSU, or was it Hopkins who lay behind this strike?

3. Mss 175/3/4/3, NSFU Correspondence with SFSSP.

4. Mss 175/6/BSU/1, BSU Minutes.

5. Mss 175/1/1/2, NSFU Minutes, Dec 1910, p. 8. .

6. Mss 175/1/2/1, NSFU Minutes of the Finance Committee, 26th Oct, 1915, 30th April, 1919. The NSFU paid 10 shillings a week for use of rooms at the Priory. On 1st June, 1920 the NSFU bought 38 Hyde Vale (the priory) for £1,220, allowing its continued use by the OSP. It now belongs to a religious order. On 1st Sept, 1920, Hopkins, chairing the Union F&GPC, presented a bill from Bolton & Hickman for £40..2s..0d for the purchase of the Hyde Vale property, and also particulars of £108 due to him as reimbursement for the purchase of land connected with the property.

7. *The Messenger* of August 1907 referred to the County Council rather than the District Council.

8. National Archive HO 144 865/156698.

9. 30th August, 1907, in Alton Abbey archives.

10. James Keir Hardie, 1856-1915, British labour leader, first working man's representative in Parliament (1892), first leader of Parliamentary Labour Party (1906).

11. This Brother John was not the original Calcutta Brother John, but joined the OSP as a probationer in 1897, aged 22, and professed in 1899. He died in 1917, being awarded a posthumous Military Cross.

12. Mss 367/ISF/1/1, ISF Minutes gives date of first meeting as 24th May, 1909 and the primary (article 12) purpose as dealing with strikes and lock-outs. See also Mss 367/TSF/1/4/1, GP Committee Minutes, 23rd Aug, 1909. Mss 367/TSF/1/1/1, Minutes, 24th April, 1908 refers to an International Federation to be formed following a conference, with a draft scheme

approved in 23rd Oct, 1908. Mss 367/TSF/1/4/2, GP Committee Minutes, 14th Feb, 1908, refers to the conference.

13. Mss 175/6/Bor/20, J.H. Borlase, *Struggle*, a typescript history of the NSFU, hereafter referred to as 'Borlase'.

14. Mss 367/TSF/1/1/1, Minutes, 18th Nov, 1910; 19th May, 1911; 29th June, 1911 etc. for the Shipping Federation view.

15. National Archive, MT 9/80 M27650.

16. Mss 159/3/B/63/1, letter from JHW dated 24th Dec, 1910. JHW was a speaker and the third was Tom Chambers.

17. Mss 159/3/B/63/1, Letters, 24th Dec, 1910; 2nd Feb, 1911; 25 Feb, 1911.

18. Mss 159/1/5/1 ITF, Report of Seafarers' Conference 1910, pp. 12, 13. The figure of 1,200 must include allied groups of workers.

19. *Ibid*.

20. Mss 159/3/B/63, General Correspondence of ITF and NSFU 1907-1911. I follow here the International Transport Federation and NSFU records in Warwick University's Modern Records Centre. However a series of reports in *The Times* of London (27th, 29th, 30th, 31st Aug, 1910) of the Copenhagen conference appears to give it greater significance. Mann and Tillett are reported as present, with Wilson taking the lead. On 26th Aug the conference agreed upon an undated strike because the owners would not agree to a conciliation board, which all participating nations had sought. However, Wilson's appeals to owners pre and post date this. Unions were also asking for better conditions, but this was the sticking point. Hopkins is not mentioned.

21. I have failed to trace this. See Mss 159/3/B/5, letter of J.V. Andersen to H. Jochade, 19th May, 1911.

22. Mss 159/3/B/63/1, General Correspondence of ITF and NSFU, 10th May, 1911.

23. G.A. Phillips, *The National Transport Workers Federation*, unpublished DPhil thesis, 1968.

24. John Chatham, *British Seafarers*, unpublished MA thesis, 1981, p. 56.

25. L.H. Powell, *The Shipping Federation*, 1950. G.A. Phillips, *The National Transport Workers Federation*, unpublished DPhil thesis, 1968. V. Marsh & A. Ryan, *The Seamen*, 1989. F.J. Lindop, *A History of Seamen's Trade Unionism to 1929*, unpublished MPhil thesis, 1972. A.P. Wailey, *A Storm from Liverpool: British Seamen and their Union 1920-1970*, unpublished PhD thesis, 1985.

26. Mss 175/6/Bor/24, Borlase. Mss 159/3/B/63, ICOSU Meeting Minutes, Antwerp, 12th-14th March, 1911.

27. Mss 175/3/ITF/6, Correspondence of Hopkins with Jochade, 1911.

28. Hopkins, writing to Jochade (29th August, 1911), said 'My secretary – Mr Anderson – suddenly disappeared, without warning, during the most critical period of the strike'.

29. Mss 159/3/B/63, General Correspondence of ITF and NSFU 1907-11.

30. *Ibid*.

Chapter Eight

1. Lord Askwith, *Industrial Problems and Disputes*, 1974, p. 149. See also G.A. Phillips, *The National Transport Workers Federation*, unpublished

DPhil thesis, 1968, pp. 81ff; H.A. Clegg, *A History of British Trade Unions since 1889*, vol. 2, 1985, p. 25.

2. Mss 159/3/B/91, General Correspondence of ITWF and NSFU 1912.

3. Mss 175/6/Bor/24, Borlase. Askwith gives slightly different details for the events in which he was not involved but dates for those which did involve him agree largely with local newspaper accounts.

4. Not to be confused with the *Cardiff Journal of Commerce*.

5. E. Tupper, *Seamen's Torch*, 1938, pp. 19f. Tupper's title was a military one (retired).

6. Mss 175/7/ITF/6, Correspondence of Hopkins with Jochade, 17th May, 1911.

7. *Hull Daily News*, 19th May, 1911.

8. *Bristol Evening News*, 24th May, 1911.

9. *Hull Daily News*, 25th May, 1911.

10. Mss 175/7/ITF/6, Correspondence of Hopkins with Jochade, 1911.

11. G.A. Phillips, *The National Transport Workers Federation*, unpublished DPhil thesis, 1968, pp. 81ff.

12. *Journal of Commerce*, 8th June, 1911; *Daily Graphic*, 9th June, 1911; *The Times*, 10th June, 1911; *Bristol Evening News*, 9th June, 1911.

13. *Justice*, 24th June, 1911; *Liverpool Echo*, 14th June, 1911; *Southampton Times*, 17th June, 1911.

14. Mss 367/TSF/1/3/2, Humber District Minutes of Shipping Federation.

15. Mss 367/TSF/1/4/2, Minutes, Shipping Federation GPC, 1908-1920.

16. Mss 159/3/B/63, General Correspondence of ITF and NSFU 1907-1911.

17. L.H. Powell, *The Shipping Federation*, 1950.

18. Glasier Papers, University of Liverpool, Special Collections Library. Diary entry for 22nd June, 1911. Glasier gives an idea of this summer's temperature when he records that after a lifetime of wearing wool next to the skin he had visited his doctor to ask if it would harm him to switch to the new cotton Aertex underwear.

19. *Hull Daily News*, 21st June, 1911.

20. Mss 367/TSF/1/3/2, Humber District Minutes of Shipping Federation, 27th June, 1911.

21. *The Times*, 27th June, 1911.

22. Mss 175/6/Bor/24, Borlase.

23. Mss 175/7/ITF/6, Correspondence of Hopkins with Jochade, 1911.

24. *The Times*, 29th June, 1911.

25. Mss 367/TSF/1/3/2, Humber District Minutes of Shipping Federation, 28th June, 1911.

26. *Ibid.*, 30th June, 1911. Lord Askwith, *Industrial Problems and Disputes*, 1974, p. 150. Askwith never refers to Hopkins by name but his 'seamen's leader' must be Hopkins.

27. Mss 175/6/Bor/24, Borlase.

28. A squadron or company (the designation indicates the type of regiment) consisted of about 100 men.

29. J. Chatham, *British Seafarers*, unpublished MA thesis, 1961, p. 23.

30. *Manchester Courier*, 8th July, 1911. Glasier recorded for 8th July: 'Almost record heat in London; temperature 85 degrees in the shade'.

31. *Lloyd's Weekly Shipping Index*, 13th July, 1911.

32. *Shields Daily Gazette & Shipping Telegraph*, 18th July, 1911.

33. *Journal of Commerce*, 22nd July, 1911.
34. For the Shipping Federation view: Mss 367/TSF/1/1/1, Shipping Federation Minutes, 21st July, 1911 where the NESSOA initiative was supported by thirty-three votes to eleven against.
35. *Shields Daily Gazette*, 20th and 21st July, 1911.
36. A. Bullock, *The Life and Times of Ernest Bevin*, vol. 1, 1960, p. 36.
37. *Shields Daily Gazette*, 24th July, 1911. W. Runciman, *Before the Mast and After*, 1924, p. 265.
38. *Journal of Commerce*, 28th and 29th July, 1911.
39. Mss 159/3/B/91, General Correspondence of ITF and NSFU, 1912.
40. Mss 175/7/ITF/6, Correspondence of Hopkins with Jochade, 1911.
41. Mss 367/TSF/1/4/2, Minutes, Shipping Federation GPC, 1908-1920.
42. Mss 367/TSF/1/1/1, Shipping Federation Minutes, 17th November, 1911.
43. Mss 159/3/B/63, General Correspondence of ITF and NSFU 1907-1911.

Chapter Nine

1. *The Seaman*, 27th Dec, 1912; 10th Jan, 7th Feb, 7th Mar, 21st Mar, 13th June, and 17th Oct, 1913.
2. Mss 159/3/B/91, General Correspondence of ITF and NSFU, 9th Feb, 1912.
3. Mss 159/3/B/91, General Correspondence of ITF and NSFU, 6th July 1912.
4. *The Seaman*, 27th Dec, 1912.
5. *Ibid.*, 21st March, 1913.
6. *Ibid.*, 17th Oct, 1913.
7. *Ibid.*, 14th Nov, 1913.
8. *Ibid.*, 3rd April, 1914.
9. *Ibid.*, 31st July, 1914.
10. This could mean no more than that he had some sea time, probably from working his passage early in life, but there is no other evidence for this.
11. Mss 175/1/2/1, NSFU F&GP Committee Minutes, 17th Feb, 1912.
12. E. Tupper, *Seamen's Torch*, pp. 100-101.
13. V. Marsh & A. Ryan, *The Seamen*, 1989, pp. 61ff.
14. Mss 175/1/1/3, NSFU Minutes, 16th Dec, 1916.
15. Alston Kennerley, 'Stoking the Boilers: Firemen and Trimmers in British Merchant Ships, 1850-1950', 2008, pp. 191-220.
16. Mss 175/3/15/1-2, NSFU Correspondence, Chinese Labour, 1920. Also Mss 175/3/16/2-3, NSFU Correspondence. K. Lunn, 'The Seamen's Union & "Foreign" Workers on British & Colonial Shipping 1890-1939', 1988.
17. Mss 175/3/4/3, NSFU Correspondence with SFSSP.
18. V. Marsh & A. Ryan, *The Seamen*, 1989, pp. 73, 78.
19. John Chatham, *British Seafarers*, unpublished MA thesis, 1981, pp. 39ff gives considerable detail of the NMB.
20. Mss 175/3/17/5, NSFU Correspondence 1912-21, iii and iv.
21. V. Marsh & A. Ryan, *The Seamen*, 1989, pp. 80ff. C. P. Hopkins, *National Service of British Seamen 1914-18*, 1920, p. 41. Records in the National Archive give details of panel meetings but little information about Hopkins, who was usually represented by his substitute.
22. Mss 367/TSF/1/4/2, GP Committee Minutes, 13th September, 1917.
23. Alston Kennerley, 'The Seamen's Union, the National Maritime Board and

Firemen: Labour Management in the British Mercantile Marine', 1997, pp. 15-28.
24. Mss 367/TSF/1/4/2, 5th December, 1918. Mss 367/TSF/1/4/2, 4th December, 1919.
25. Mss 367/TSF/3/4/5, 1920 letter from C.P. Hopkins.
26. Mss 175/6/NMB/1, NMB *Circulars*.
27. Mss 175/3/4/3, NSFU Correspondence with SFSSP. Few details survive beyond this brief reference.

Conclusion

1. A.P. Wailey, *A Storm from Liverpool: British Seamen and their Union 1920-70*, unpublished PhD thesis, 1985, p. 7.
2. M. Gee (ed.), *Captain Fraser's Voyages*, 1979, p. 100.

Bibliography

Manuscript Sources

University of Warwick Modern Records Centre

Mss

126/S&FU/4/1, AGM Reports 1912-16
159/1/5/1, ITF Report of Seafarers' Conference, Antwerp 1910
159/3/B/5, Danish Seamen's Union
159/3/B/25, Belgian Dockers' Union
159/3/B/41, Dutch Seamen's Union
159/3/B/63, General Correspondence of ITF and NSFU 1907-1911
159/3/B/78, NSFU
159/3/B/81, Antwerp Seafarers' Conference
159/3/B/91, General Correspondence of ITF and NSFU 1912
175/1/1/1, NSFU Minutes
175/1/1/2, NSFU Minutes 1911-1915
175/1/1/3, NSFU Minutes 1915-1920
175/1/2/1, NSFU F&GP Committee Minutes 1911-1913
175/3/4/3, NSFU Correspondence with SFSSP
175/3/15/1-2, NSFU Correspondence, Chinese Labour 1920
175/3/16/2-3, NSFU Correspondence.
175/3/17/5, NSFU Correspondence & Minutes 1912-1921
175/6/Bor typescript, J.H. Borlase, *Struggle, Seamen through the Ages.*
175/6/BSU/1, BSU Minutes
175/6/NMB/1, National Maritime Board Joint Supply Office circulars
175/7/ITF/6, Correspondence of Hopkins with Jochade 1911
367/ISF/1/1, ISF Minutes
367/TSF/1/1/1, Shipping Federation Minutes
367/TSF/1/3/2, Humber District Minutes of Shipping Federation
367/TSF/1/4/2, Shipping Federation General Purposes Committee 1908-1920
367/TSF/1/4/1, Shipping Federation General Purposes Committee 1890-1907
367/TSF/3/2/1, 1893-1910 Letter from J. H. Wilson
367/TSF/3/4/5, 1910 Letter from E. Cathery
367/TSF/3/4/5, 1920 letter from C. P. Hopkins

The National Archive
H0 144 865/156698, Hopkins's application for British Citizenship
MT 9/80 M27650

Greater London Records Office
A/FWA/C/D251/1&2, Family Welfare Association Records

Lambeth Palace Library
Davidson 57, 65, and 129, Archbishop Davidson's Papers

Rhodes House Library, Oxford
Bodleian USPG CLS47, Papers relating to USPG

The Mission to Seafarers, London
SAWM Records

Alton Abbey, Hampshire
Various papers
Dom Andrew Johnson OSB, part typescript, *For God and Our Sailors*
Copies of *The Messenger*

Ipswich County Records
HB1/5A/1, Mr & Mrs R.A. Horn, correspondence

Community of the Resurrection, Mirfield, W Yorks.
Chronicle
CR Quarterly

Nottinghamshire County Records
PR 18,676 Registers of St Paul's Church, Carlton

University of Liverpool, Special Collections Library
Glasier Papers

Newspapers and Periodicals

Bristol Evening News
Cardiff Citizen
Cardiff Journal of Commerce
Catholic Times & Catholic Opinion
Church Intelligencer
Church Times
CR Quarterly Review
Daily Graphic
Daily Mirror
Daily Post
Daily Telegraph
Études
Fairplay
Falmouth and Penryn Weekly Times
Falmouth Grammar School, *Magazine*, Falmouth, 1922.
Hampshire Express

Hastings & St Leonard's News
Hastings & St Leonard's Times
Hereford Times
Hull Daily News
Indian Churchman
Indian Church Quarterly Review
Indian Daily News
Journal of Commerce
Justice
Labour Leader
Liverpool Echo
Lloyd's Weekly Shipping Index
Manchester Courier
Rangoon Gazette Weekly Budget
Rangoon Times
Shields Daily Gazette and Shipping Telegraph
Shipmates
Southampton Times
The English Churchman
The Englishman (Weekly Summary)
The Messenger
The Nautical Guildsman
The Seaman
The Seamen's Chronicle
Shipmates
The Times
The Times of India (Overland Weekly Edition)
West of England Observer

Printed Sources

Place of publication is London unless indicated otherwise.

Anson, P.F., 'Father Hopkins – Sky Pilot', *The Irish Monthly*, October 1922.
---, *The Church and the Sailor*, 1948.
---, *The Call of the Cloister*, 1964.
---, *Bishops at Large*, 1964.
---, *The Sea Apostolate in the Port of London*, 1991.
Askwith, Lord, *Industrial Problems and Disputes*, reprinted 1974.
Bagwell, P.S., *The Railwaymen*, vol. 1, 1963.
Barnett, H.O., *Canon Barnett, His Life, Work & Friends by His Wife*, 1918.
Barnett, S., *Towards Social Reform*, 1909.
Bell, G.K.A., *Randall Davidson, Archbishop of Canterbury*, 3rd edition, 1952.
Binyon, G.C., *The Christian Socialist Movement in England*, 1931.
Black, A., *Guilds & Civil Society*, 1984.
Boase, F., *Modern English Biography*, 1965.
Bonham, V., *A Joyous Service*, privately printed by the author and the Community of St John the Baptist, Clewer, 1989.
Booth, C., *Life and Labour of the People in London*, Series One, Two and Three, 17 vols., 1886-1903.

British Parliamentary Papers, 1873, XXXVI and 1874, XXXIV.

Brown, K.D., *John Burns*, 1977.

---, *The English Labour Movement 1700-1951*, 1982.

Brown, R. Grant, *Burma as I saw it, 1889-1917*, 1926.

Bruce, G., *The Burma Wars 1824-1886*, 1973.

Budd, George, *Remarks on the Cause of Scurvy*, 1843.

Bullock, Alan, *The Life and Times of Ernest Bevin*, vol. 1, 1960.

Burton, V.C., 'Apprenticeship Regulation & Maritime Labour in the Nineteenth Century British Merchant Marine', *International Journal of Maritime History*, 1:1, (June, 1989), pp. 191-220.

Cameron, A.T., *The Religious Communities of the Church of England*, 1918.

Chevers, N., *On the Preservation of the Health of Seamen, especially of those frequenting Calcutta*, Calcutta, 1864.

---, *A Manual of Medical Jurisprudence for India*, 1870.

---, *Diseases of India*, 1886.

---, *A Manual of Medical Jurisprudence for Bengal and the North-West Provinces*, Calcutta, 1886.

Church of England Year Book, 1904.

Clegg, H.A., *A History of British Trade Unionism since 1889*, vol. 2, 1985.

Clegg, H.A., Fox & Thompson, *History of Trade Unionism*, vol. 1, 1964.

Cole, G.D.H., *Introduction to Trade Unionism*, 1953.

Committee of the Society for Improving the Condition of Merchant Seamen Report, 1867.

Crawford, D.G., *Roll of the Indian Medical Service 1615-1930*, 1930.

Crockford's Clerical Directory, 1885-1922.

Cross, F.L. (ed.), *Oxford Dictionary of the Christian Church*, 1963.

Dawson, Cdr., *Merchant Sailors' Wants*, 1863.

de Mierre, H.C., *The Long Voyage*, 1963.

Dictionary of Labour Biography, vol. 4, 1977.

Down, W.J., *On Course Together*, Norwich, 1989.

Evans, S.G., *The Social Hope of the Christian Church*, 1965.

Fabri, F., *Wanderings*, Palestine Pilgrim Text Society, 1892.

Falkus, H., *Master of Cape Horn*, 1982.

Farmer, H.F., *Log of a Shellback*, 1925.

Flanders, A., *Trade Unions*, 1968.

Fletcher, R.A., *Guide to the Mercantile Marine*, 1912.

Gee, M., *Captain Fraser's Voyages*, 1979.

Gilje, Paul A., *Liberty on the Waterfront*, Philadelphia PA, 2004.

Gray, D., *Earth and Altar*, 1986.

Grosjean, E., *Les Missions Protestantes d'Angleterre en Façeur des Marins, Études*, Paris, Feb 1894.

Harris, J., *Britannia*, 1837.

Hawkins, K., *Trade Unions*, 1981.

Hopkins, C.P., 'The Church and Our Sailors', *Indian Church Quarterly Review*, (April, 1890), pp. 162-171.

---, *Prayer Book for Catholic Seamen*, 1903.

---, *Altering Plimsoll's Mark*, 1913.

---, *National Service of British Seamen 1914-18*, 1920.

---, *Seafarer's Annual*, 1921.

Hughes, T., *James Fraser*, 1887.

Hyndman, H.M., *The Murdering of British Seamen by Lloyd George*, British Socialist Party, 1913.

Inglis, K.S., *Churches and the Working Class in Victorian England*, 1963.

Jay, A.O., *Life in Darkest London*, 1891.

---, *The Social Problem: Its Possible Solution*, 1893.

---, *A Story of Shoreditch*, 1896.

Jones, S., *Trade & Shipping: Lord Inchcape 1852-1932*, Manchester, 1989.

Kendall, G., *Charles Kingsley and His Ideas*, 1946.

Kennerley, Alston, 'The Seamen's Union, the National Maritime Board and Firemen: Labour Management in the British Mercantile Marine', *The Northern Mariner/Le Marin du Nord*, 7:4, (1997), pp. 15-28.

---, 'Ratings for the Mercantile Marine: The Roles of Charity, the State and Industry in the Pre- Service Education and Training of Ratings for the Mercantile Marine, 1879-1939', *History of Education*, 28:1, (1999), pp. 31-51.

---, 'The Shore Management of British Seafarers in the Twentieth Century', in David J. Starkey and Hugh Murphy (eds.), *Beyond shipping and Shipbuilding*, Maritime Historical Studies Centre, University of Hull, 2007.

---, 'Stoking the Boilers: Firemen and Trimmers in British Merchant Ships, 1850-1950', *International Journal of Maritime History*, 10:1, (June, 2008), pp. 191-220.

---, 'Joseph Conrad at the London Sailors' Home', *The Conradian*, 33:1, (2008), pp. 70-102.

Kverndal, R., *Seamen's Missions*, Pasadena, California, 1986.

---, *The Way of the Sea*, Pasadena, California, 2008.

Lambert, J.M., *Two Thousand Years of Guild Life*, Hull, 1891.

Leeson, R.A., *Travelling Brothers*, 1979.

Lloyd's *Register of Shipping*, 1884.

Lunn, K., 'The Seamen's Union & "Foreign" Workers on British and Colonial Shipping 1890-1939', *Bulletin*, Society for the Study of Labour History, 1988.

MacGregor, D. R., *The China Bird*, 1961.

MacKenzie, Compton, *My Life and Times: Octave Two*, 1963.

---, *The Altar Steps*, undated.

Mann, Tom, *Memoirs*, 1923.

Marks, J.E., *Forty Years in Burma*, 1917.

Marsh, V. and A. Ryan, *The Seamen*, Oxford, 1989.

Martin, H. (ed.), *The Christian Social Reformers of the Nineteenth Century*, 1927.

Masterman, C.F.G., *Frederick Denison Maurice*, 1885.

Mayor, S., *The Churches and the Labour Movement*, 1967.

McCleod, H., *Religion and the Working Class in Nineteenth Century Britain*, 1984.

Miller, R.W.H., *From Shore to Shore*, privately printed, Nailsworth, Glos., 1989.

---, 'Seamen's Welfare', *International Association for the Study of Maritime Mission Newsletter*, Autumn 1991.

---, 'An Anglican Contribution to the Catholic Maritime Apostolate', *Mariner's Mirror*, Feb 1996.

Mudie-Smith, R., *The Religious Life of London*, 1904.

Paget, S., (ed.), *Henry Scott Holland: Memoirs and Letters*, 1921.

Parkhurst, P.G., *Ships of Peace*, privately printed, 1962.
Patterson, A.Temple., *A History of Southampton 1700-1914*, vol. 3, Southampton, 1975.
Pelling, H., *A History of British Trade Unionism*, 4th edition, 1987.
Peters, G., *The Plimsoll Line*, 1975.
Pimlott, J.A.R., *Toynbee Hall*, 1935.
Plimsoll, S., *Our Seamen – an Appeal*, 1873. Powell, L.H., *The Shipping Federation*, 1950.
Press, J., 'Philanthropy and the British Shipping Industry 1815-1960', *International Journal of Maritime History*, 1:1, (June, 1989), pp. 107-127.
Proceedings of the Government of India, India and Burma (India Office Library).
Raven, C.E., *Christian Socialism 1848-1854*, 1920.
Reckitt, M.B., *Faith and Society*, 1932.
---, *Maurice to Temple*, 1947.
---, (ed.), *For Christ and the People*, 1968.
Report of the Committee of the Society for Improving the Condition of Merchant Seamen, 1867.
Runciman, W., *Before the Mast and After*, 1924.
Schneer, J., *Ben Tillett*, 1982.
Shalimar (F.C. Hendry), *Ships and Men*, 1946.
Shinwell, E., *Conflict Without Malice*, 1955.
Taylor, B., 'Founders and Followers: Leadership in Anglican Religious Communities' in (ed.) J. Loades, *Monastic Studies*, Headstart, Bangor, 1990.
Thacker's Indian Directory.
The Lambeth Conferences (1867-1930), 1948.
Toynbee, H., *The Social Condition of Seamen*, 1863.
Tuchman, B., *The Proud Tower*, 1962.
Tucker, H.W., (ed.), *Records of the S.P.G., 1701-1892*, 1893.
Tupper, E., *Seamen's Torch*, 1938.
Wagner, D.O., *The Church of England and Social Reform since 1854*, 1930.
Walker, H., *East London – Sketches of Christian Work and Workers*, 1896.
Walker, T., *The Original*, Glasgow, 1887.
Webb, S.& B., *The History of Trade Unionism*, reprinted 1973.
Williams, D.M., 'Mid Victorian Attitudes to Seamen and Maritime Reform', *International Journal of Maritime History*, 3:1, (June, 1991), pp.101-106.
Wilson, J.H., *My Stormy Voyage Through Life*, vol. 1, 1925.
Wise, Sarah., *The Blackest Streets*, 2008.
Woodhams, D., *The Making of Burma*, 1962.

Unpublished Theses

Bovill, D.G., *Education of Mercantile Mariners in the North East Ports (1840-1902)*, University of Durham DPhil, 1987.
Chatham, J., *British Seafarers: the opposition to collaboration, 1911-1927*, University of Warwick MA, 1981.
Kennerley, A., *British Seamen's Missions & Sailors' Homes: Voluntary Welfare Provision for Serving Seafarers, 1815-1970*, CNAA PhD, 1989.

Lindop, F.J., *A History of Seamen's Trade Unionism to 1929*, University of London MPhil, 1972.

Miller, R.W.H., *Charles Plomer Hopkins and the Seamens' Union with Particular Reference to the 1911 Strike*, University of Warwick MA, 1993.

---, *Ship of Peter: The Catholic Sea Apostolate and the Apostleship of the Sea*, University of Plymouth MPhil, 1995.

Phillips, G.A., *The National Transport Workers Federation*, University of Oxford DPhil, 1968.

Wailey, A.P., *A Storm from Liverpool: British Seamen & their Union 1920-1970*, University of Liverpool PhD, 1985.

Index